VIETNAM

Publisher:	Aileen Lau
Editorial Manager:	Bina Maniar
Editors:	Bina Maniar
	Emma Tan
	Aileen Lau
Design/DTP:	Sares Kanapathy
Illustrations:	Eric Yeo
Cover Artwork:	Susan Harmer
Maps:	Rebecca Fong

Published in the United States by
PRENTICE HALL GENERAL REFERENCE
15 Columbus Circle
New York, New York, 10023

ISBN 0-671-87907-3

Titles in the series:
Alaska - American Southwest - Australia - Bali - California - Canada - Caribbean - China - England - Florida - France - Germany - Greece - Hawaii - India - Indonesia - Italy - Ireland - Japan - Kenya - Malaysia - Mexico - Nepal - New England - New York - Pacific Northwest USA - Singapore - Spain - Thailand - Turkey - Vietnam

USA MAINLAND SPECIAL SALES
Bulk purchases (10+copies) of the Travel Bugs series are available at special discounts for corporate use. The publishers can produce custom publications for corporate clients to be used as premiums or for sales promotion. Copies can be produced with custom cover imprints. For more information write to Special Sales, Prentice Hall Travel, Paramount Communications Building, 15th floor, 15 Columbus Circle, New York, NY 10023.

Printed in Singapore

VIETNAM

Text by Joseph R Yogerst

With contributions by:
Morten Strange
Laure Lau

Editors:
Bina Maniar
Emma Tan
Aileen Lau

Prentice Hall Travel

New York   London   Toronto   Sydney   Tokyo   Singapore

C O N T E N T S

C O N T E N T S

C O N T E N T S

WHAT TO DO

C O N T E N T S

Vietnam the vigorous;

the latest little dragon of

that was always there anyway.

Asia today ... a dragon

After the deluge of war

the spirit of Vietnam

is renewed and uplifted. Smiles abound throughout the country.

all over Vietnam as if it were an ever-evolving drawing board for layers of future events.

Natural beauty, another bounty

of the country was thankfully not entirely looted by time and war ... so much remains to be enjoyed.

Introduction

The airplane appears to drift across an endless emerald plain, spotted with thatched-roof hamlets as it approaches the ground at Tan Son Nhut Airport, Ho Chi Minh City. The door swings open to a mulchy tropical aroma and you walk across a tarmac so hot, it seems to burn the soles of your shoes. You might expect problems at customs and immigration, but the formalities are a breeze. A young women in uniform says, "Welcome to Vietnam" with a broad grin and any preconceived notions about the country begin to thaw, as they will again when the complex layers that mark modern Vietnam are peeled back during the rest of your visit. Hundreds of faces are pressed against the terminal windows, anticipation almost getting the better of them, anxious to get a look at their long-lost relatives from overseas. Some of them

1

A rural welcome by a Vietnamese Montagnard girl .

Fantasy becomes reality amisdst the rolling hills and the azure blue seas.

are dressed in black "rice paddy pajamas" and conical straw hats, while others sport designer jeans and snappy sports coats. There's grandmother with betelnut-stained teeth, and standing next to her, grandson with his Sony boom box and high-top sneakers.

Beyond the human throng is a crowd of cars, shiny new Japanese models that seem to keep their distance from the old American clunkers – patriarchal vehicles that should have been consigned to a museum.

Mix of Old & New

It is a curious mix of old and new especially in big cities like Hanoi and Ho Chi Minh (Saigon), which is slowly seeping into every corner of the country. Everyone wants to tell you how life is chang-

oppression, the 50 years of almost continual warfare and a post-war history of imprudent economic reformation, have set her back but it will not be long before Vietnam lands on her feet again.

In the midst of this great change, it would be difficult to find a more exciting destination in all of Asia.

Visions of War & Violence?

Most tourists who visit Vietnam today may be too young to remember the Vietnam War, but they probably grew up with images of Vietnam screened on television and published in the papers. Hollywood has reinforced such images through the combat movies of the 70s in films like "The Deer Hunter" and "Apocalypse Now!"

Mention the word "Vietnam" to most people and more often than not the name conjures visions of war and violence.

ing, from government economists and tour guides, to rice farmers and Buddhist monks.

A Dramatic Evolution

But, in essence, that is what Vietnam is all about: a country undergoing a dramatic evolution and embarking on a great leap forward to traverse the gap between the third and the first worlds.

However, the ravages of colonial

A Land of Mystery

It would seem that little is known about current life and times in Vietnam other than the fact that it is part of one of the last remnants of communism in the world. Little too is known of her pre-colonial and pre–invasion history. In short, Vietnam remains a great mystery.

But all of this is about to change. Vietnam is finally opening its doors to the outside world again after nearly two

Fun in the marshes on the back of a water buffalo.

decades of introspection.

Open Doors

Alterations to the fabric of government and society, known as *doi moi* ("renovation" – the Vietnamese version of *perestroika* – a system of unilateral economic reforms in agriculture, industry, business and trade) set peasants free to own their own land and sell in a market economy.

With private enterprise, almost overnight millions of small businesses (from restaurants to corner cigarette vendors) sprang up from Hanoi to Saigon. In natural succession, religious tolerance has opened the way for worship in Bud-

dhist monasteries as well as Catholic churches once again.

Tourist Revolution

Tourism is undergoing a revolution and is expected to be a top foreign exchange earner.

The Vietnamese, and even foreign investors, are constantly planning and developing the country's assets – places, people and activities – to form Vietnam into a great Southeast Asian destination, possibly to rival that of Thailand and Bali.

Some parts of the country are still off-limits for "security" reasons – especially areas of the Central Highlands –

but for the most part Vietnam is now as easy to visit as other great tourist destinations of Southeast Asia. The number of international flights into Hanoi and Ho Chi Minh has also increased tremendously in recent years.

You can join any of the hundreds of package tours offered by some of the world's best operators, or wander around the country on your own, using public transport. Cruise ship lines are starting to add Vietnamese ports to their Asian itineraries, while adventure travel enthusiasts will soon be able to hike or mountain bike down the Ho Chi Minh Trail.

The touristic infrastructure also includes an improvement in the standard of hotels and restaurants, the installation of modern international telephone links and the growth of a credit card culture.

A hardy but happy flower vendor.

Sights, Smells & Sounds

People often visit to see at first hand the legacy of war, the battlefields, the tunnels and the military museums. But what they find instead is a different country... pristine tropical beaches where the only footprints are those of the water birds, zesty Vietnamese food and splendid continental cuisine, ancient Imperial cities and marvelous French quarters that have remained unchanged over the centuries; hilltribes living in their own cultural cosmos, protected and nurtured by the great backbone of mountains that runs down through the center of Vietnam.

Beauty & Poignancy

This is a poignant and beautiful nation that raids your imagination with a variety of sights, sounds and smells, a place that quickly overwhelms even the most jaded traveler.

So cast yourself away on Ha Long Bay in a red-sailed junk, walk along isolated white sand coves north of Danang, plunge into the primeval depths of Cuc Phuong National Park, where tigers and other jungle creatures still roam, make a pilgrimage to the Imperial tombs along the Perfume River,

Rice planting in Nghia Binh Province.

or explore the massive ruins of the royal Citadel in Hue.

The "Human" Experience

There is also the "human" experience: the Tet Festival – the lunar new year – which is ushered in with an aroma of mandarin oranges and plum blossoms; Christmas Eve as celebrated in old Saigon, as thousands of Vietnamese Catholics pour into the streets in a spirited demonstration of their faith.

Experience The Charm

Do not be afraid to get your feet wet in the multitude of rice paddies when you visit the emerald patchwork of paddy fields that mark the Red River Valley and the vast Mekong Delta.

Here the peasants are more than willing to show you the best way to plant young rice stalks. Likewise when you visit any of the Buddhist temples and monasteries that have thrown open their doors to the outside world, you will find that the hordes of saffron-robed monks are just as curious about tourists as tourists are about them.

An Innate Charm...

Visitors will quickly uncover the innate charm of the Vietnamese people. One

Vietnam Fast Facts

Area: 331,689 square kilometers (128,401 square miles), about the size of Norway or New Mexico.
Population: About 70 million (1993), roughly 50 percent under age 21; growth rate of 2.2 percent annually.
Capital: Hanoi (population: 2 million)
Government: Socialist republic under the aegis of the Communist Party, based on a Marxist-Leninist political philosophy; the Politburo is the most powerful government body, the National Assembly comprises about 500 deputies drawn from the 40 provinces.
Religion: The major faith is Mahayana Buddhism, with strong Confucian and Taoist influences. There are about six million Roman Catholics, as well as small groups of Muslims, Hindus and Protestants. Indigenous sects include the Cao Dai and Hoa Hao.
People: About 90 percent of the population is ethnic Vietnamese, but there are 57 minority groups including Chinese, Cham, Khmer, Thai (Zao), Hmong and Muong.
Economy: Over 70 percent is agrarian, largely based on rice farming; the per capita income is about US$200 per year which makes Vietnam one of the world's poorest nations.
Language: Vietnamese is the official language, spoken by almost the entire population. There are 57 minority languages drawn from the Austro-Asian, Sino-Tibetan, Tai-Kadai, Malayo-Polynesian and Mon-Khmer language groups.
Currency: Vietnamese Dong; US$1.00 = 10,000 Dong (January 1993).
National Anthem: "Marching to the Front" (*"Tien Quan Ca"*).
Highest Point: Phan Si Pan, 3,143 meters (10,311 feet).

would think that after more than 50 years of war, in the wake of terrible suffering and deprivation, they would not feel compelled to smile at a foreigner, or engage in a casual chat.

But, there is a freshness, an innocence of sorts that permeates the Vietnamese soul, that transcends and seems to contradict their horrible war experience.

There is little lingering animosity, even against the Americans, rather the experience is just the opposite – an outpouring of affection and curiosity more reminiscent of bygone Asia.

A New Era

With the end of the American embargo, Vietnam will enter an era of unprecedented change. Her economy will blossom, the standard of living will gradually rise and observers have little doubt that she will take her place amongst the Little Dragons of Southeast Asia.

Political Osmosis

The communist government may also dissolve, not through revolution, but through a sort of political osmosis brought about by "market forces" such as capitalism and grassroots human rights movements.

A generation from now, the Vietnam War will finally be history, as distant and dim as the French colonial period now seems.

It will have been a long and, at times, exasperating road, but in the end Vietnam will succeed in its goal of making people think of her as a country rather than a war.

BURMAH
SIAM
AND
ANAM.

Geographical Miles 60 = One Degree.
English Miles 69·1 = One Degree.
British possessions coloured Red.

Vietnam within its present boundaries is a relatively new creation that only stretches back as far as the end of French colonial rule in 1954. But this is not to say that Vietnamese history is young. The nucleus of the current culture is much older than the nation itself, nearly as old as the great heartland civilizations of China and India and certainly far older than most North American and European nation states. Although, during all those years, the land was rarely known as Vietnam.

Anam, of old.

The first inklings of human occupation can be traced back to the Paleolithic period or the old Stone Age, when cave dwellers lived on the edge of the Red River Delta. Then, the great rice plains of today were no more than swamps, surrounded by porous limestone hills and thick subtropical forest. There were also small settlements of primitive fisherfolk who lived off the bounty of the nearby sea along the Gulf of Tonkin. By the end of the Neolithic period (4,000 BC) rice culture had infiltrated southwards from China which resulted in the evo-

History

9

In the Beginning...

According to Vietnamese legend, about four thousand years ago, a powerful dragon king, Lac Long Quan, married the beautiful fairy princess Ao Co. She bore him 100 sons. Because they were so different, the marriage was doomed to failure. So Ao Co took 50 of her sons and fled to live in the hills, while the father took the remaining boys and went to live on the plains. The descendants of the fairy princess became the hilltribes; the descendants of the dragon became the Kinh people (the primary ethnic group of modern Vietnam). One of the lowland sons was said to have become the first king of the Hung Dynasty, a royal lineage which ruled over the land of Van Lang until 1954.

lution of the various tribes of the Red River region from semi-nomadic hunters and gatherers into sedentary farmers with an interest in enforcing order on the land.

Myth and legend aside, we know that a group of 15 tribes called the Lac Viet organized themselves into a loose confederation around 2,000 BC. Their rulers were known as the Hung Kings and their civilization was called the Kingdom of Van Lang, the first of a long sequence of Imperial dynasties that would stretch into the middle of the 20th century. Excavations show that they grew rice, had developed a primitive form of irrigation and decorated their skin with animal tattoos.

The Lac Viet were also fierce warriors, but not as fierce as the mountain people – the progeny of the legendary fairy Ao Co – who swept across the plains in 258BC to become the new masters of the Red River Valley. An

Duong, the mountain chieftain, became the earliest ruler of the Au Lac Kingdom and essentially the first person to mould northern Vietnam into a single political unit. He established a splendid capital at Co Loa, on the northern fringe of present-day Hanoi, with three concentric walls and a thriving Bronze Age society that produced metal arts and crafts, tools and weapons.

Chinese Occupation

As the prologue to a pattern that would mark nearly two thousand years of Vietnamese history, the Au Lac kingdom was brought to its knees by foreign invaders. In keeping with their "manifest destiny" to vanquish all of east Asia, the armies of the Chinese Han Dynasty marched into the Red River Valley near the end of 2BC. With overwhelming numbers and better weapons, the Chinese conquest was easy and they had no trouble imposing a political and military occupation that would last for more than a millennia.

As northern Vietnam was a distant province of China for over a thousand years, a certain amount of assimilation was bound to take place. Modern Vietnamese historians, with an understandably nationalistic slant, prefer to minimize the record of foreign influence. But it would be more accurate to say that the frail Red River society was deluged by Chinese culture, as effectively as modern Asia is being overwhelmed by West-

History and art off the walls of the Cham Museum in Danang.

ern-style business and living standards.

The Han ruled by means of powerful functionaries called *mandarins* who were responsible for dispensing law and order, collecting taxes and recruiting "voluntary" labor for state construction projects. This spurred the creation of a feudal system of powerful lords who ruled over the peasant class and the restriction of independent entrepreneurs to the cities. The Chinese dialect Mandarin became the language of government and education.

At the same time, Confucianism was introduced as a handy adjunct to Buddhism (that had been earlier introduced from India). Perhaps even more than the *mandarins*, Confucius' doctrine with its emphasis on respect for author-

ity (especially for the Han emperor), elders and teachers imparted discipline on the ordinary citizenry. The philosophy basically codified social mores and hierarchy by systematically setting out doctrines of behaviour such as, how the Vietnamese should treat one another as well as their Chinese masters, thereby fracturing society into a pyramid of distinct tiers, with Imperial authority sitting at the peak and the peasant at the base. Today, the empire has crumbled and the *mandarins* are long gone, but the basic tenets of Confucianism still prevail in Vietnamese society, where they have intertwined and now co–exist in a somewhat complementary relationship with the communist system.

Yet, the Chinese were also responsible for many technological, artistic and commercial innovations. They carried the Iron Age to the banks of the Red River, which, together with better irrigation techniques made the delta one of Asia's most fertile regions. They introduced new food plants and advanced sericulture (a harbinger to the development of the silk *ao dai* which is so much a symbol of Vietnam today). They revolutionized architecture, taking it from the adobe age into a state of amazing Imperial grace and refinement and they incorporated Northern Vietnam into a thriving Chinese trade network that included the Spice Islands, India, Persia, East Africa and the Roman Empire.

But, in spite of this, the ugly head of popular resistance rose against Chinese political and cultural hegemony and gave birth to the Vietnamese penchant towards armed resistance, especially to peasant guerilla movements willing to fight against overwhelming odds. Brief and bloody rural insurrections resulted from the advent of Chinese rule. The most famous of these was a brief revolt by the Trung Sisters who managed to retake the region for three years before being crushed by the Han emperor aided by his best general (see box p 14).

Even after the Han Dynasty broke into three separate kingdoms in AD 220, Chinese domination over the Red River region continued. The fall of the Tang Dynasty in AD 906 plunged China into chaos and gave the Vietnamese the chance that they had been waiting and hoping for. It took another 30 years and

numerous rebellions, before the Chinese were successfully routed at the Battle of Bach Dang in AD 938. Bach Dang was a classic naval confrontation fought in the spirit of Salamis and Lepanto. Hundreds of Vietnamese and Chinese junks gathered to face one another at the Bach Dang estuary which unbeknown to the enemy had been sabotaged by the Vietnamese by the placement of iron-tipped stakes at the estuary's mouth. The Chinese attacked on the high tide, but later, as they tried to make a tactical retreat into Ha Long Bay, their junks were ravaged by the metal stakes. The battle turned into a rout and Vietnam was free of foreign domination – for the time-being.

Feudal Kings & Lords

A period of internal anarchy followed during which warlords such as the Twelve Lords fought for the control of the Red River Valley. A mighty warlord named Dinh Bo Linh emerged. He united the country in AD 967, renamed the nation Dai Co Viet and built a splendid little capital at Hoa Lu in what is now Ha Nam Ninh province. But, within fifty years power had passed to Ly Thai To, who founded the Ly Dynasty and moved the capital to Thang Long on the Red River – an Imperial bastion that would later grow into the great city of Hanoi. The Ly epoch lasted for just over two hundred years. It was a period of transition during which the Vietnamese re-

Cham Temple remains at Phu Khanh Province, Nha Trang.

claimed their hold on native culture, religion, education and government. Numerous Chinese attacks were foiled and the Vietnamese felt confident enough to expand the boundaries of their own empire, albeit in a southwardly direction, against the highly refined Cham kingdom (a kin of the Khmer civilization that was building Angkor Wat at about this time). By the end of the Ly period, the state boundary had been pushed to the outskirts of present-day Danang.

Tran Dynasty

The Tran Dynasty emerged in 1225 at the head of a much more mature nation than had existed at the end of Chinese rule. The Tran rulers consolidated most of the groundwork laid by their predecessors including the refinement and expansion of irrigation projects; the propagation of feudalism and slavery; the development of a strong military and the centralization of authority. No one could ascertain whether the average citizen was any better off than under Chinese rule, but the seeds of Vietnamese nationalism were being sown. The greatest challenge faced by the Tran was the Mongol threat. The Mongols organized three separate incursions, each of which were successfully repulsed by the Vietnamese, but, many lives were lost. The Chinese armies also invaded, returning in 1407 and briefly recon-

The Trung Sisters

Women have always played a part in Vietnam's liberation movements, an example set by the famous Trung sisters – Trung Nhi and Trung Trac – who sparked a rebellion against the Chinese in AD 40. Although the line between fact and fiction is somewhat obscure, records reveal that they rose to arms after the Chinese governor To Dinh executed Trac's husband, a prominent landowner.

Using a number of female lieutenants, the Trungs won the Battle of Luy Lau and eventually captured 65 enemy citadels successfully driving the invaders from northern Vietnam. They reigned for a mere three years until a huge Han Dynasty army squashed their independence movement. After their defeat, they drowned themselves in a tributary of the Red River to avoid torture at the hands of the Chinese.

The sisters ran their headquarters at a place called Me Linh in the Red River Valley (about an hour's drive from modern-day Hanoi). You can still see the ruins of their fortress, the Citadel with Three Ponds and a pagoda dedicated to their memory. There is another pagoda dedicated to the Trung sisters on the south side of Hanoi. The sixth day of the second lunar month (usually in February) has been proclaimed a national holiday and is called *Trung Sisters Day*.

quering Dai Viet. The twenty-year interval that followed is called the Ming Occupation – a period of brutal subjugation in which nearly every Vietnamese male was pressed into military service or slavery; personal property was confiscated; the wealth of Dai Viet was channelled back into China and craftsmen, architects and artists were spirited away to serve the imperial court in Peking. So in less than two decades, the Chinese managed to rape the nation of much of its physical and intellectual wealth!

Lord Le Loi

The seeds of resentment were swiftly being sowed when a charismatic feudal lord named Le Loi proclaimed himself king in 1418 launching the great war of independence. Aided by his most trusted advisor Nguyen Trai (now regarded as one of the great scholars of Vietnamese history) and controlling the action from a base in Thanh Hoa province, his followers launched guerrilla attacks against Ming outposts and convoys. After years of inconclusive fighting, Le Loi launched his final assault. His forces swept through the Red River Delta and besieged the Ming troops inside the walls of Thanh Hoa. The Chinese sent massive reinforcements, but they were ambushed in the mountains north of the valley, routed and driven back to China.

One of Le Loi's first tasks was land reform (or a less perverse form of feudalism), which is said to have greatly improved the plight of the average peasant. The urban middle class began to flourish with the formation of craft guilds similar to those found in Europe at the same time. Le Loi also introduced a codified legal system (the Hung Duc Code), standard weights and measures and a new copper currency. At the same

Port scene of the 1880s when sea-going vessels stopped along the Vietnamese coast.

time, the royal court encouraged creativity and thinking through the works of great Confucian scholars such as Le Loi's friend and confidante Nguyen Trai. So while Shakespeare was producing his great plays across the world in England, the bards of the Le Dynasty were laboring to produce great classics of Vietnamese literature and poetry.

Although the Le Dynasty only lasted until 1789, the central monarchy became impotent from the early 17th century onwards as two aristocratic clans – the Trinh in the north and the Nguyen in the south – began to dominate the country. The golden era was slowly fading into a quagmire of greed and corruption as land reform and codified laws were scorned by an increasingly powerful aristocracy who taxed and extorted the peasants to the point of poverty and indigence.

Tay Son Rebellion

The peasants began to revolt in sporadic patches throughout the country. However, the small bands that were first formed were easily crushed by the imperial army. But, as the century progressed the central authority became listless, the royal court more insular and the attitude gradually prevailed that these troubles would go away if they were ignored. But the troubles did not fade away and the country tumbled towards chaos and despair. However, full-blown

Problems with the neighbours – Laotian Soldiers on guard.

revolution did not strike until 1771 when three brothers banded a small peasant army together in a village called Tay Son on the central coast. Nobody could have predicted it at the time, but the three brothers would change the entire fate of Vietnam!

As with most revolts, the Tay Son rebellion started small – with the overthrow of the despised local *mandarins*. Within two years Tay Son forces organized under Nguyen Hue (the youngest brother) had captured both Quang Ngai and Quang Nam province. They soon grew strong enough to challenge the authority of the Nguyen lords. The Trinh lords saw this as their chance to reunite the nation, so they in turn retaliated. Caught in a pincher between two pow-

erful armies, the Nguyen forces collapsed and the remnants of the regime fled to the Mekong Delta. In desperation, Nguyen Anh, the last of the southern lords, called upon the King of Siam for help. A huge Siamese fleet sailed up the Mekong in 1784, confident of an assured victory over the ragtag peasant legions. But, they sailed right into an ambush and the vaunted Battle of Rach Gam in which the Tay Son forces – despite their inexperience at naval engagement – totally overwhelmed the foreign invaders. Having secured the south, the Tay Son turned their attention to eliminating the Trinh lords of the north. In 1786, they marched through the Pass of Clouds above Danang at the start of a campaign to capture the Red

River Valley. With the support of the local peasants, the Tay Son easily captured Thang Long (Hanoi) and vanquished the Trinh. Once again, the skeletal crew of royals appealed to foreign aid – in this case the Chinese, who proved more than willing to dispatch 200,000 men in what they figured would be a golden opportunity to draw Vietnam back into the Middle Kingdom. Appealing to the entire nation, the Tay Son recruited their own huge army and marched north once again.

In one of the most brilliant campaigns in Asian military history, Tay Son forces advanced 80 kilometers over a span of six days in January 1789. What resulted was a lightning attack by mammoth elephants and foot soldiers that threw Chinese forces into disarray. The Imperial Palace in Peking urged for

peace and Vietnam was once again reunited under its king, Nguyen Hue.

Emperor Gia Long

Another golden age should have followed. But Nguyen Hue died just three years later in 1792 and his brothers had neither the military skill nor the political potency to keep their adversaries at bay.

Unfortunately for the regime, the Tay Son troops had never been successful at ousting the refugee Nguyen Anh from his lair in the Mekong Delta. Although his first appeal for foreign military intervention had ended in crushing defeat, Nguyen Anh took his case to a French missionary who arranged an audience with Louis XVI. This eventu-

HANOÏ. — LA

Refinement and sophistication of old Hanoi.

DE DES SUPPLICES.

Dynastic urns in the Imperial City, Binh Tri Thien, Hue.

ally led to a treaty in which Paris promised military assistance in return for territorial and trade concessions. Although Louis XVI was beheaded in the French Revolution of 1789, French venturism into Asia did not stall. The next phase of the Vietnamese civil war was a long and bloody fourteen years of strife that culminated in Nguyen Anh capturing Thang Long in July 1802. He proclaimed himself king and took the Imperial name Gia Long for himself. The second Nguyen Dynasty had begun, but more important than that was the fact that the French had entered the Vietnamese political fray.

Gia Long moved the capital to Hue and inaugurated a massive building program that would soon transform the city sitting on the Perfume River into a miniature version of the Imperial court in Peking. French missionaries and merchants were allowed into the country, while at the same time Gia Long paid annual tribute to the Qing Emperor of China in return for a pledge to respect Vietnamese sovereignty. His successor, Ming Mang, attempted to curtail the rapidly growing French power within the kingdom. But, his execution of Catholic missionaries did not go down well in Paris, where it was used as an excuse for invasion.

French Colonial Rule

When French forces landed at Danang

in August 1858, Ming Mang tried to appease the invaders through *hoa nghi* (peace and negotiation) but he greatly misread French intentions and failed to appreciate the geopolitical games occuring in Europe that had prompted Paris to stake a permanent claim to this part of the Asian coast as a means of counterbalancing the growing British influence in the region. By 1867, the French had captured the southern third of the country, carving out a colony called Chochinchina and establishing a capital at the river port of Saigon. French forces then marched into adjacent Cambodia, transforming the ancient kingdom into a protectorate. After the death of Emperor Tu Duc in 1883, the French usurped Hue, the central coast (Annam) and the Red River region (Tonkin). However they left the Nguyen monarchy untouched in a veiled attempt to make it seem that the Vietnamese still ruled their own country. But, guerrilla resistance against the foreign invaders continued in various pockets of the country until 1896 by which time the whole of Indochina had fallen to the French.

French colonial rule can be construed as a century of great cultural infusion and economic development. The French introduced the likes of Voltaire, Debussy and Toulouse-Lautrec to a previously unenlightened populace. They organized the wealth of the land into a highly efficient plantation system geared for exports and they made sure that fresh *baguettes* could be found in every town and village from the Chi-

nese border to the Mekong Delta! The period can also be viewed as a period of national rape and pillage, a brutal century during which the French stripped Vietnam of much of its natural wealth, subjugated and often tortured its people and generally mocked and humiliated one of the greatest Southeast Asian civilizations.

On the more positive side, the French developed the foundation for modern infrastructure with the construction of highways, railroads, port facilities, telegraph networks, post offices and banks. They also introduced modern medicine, built schools and pushed the frontiers of agriculture far into the Mekong Delta. But, one should not forget that their intentions were not totally altruistic, much was done to facilitate French trade and industry, with scant regard for the physical and emotional well-being of the average Vietnamese citizen. French authorities continued to export rice even while the peasants were starving. They strove to restrict peasants from any sort of formal education, whilst at the same time making the *mandarins* and intelligentsia as "European" as possible so that they would never turn on their colonial masters. They levied exorbitant taxes, encouraged monopolies on basic consumer goods and forcibly resettled thousands of people to make way for French economic schemes.

Only the Imperial court at Hue and a few elite benefited from this inequitable system as the vast majority of Vietnamese were considered to be little more

At the Tomb of Khai Dinh, Hue.

than beasts of burden. This situation was ripe for rebellion, as despite their French education many Vietnamese intellectuals became harsh critics of the colonial regime. Many were thrown into prison, some were executed, others went underground or into exile abroad. Their requests were simple: they wanted enough food to keep their families alive, lower taxes and an end to the virtual slave labor of the plantation system.

There was a revolt in 1908 and then later in 1917, as native troops took advantage of the French involvement in World War I to stage a bloody mutiny in the Red River Valley. But, the French were simply too strong and the opposition too fragmented.

Ho Chi Minh

The Great Depression prompted the French to extort even more tax revenue and to exploit natural resources from Indochina to make up for economic shortfalls at home, which resulted in a further strain upon the peasants, many of whom died from malnutrition and disease during this period. Inspired by the success of the Bolshevik Revolution in Russia, a group of Hanoi-based intellectuals formed the first communist cell in March 1929. A year later, a unified Vietnamese Communist Party was unveiled at a meeting in Hong Kong – a meeting chaired by an eager young patriot called Nguyen Ai Quoc (born Nguyen Tat Thanh), who later changed his name to Ho Chi Minh.

During World War II, the Japanese promised liberation from colonial oppression when they invaded Southeast Asia in 1942, but the Vietnamese and other subjugated peoples soon discovered that it was no more than a ploy on the part of Tokyo to gain their own mastery over the region.

The Vichy French – who were allies of Nazi Germany were left in charge of Indochina. Unfortunately without the prying eyes of French humanitarians, the colonial regime in Vietnam became even more brutal and the peasants were forced to work that much harder to equip and feed the Japanese war machine.

The American victory in the Pacific brought a new ray of hope to Vietnam. Hot on the heels of the Japanese surrender, Ho Chi Minh and his forces proclaimed their country as the Democratic Republic of Vietnam and asked for US recognition. This was a crucial moment in the modern history of both Vietnam and America. If President Truman had acceded to Ho's request, Vietnam probably could have been cajoled into the capitalist camp.

But, as it was, Truman sided with France (more out of consideration over what was happening in post-war Europe than as a reflection on the future politics of Asia). Vietnam's fate was sealed and it was up to the Vietnamese to drive the invaders from their land again.

In 1946, guerilla warfare broke out

Anti-Foreign Insurrection Episodes

The Vietnamese people have a long tradition of insurrection against foreign intervention, revolts that were often staged on the back of ragtag peasant armies with little military training and grossly inferior weapons. More often than not, the Vietnamese have succeeded in driving invaders from their land.

Historical episodes reveal :
• The Trung Sisters – the first in a long line of Vietnamese women warriors – defeated the mighty troops of Han China in AD 40 using guerrilla tactics and many female commanders.
• Vietnamese forces whipped a superior Chinese fleet at the Battle of Bach Dang in AD 938, ending nearly a thousand years of Chinese rule in Vietnam.
• The Mongol hordes swept out of the plains of Central Asia in the early 13th century on their way to conquering China, Russia, Persia, the Ottoman Empire and half of Europe – the largest land empire in world history – yet they failed in three attempts to invade Indochina. In fact, the Vietnamese were one of only two nations to defeat the Mongols on the field of battle (the other was Egypt).
• Emperor Le Loi, one of the nation's greatest military commanders, expelled a Ming Chinese invasion in 1427 with a devastating victory in the Battle of Chi Lang Pass.
• Tay Son rebels under General Nguyen Hue ambushed and routed a Siamese invasion fleet at the Battle of Rach Gai in the Mekong Delta in 1785. Four years later, Nguyen Hue led a legendary lightning assault against superior Chinese forces in the Red River Delta, a campaign that reunified Vietnam.

as Viet Minh communist troops under General Vo Nguyen Giap staged their first commando attacks against French targets. The fighting would last for more than eight years as the Viet Minh secured training, arms and sanctuary from their comrades in China and as French forces began to rely more and more on Washington to underwrite "the struggle against communist aggression" in Indochina. In 1954, hostilities reached a climax at Dien Bien Phu (an isolated French outpost in the northern highlands) which came under siege.

The battle waged on for nearly two months before the French capitulated. A subsequent peace conference in Geneva divided Vietnam in half at the 17th parallel with a stipulation that free elections be held within two years to reunite the country. Communist forces were given control of the northern zone, while the French helped establish a "free" Vietnamese regime in the south. Meanwhile, the Nguyen Dynasty crumbled with the abdication of Bao Dai, (the last emperor of Vietnam) who fled to France.

American Intervention

Under Prime Minister Ngo Dinh Diem and his American backers, the South chose to disregard the Geneva accord. Diem nixed the elections and accused the communists of fermenting revolution in the South, once it became clear that the Geneva treaty was practically invalid. From a military perspective, Diem was able to hold his own against the communists until the early 1960s, when increasingly large numbers of American military "advisors" came into play. In fact for all intents and purposes,

US troops were involved in full-scale war as early as 1962. But it was only after another three years – after the Tonkin Gulf incident sparked an outcry in Washington – that vast American ground forces were dispatched to Indochina.

The first Marine units hit the beach at Danang in March 1965 and by the end of the year there were more than 200,000 US troops in Vietnam. From the very start it was tough going, fighting against guerrilla forces in difficult terrain, in a hostile tropical climate alongside South Vietnamese forces who seemed to have the skill and stomach for a fight.

The Americans soon resorted to mass weapons of destruction: carpet bombing in the North and along the Ho Chi Minh Trail and the use of napalm and chemical defoliants to destroy enemy hideouts in the South.

Cham culture depicted in the My Son ruins outside Danang.

The Tet Offensive

The Tet Offensive of 1968 was a turning point in the war for both sides. The communists launched their sneak attack in the belief that the ordinary people of South Vietnam would spontaneously arise and support them in one bold effort that would push the enemy into the sea. They were wrong as local support was lukewarm and, they also underestimated the fury of the Americans who decimated Viet Cong forces in the counter-offensive.

In military terms it represented an overwhelming victory for US forces. But the brutal nature of the fight demoralized the Americans and television reports depicting the bloody destruction turned the American public against the war effort. Washington wasted another five years and tens of thousands of lives trying to disentangle itself from the conflict.

The Americans pulled out in 1973 and Saigon fell on March 30th, 1975 to the communists. Vietnam was again free of foreign domination. It was united again, but at the price of almost total destruction.

The dominoes have started to fall, but in a different direction than Cold War pundits predicted in the 1950s and 1960s. Communism has crumbled in the Soviet Union and Eastern Europe. Marxism has collapsed in Ethiopia, Nicaragua and Cambodia. Socialism is on its way out in Laos, Angola and the Congo. The Socialist Republic of Vietnam remains among a dwindling club of die-hard communist states that include China, North Korea and Cuba.

Government

27

Ho Chi Minh, remembered by Diep Minh Chan in the capital city.

The Communist Party

The Communist Party is still part of everyday life in Vietnam. There are nearly two million cadres (over three percent of the population) and the party continues to dominate the government from the national level right down to villages and hamlets.

The party is still the primary purveyor of Vietnamese nationalism. It determines foreign

The flag tower near the Army
Museum in Hanoi.

trenched in the national constitution.

Party Policy

As in most communist systems, the most powerful political body is the Politburo, (a group of 14 well-connected individuals led by the party general secretary) which is largely responsible for determining domestic and foreign policy, as well as managing the country in times of crisis. Basically, the Politburo advises bureaucrats on the course of action to take. It can even issue its own policy statements and directives independent of formal government channels.

Members of the Politburo are elected by the party's Central Committee, which meets twice a year to approve decisions already made at a higher level. Theoretically, a chairman should rule over the Central Committee, but the position has been vacant since 1969 when Ho Chi Minh died. A Party Congress is now held once every four years to debate major policy changes like the *doi moi* (renovation) economic reforms that were introduced after 1986.

Party policy is carried out by the national administration; specifically the Council of State and the Council of Ministers. The former, comprising of 15 members is a collective presidency which acts as a public mouthpiece for the party. The latter is the executive branch or cabinet embracing the heads of various ministries and state commissions and is headed by the Prime Minister.

policy and controls the armed forces and there is no doubt that party membership has its value, not measured in terms of material benefits such as cars, flats and caviar but for more practical things like access to better health care and education.

Outsiders are often perplexed by the Vietnamese government, perhaps because there is no single symbol of authority, no obvious cult of the personality – at least not for living leaders – no local version of Fidel Castro or Kim Il-Sung. Rather, the country is run by the committee.

In simple terms, the various government departments enforce and manage various policies set by the Communist Party whose ultimate power is en-

Veterans celebrating Dien Bien Phu victory over the French.

Both councils are elected by the National Assembly – the Vietnamese equivalent of a parliament or congress – of roughly 500 deputies who meet twice a year. The deputies must stand for election every five years for each constituency which contains about 100,000 voters. They must be Communist Party members and the National Assembly rarely departs from party doctrine.

Winds of Change

However, the winds of change are blowing. A new constitution was passed in April 1992 which attempted to curb the power of the Communist Party while at the same time strengthening the role of the National Assembly and cabinet. Criteria necessary for freer elections and a solid legal base for free-market economic reforms like private enterprise and foreign investment were also set out.

However, the party retains control over the army and all land remains the property of the state.

Following the new constitution, 37 million Vietnamese voters went to the polls in August 1992 to chose new members of the National Assembly. The elections were hailed as "truly democratic" by the Communist Party leader Doi Muoi because it was the first time that independent candidates were allowed to run under the communist regime.

However, only ten percent of the

Ho Chi Minh

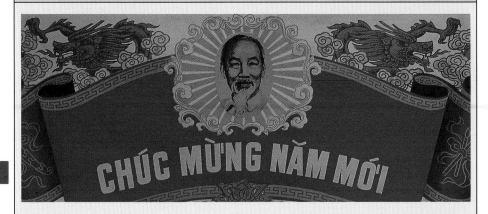

A temple reveres their leader.

History will show that Ho Chi Minh (1890-1969) was one of the few communist leaders of the 20th century who truly strived to improve the lot of the common man. A humble man, he was never completely comfortable when thrust into the spotlight as the father of his country. Contrary to the US governments' unfavourable view of Ho Chi Minh many of his deepest beliefs were inspired by the American Revolution.

Born Nguyen Tat Thanh, the son of a school teacher in Chua (a tiny hamlet in Nghe Tinh province, a region often called the "cradle of revolutionaries" because so many Vietnamese leaders were born there), his father infused him with a hatred of French colonial rule and of the local *mandarins* who conspired with their colonial masters. He left Vietnam aboard a French ocean liner – not as a passenger, but as a mess boy! His travels took him to America, England and then Paris, where he joined the French Socialist Party and began to work towards Vietnamese independence. It was during his time in France that young Ho came to admire American democracy.

However, despite an affection for Western ideals and pleas to support a liberation movement against colonial repression, Ho's pleas were rejected by the Americans who did not want to upset their long term allies, the French. Ho then took his plea to communist Russia where he found people who were more than eager to help establish a budding liberation movement. By 1930 he was back in Asia. He changed his name to Ho Chi Minh ("He Who Enlightens") and founded the Communist Party of Indochina at a meeting in Hong Kong. But he did not return to Vietnam until 1941 (under the escort of American government officials who wanted to use him as a bulwark against the growing Japanese power in Asia). Throughout the war, Ho and his Viet Minh guerrillas fought the Japanese with the aid of clandestine US supplies and ammunition. When the Japanese surrendered, he rushed to Hanoi and using words adopted from the American Declaration of Independence he declared Vietnam's liberty from France.

But Washington decided to back Paris and French troops flooded back into Indochina. Rejected by the West for the second time, Ho became the leader of a fierce guerrilla movement which had little choice but to accept aid from the Soviet Union and China. In doing so, he became a pawn of superpower politics and a central figure in the Cold War.

Ho Chi Minh finally achieved his goal of expelling the French in 1954. He died in the midst of a long and bloody struggle against the Saigon regime and their American allies six years before the reunification of Vietnam.

In the final analysis, one must view Vietnam not so much as a textbook communist state, but as a patchwork quilt of special interests that hardly varies from the old feudal system which prevailed in dynastic days.

Part of the fun of Vietnam is feeling your way through the labyrinth of statecraft.

Foreign businessmen, of whom there are growing numbers nowadays, often have to pick their way through government policies, usually interpreted or implemented differently, between provinces.

candidates were non-party members. Still, the poll produced some unexpected results: voters opted for younger, better educated, more professional politicians, especially doctors and teachers (people who were outside the traditional political system) who were running for the first time.

The big losers in the election were the heads of state factories and collectives, another sign that people were disenchanted with the old-style socialist system.

The party-government affiliation continues at a local level although individual provinces exercise a certain degree of autonomy when it comes to economic and development issues. Vietnam is divided into 40 provinces, three municipalities (Hanoi, Haiphong and Ho Chi Minh City) and one special economic zone (Vung Tau) which is ruled directly from Hanoi. Provinces are further divided into rural districts and communes, while the three big cities are split into urban districts and wards. Party officials control each of these units.

Elegance of the former Governor's Residence, Hanoi.

Economy

Vietnam is the ultimate oxymoron: a communist country with a capitalistic bent. That may seem like a contradiction in terms, but rigorous state control and unfettered free-market commerce are both facts of life in modern Vietnam.

Industry – the so-called "state enterprises" – are still very much under central government control. A constant lack of investment is one of the many causes of industry's starvation. On the other hand, there are millions of budding entrepreneurs at street level, people who run restaurants, shops, market stalls, corner stands and small hotels and the black market which thrives on goods smuggled in from Thailand, China and Hong Kong resulting in an escalation in major urban areas. In fact, it is a very safe bet to say that today the number of die-hard capitalists far outnumber the communists in Vietnam.

Harvesting rice, a great player in the domestic economy of Vietnam.

33

Birth of Small Enterprise

In 1986 there

Main ferry boat of labourers with its attendant "basket" boats in Hong Gai, a coal mining area.

was little in the way of private enterprise. But in 1992 enterprise is now regarded as a watermark in the Vietnamese economic cycle. Nearly everyone used to work for the state, which controlled all forms of industry, business and agriculture. But, chronic unemployment, savage inflation, rural famine and a massive drain on the treasury to support the war in Cambodia forced Vietnam to the brink of civil unrest. At the same time, high-ranking members of the government could clearly see that Vietnam was being "left in the dust" by the booming economies of Thailand, Malaysia, Singapore and Indonesia – that had opted for the capitalist route. With their backs against the wall coupled with fears that Vietnam would fall

even further behind its neighbors, the government decided to back away from its fierce adherence to Marxist-Leninist dogma. The Sixth Party Congress in December 1986 was the turning point, as Communist Party delegates passed sweeping *doi moi* (renovation) economic reforms. They chose to allow small-scale private enterprise, reduce the suffocating chokehold of state collectives on agriculture and open up the industrial and service sectors to foreign investment through deregulation, tax incentives and more relaxed investment laws.

The Economic Soul

Almost overnight, the economic soul of

Rattan chairs leaving a factory in Ho Chi Minh City.

the country sprung to life. Today, you can see it on the streets, in the thousands of small enterprises, the sudden feast of consumer goods, and in the country-side, where crop yields are again rising. Increasingly, a growing number of international firms have embarked on business ventures with Vietnam.

Investment funds are beginning to flood the country as foreigners pour money into a number of areas including oil and mineral exploration, the hotel industry and light manufacturing.

Even the Communist Party has jumped onto the business bandwagon with an announcement that it will create its own limited and joint-venture companies to fund the party budget.

Economic Reform

During the first five years of economic reform, the government approved more than 400 foreign investment projects worth US$3.4 billion.

In early 1992 the government has also approved the investment of more than US$700 million in new projects – almost double the amount pledged during the same period in the previous year. Taiwan has emerged as the single biggest investor with a US$742 million stake in 1992, followed by Hong Kong (US$529 million) and France (US$391 million).

Meanwhile, the country's financial sector has started to mature: Visa and

Tender loving care and lots of leaves for silkworms in a Muong village.

other international card companies have started to open offices and foreign banks are obtaining licenses. Seven state-owned firms went private in 1992 and became joint-stock companies selling their shares to private investors.

At least one of these companies has applied for permission to sell at least 55 percent of its stock to foreigners and many more may follow suit.

in exports and US$1.7 billion in imports. Main export products include crude oil, rice, coal, seafood, rubber, coffee and tea. The primary imports are processed petroleum products, chemicals, fertilizers, iron and steel.

Yet a full-scale boom has yet to materialize because the world's two largest investors – the US and Japan – adhered to most of the tenets of the embargo. For the same reason, Vietnam has been banned from receiving World Bank and Asian Development Bank loans in addition to IMF funds that could have helped develop a modern infrastructure. At the same time, the country is striving to rise above a number of self-generated problems of the past, including bureaucratic red tape and ambiguous legal protection for foreign investment and a work force which still requires technical training.

Another problem that Vietnam must deal with is the disparity between North and South. According to a modern Vietnamese proverb, "the tail (Saigon) wags the dog (Hanoi)". People in the North have lived in the midst of austere communist economics for nearly 40 years; they have little experience in the ways of the free–market world, their basic infrastructure has never recovered from the war and many public officials have yet to adjust to necessary reforms.

The South is a dramatic contrast. People still remember the "good old days" of the American occupation when you could sell anything to just about anyone. The entrepreneurial spirit sur-

Trade

Trade is still relatively modest, but heading in the right direction. Vietnam posted an estimated trade surplus of US$400 million in 1992, based on US$2.1 billion

Panning for gold in Lai Chau Province.

vives and thrives in places like Danang, Nha Trang and Cholon. The Americans endowed the South with the finest infrastructure in Southeast Asia and many of their airports, roads and bridges still survive. Foreign businessmen also seem more attracted to the bright lights of Saigon city, than the languid, somewhat dowdy façade of Hanoi and Haiphong.

Industry & Minerals

State subsidies dropped in 1986, which meant that the government factories should theoretically have been exposed to the same free-market forces as everybody else. If that had actually been the case, they would all have gone under. As it is, though still supported by the state, most of these factories, now virtually bankrupt, will start to survive and improve after the lifting of the American embargo, when sufficient foreign investment can work towards retooling and reorganizing them.

But, while industry is perhaps the most chronically ill of all economic sectors, it has one of the best chances for rapid resuscitation in future. Some of the biggest names in the capitalist world have staked claims in Vietnam. The Japanese giant, Sumitomo has invested in a huge plastics factory while further investments pour in from Taiwan, Singapore and Malaysia. Coca Cola's entry came by way of a Singapore partner;

Bark-binding in Hanoi.

AT&T has used the partial relaxation of the embargo to help jump-start the telecommunications industry; Heineken® beer, Daewoo® trucks and buses and Rothmans® and British-American cigarettes will all be locally manufactured.

Vietnam is thought to possess a bounty of mineral resources. Coal has been a major commodity for many years. The largest mines are in the north, especially at Hon Gai in Quang Ninh province near the Chinese border and in Nghe Tinh province below the Red River Delta. Most of the nation's power plants run on coal, which is both a cheap source of energy and a rich source of pollutants. No one is quite sure how much natural gas and oil lies beneath the South China Sea because offshore deposits are only now being exploited. But Vietnam's reserves are thought to be enormous. European and Asian oil companies have stumbled over one another in a mad dash to ink exploration contracts, while the American giants are coming into the play post–embargo. The old French customs port at Vung Tau has transformed itself into Vietnam's oil exploration center. In 1992, Vietnam exported roughly five million tons of crude oil. But, the country badly needs more refinery capacity if liquid energy resources are to be exploited to their full potential.

Australian mining experts have recently found large deposits of precious metals in the Northwest Highlands including bauxite, copper, gold and rare earths, plus new reserves of oil, coal and natural gas. The government wants to renovate the old French railway line through the Red River Gorge in order to take advantage of these deposits, but a severe lack of funds has hampered any moves in this direction.

Agriculture & Fishing

Agriculture remains the nation's largest employer – over 80 percent of the work force – a situation that will continue well into the 21st century. The largest crop is rice which is grown for both domestic consumption and trade. Vietnam is now the world's third-largest rice exporter. Other major crops include bananas, cassava (manioc), citrus, coconuts, coffee, maize, mangoes, melons, pineapples, rubber, sugar cane, sweet potatoes, tea, tobacco and assorted vegetables.

The fertile Mekong Delta is considered the "rice bowl" of Vietnam with many of its farms producing two or three crops per year. Hau Giang province is the single largest producer with an annual yield of more than 1.5 million tons.

Most of the peasants are benefitting from the free market agricultural reforms. Introduced in 1988, they have led to an immediate jump in production. Today, farmers are allowed to grow what they want and sell their produce and livestock to whoever they wish (be it state collectives or private commodity traders). Land remains the property of the state, but each family is "leased" a certain amount according to their needs. In order to prevent accumulation by large landowners, farmers are not allowed to sell or trade their leases, although officials admit that illegal land transfers do take place.

Farmers pay a land tax in rice that amounts to about ten percent of their annual yield. This tax revenue is split between the national and provincial governments, with some of the money going to support families who farm s w a m p or jungle land.

Fishing in An Giang Province, Chau Doc.

Nowadays old collective farming practices function as agricultural supply markets, selling seed, fertilizer, pesticides, machinery and advice. Old–style communist cooperatives have remained entrenched in the North for the past 40 years. The fishing industry is also in a period of transition. Thirty years ago, the Mekong Delta was a rich fishing ground. But, pollutants from the widespread use of chemical defoliants during the war coupled with the destruction of mangrove swamps and the increased use of chemical fertilizers in recent years, has severely depleted the freshwater fish population. Attention is now being focused on the rich deep-water fishing grounds of the South China Sea and on developing a thriving fishing industry

in most ports along the coast. Phan Thiet has become a center for fish sauce production, while Ho Chi Minh City has developed a small but thriving industry engaged in the exportation of frozen shrimp and other seafood.

Tourism

Given the innate natural beauty and charm of Vietnam, tourism will be one of the great industries of the future. But, for the time being, growth takes time. Less than 100,000 foreign visitors (excluding Vietnamese migrants) visit the country each year, a pittance compared to those visiting nearby Thailand, Hong Kong and Malaysia, which attract more than five million visitors annually.

The government has made it increasingly easy for tourists to visit Vietnam, with a slick visa operation at overseas missions and the relaxation of the restrictions that previously limited visitors to package tours. A growing net-

Vital Statistics

Population	70 million
Population Growth	2.2% pa
GNP	US$200/person
GNP Growth	3% pa
Foreign Debt	US$14 billion
Inflation	approx 100%
Exports	US$2.1 billion
Imports	US$1.7 billion
Trade surplus	US$400 million

Figures are 1992 estimates.
*Source: **Asiaweek, Associated Press** & **World Bank**.*

The Life of Van – A Rice Paddy Peasant

Planting time is no time to grumble about wet feet.

when we worked in the big cooperative. Now under the new system we work for ourselves. This makes things better... Our village has a number of television sets. That's the main form of entertainment. We don't sing or dance – except during wedding ceremonies, or during the village festival each March. The festival takes place after Tet to honor the village god. The most exciting thing that has happened to me in my lifetime was my wedding day."

Van is the 39 year-old wife of a rice farmer. The mother of six children, she lives in a tiny hamlet called Truong Yen in Ha Nam Ninh province on the southern fringe of the Red River Valley. Van describes her life as a rice paddy peasant:

"I work seven days a week, from when the sun comes up in the morning to when the last job is done at night. Most of our time is for working. There isn't much time for entertainment or talk. When I do talk to my friends, we talk about work and harvesting. Whether the harvest is good or not. If there are shortages...

We have two main rice crops each year – winter and spring. We also grow some vegetables for our own use. But we don't have any farm animals. To buy a young pig costs 100,000 dong. But the pig can die and then your investment is gone... In the old times, we worked together in the cooperative. But now each family has its own rice fields. The size depends on how many people are in the family. Each family supervises its own work, like preparing seeds, ploughing, planting, organizing insecticides, then harvesting the rice from the starting point to the end...In recent years life has been getting a little better. There were hard times

Typical rural landscape.

work of international air connections also helps to facilitate the once cumbersome wheels of tourism. But, what Vietnam is trying to build is a solid infrastructure. Hanoi and Ho Chi Minh City suffer from a chronic shortage of hotel rooms and most provincial centers offer nothing more than rudimentary guest house accommodation. There are also no true international beach resorts. Domestic transportation is sometimes slow and crude, ranging from belching country buses to the derelict Soviet-built planes flown by the national airline. Funds are still sadly needed to refurbish museums, rebuild ancient monuments and establish new tourist attractions. Soon Vietnam's vast adventure travel potential, from scuba diving and white-water rafting, to treks down the Ho Chi Minh Trail will start to be tapped by investors.

The lifting of the American embargo, will undoubtedly pour millions of foreign investment dollars into the development of Vietnam's tourist industry.

A potter tends his products by the Red River.

FRENCH DISHES

REX SHOP

MUA & BA'N
SELLING & PURCHASING
CÁC MẶT HÀNG
ALL KIND OF SPECIAL
THỰC PHẨM
FOODSTUFF
ĐẶC BIỆT.

● NHẬN GIỮ XE
CHO QUÝ KHÁCH.
VEHICLE KEEPING

Bilingual signs sums up the business.

One of the world's longest, thinnest countries, Vietnam stretches more than 1,650 kilometers (1,000 miles) from north to south, but is just 50 kilometers (31 miles) at its slimmest point, a narrow isthmus of land on either side of the former demilitarized zone.

Roughly S-shaped, Vietnam is bounded by China to the north, Laos and Cambodia to the west, the South China Sea to the east and the Gulf of Thailand to the south. Her total land area is 331,689 square kilometers (128,401 square miles), about the same size as Norway or New Mexico. Three great geographical features dominate the country: the Red River Delta in the north, the Mekong Delta in the south and the Central Highlands in–between.

Rivers deep, mountains high at Son La, North Vietnam.

Geography & Climate

45

Red River Delta

The Red River Delta is the cradle of Viet-nam-ese civilization, a

Danta Jn Falls, Dalat.

square kilometers (5,700 square miles).

The Mekong Delta

At the opposite end of the nation is the famous Mekong Delta, the "rice bowl" of Vietnam and terminus of one of the world's greatest rivers. The Mekong begins its journey in the Tibetan Highlands and flows 4,200 kilometers (2,600 miles) before disgorging itself into the South China Sea. It is much longer and wider than its cousin to the north and breaks into nine distinct branches in the delta, collectively known as the Nine Dragons (Cuu Long). The two largest branches are the Tien Giang and the Hua Giang, both of which are muddy and slow-moving tropical rivers – not unlike the Amazon or Congo at first glance. The Mekong Delta is nearly three times the size of the Red River Delta with a land stretch of more than 15,000 square miles (40,000 square kilometers).

Despite its veneer of cultivation, the Mekong Delta continues to embrace some of the great wilderness areas of Vietnam including the swampy Ca Mau region, the dense U Minh forest and marshy areas like the Plain of Reeds along the Cambodian frontier. The mangrove swamps and jungle wilds managed to keep civilization at bay for countless centuries and proved to be perfect hideouts for Viet Cong forces during their long struggle against the French and Americans. Contrary to popular belief Ho Chi Minh City (Sai-

massive V-shaped plain that continues to spread its muddy tentacles into Ha Long Bay and the Gulf of Tonkin. The Red River (Song Hong in Vietnamese) starts in the isolated highlands of southern China, running roughly 1,159 kilometers (1,900 miles) before pouring into the sea beyond Nam Dinh. Along the way the river and its tributaries pick up billions of tons of sediment which they deposit in the delta, making the valley one of the most fertile regions of Asia. In former times the rivers flowed as they pleased, often spilling over into croplands.

Today, the Red River region is a patchwork quilt of canals, dykes, irrigation ditches and flooded paddy fields which spread across more than 15,000

The lazy hazy coast of Hon Com Peninsula.

gon), does not lie on the banks of the Mekong, but on the Saigon River, which feeds into the northern part of the delta.

The Central Highlands

The Central Highlands are actually part of a huge mountain range, an outrider of the Himalayas that runs down through the heart of Indochina, comprising about 75 percent of Vietnam's land area. The French named these mountains the Chaine Annamitique, but the Vietnamese name is the Truong Son Mountains. In the far north, the chain fans into steep parallel ridges that connect with the twisted knot of mountains in southern China, a region some-times called the Northern Highlands or the Northwest Frontier.

Vietnam's highest peak is Phan Si Pan, 3,143 meters (10,311 feet) high, which straddles the Chinese frontier. The highest summit in the south is Ngok Linh 2,598 meters (8,624 feet) which occurs in Gia Lai Kontum province. The Central Highlands are actually an elaborate network of basins and ranges which spill to the very edge of the sea. Among the lofty tablelands are the Pleiku, Kontum, Darlac and Mnong plateaus.

The Coast

Although it is not a geographical region as such, the coast forms a distinct part of

Tranquil geo-scenery at Hoa Lu.

Vietnam. It stretches for about 3,000 kilometers (1,800 miles) between the Gulf of Tonkin and the Gulf of Siam, encompassing some of the finest harbors and most stunning scenery in the whole of Asia. The coastal plain (excluding the deltas) is very narrow in most places, yet it supports a hefty population of fisherfolk and rice farmers, in addition to major cities like Hue, Danang, Nha Trang, Vinh and Quy Nhon. There are also quiet ample coastal valleys carved by meandering rivers like the Song Ca in Nghe Tinh province and the Ha Giao in Nghia Binh province.

Ha Long Bay, just east of Haiphong, is a classic *karst* landscape of sheer limestone cliffs and islands that seem to rise straight from the sea. Many people consider it the most beautiful spot in Vietnam. But, the coast also has its fair share of beautiful beaches, many of them still empty and very undeveloped.

Probably the most famous strand is China Beach in Danang, a popular wartime R&R (rest and recuperation) resort for American GIs and later the focus of a popular American television series. But, there are many other beach resorts including Sam Son, the sandy Cua Lo peninsula, Quy Nhon, Nha Trang, the old French customs port of Vung Tau (Cap St Jacques) and Rach Gia on the Gulf of Thailand. In total Vietnam claims more than a million square kilometers of coastal waters with hundreds of islands ranging in size from sand bars and reefs to huge chunks of land like Phu Quoc in the Gulf of Thailand. Many of the offshore possessions have strange names left over from colonial days such as the Pirate Islands, Royal Bishop Bank, Ile Chateau Renaud and the Norway Islands. The most famous is Con Son, called Poulo Condor in colonial days when it was a notorious French prison. Vietnam also lays claim to two distant archipelagoes in the South China Sea – the Paracel and Spratly Islands – where large oil and gas deposits are known to lie. The Spratlys in particular have become a source of regional tension, as they are also claimed by China, Malaysia, the Philippines, Brunei and Indonesia. Both Vietnam and China have a semi-permanent military presence in the Spratlys and Malaysia has staked its claim with the development of the first tourist resort in this chain of islands.

Weather Worries

Lying between 8° and 23°N latitude with a great range of altitude, the Mekong Delta and most of the south are distinctly tropical.

The north is more subtropical, with distinct seasons and a greater range of temperatures. Highland areas are predictably unpredictable: they can be cool and misty or clear and hot!

Visit Ho Chi Minh City (Saigon) between November and January, during the early part of the dry monsoon, when there are usually clear skies and

Coastal scenery of Halong.

reasonable temperatures with daytime highs of between 29-32°C (85-90°F). The southern "spring" between March and May can be extremely hot, with temperatures reaching above 38°C (100°F) daily. Heavy rains normally arrive in June (the rainy season) usually lasting until October. Even during the dry season, humidity is high.

Hanoi is cold, gray and depressing in winter, when the temperature can dip as low as 6°C (42°F). Summers in the north reach the other extreme, with oppressive heat and humidity which is often even higher than in the south. During spring or fall, you can expect blue skies, minimal rain and moderate temperatures with daytime highs ranging from 21-29°C (70-85°F).

Vietnam's environment has taken a severe beating over the last 50 years as three successive wars pounded the plants and animals with even more ferocity than was unleashed on the cities. Carpet bombing, napalm, chemical defoliants, mines and military bulldozers unleashed an almost systematic destruction that scarred the landscape from north to south.

Unfortunately, post-war policies have only added to Mother Nature's agony. In the rush to rebuild, the Vietnamese may have destroyed much of what was left of the tropical rainforest; polluted many of the rivers, marshes and estuaries with chemical fertilizers and pesticides; pushed the frontier of agriculture further and further into wilderness areas and depleted rare animal populations in a quest for food, folk medicines and general development.

Blossoms that bring colour and cheer to Vietnamese life.

Flora and Fauna

Natural Depletion

The catalogue of flora and fauna in Vietnam is a shadow of what it was prior to World War II. But then again, the same could be

Birding in Vietnam

After years of international isolation Vietnam is now opening its doors to the outside world. Fortunately this also includes the world of ornithology, or the study of birds. Since 1988, joint scientific expeditions have been regulary organised with both local and overseas participants surveying the country's best birding locations. In 1991 the first commercial bird tour for foreign birdwatchers was arranged to be followed by many more.

The bird fauna in Vietnam is unusually varied. Vietnam is part of the Oriental zoogeographical region and many birds are shared with Southeast Asia, the Indian subcontinent and South China. However, Vietnam is a large nation with a great diversity of habitats ranging from north to south. There are five subregions within the country, each containing a different composition of bird species. Of the over 600 species of birds that occur, nine are local endemics that cannot be found anywhere else in the world. These nine and 33 others are very rare and are regarded as threatened by extinction. When an expedition held from April to July 1988 visited forest locations in Vietnam they recorded no less than 326 different species of birds – a number which successfully shows Vietnam's great potential in the field of nature tourism.

While birding you will be able to see many different woodpeckers, flycatchers, cuckoo-shrikes, leafbirds, bulbuls, babblers and sunbirds. These are typical Oriental bird families well represented in this part of the world. A few bird species have Palearctic affinities, like the Blackbird, Wryneck, House Martin and European Nuthatch. Any birder from Europe will be able to recognize these species as they are not typical Oriental birds and do not occur any further south in tropical Southeast Asia.

top: Chinese Pond Heron; middle left: Streaked Spiderhunter; middle right: Green-winged Pigeon; bottom: Pied Hornbill.

In the last few years the pheasants of Vietnam have been the focus of special interest and study. This family of beautiful forest birds has its centre of distribution in the Indochinese area and several of its species do not occur anywhere else in the world. The largest population of Crested Argus can be found in Vietnam, although rarely seen in its remote forested hills habitat (its booming call makes it relatively easy to survey); The Green Peafowl (known as the Peacock) and the Siamese Fireback are still relatively numerous. Other species are in decline and are facing possible extinction – the Vietnamese Pheasant was only discovered in 1964, (rarely recorded and the female has never been seen!) The Imperial Pheasant and Edward's Pheasant are also extremely rare and are listed as endangered species.

Surprisingly some birds adapt to human disturbance, benefitted from forest clearances and thrive near human settlements. In Vietnam, Oriental region birds like the Spotted Dove, Red-whiskered Bulbul, Magpie Robin, White-rumped Munia, Long-tailed Shrike, Cinnamon Bittern and Chinese Pond Heron can be seen all over the country.

In Vietnam ecotourism is still at an early stage of development but, there are still a number of national parks and other locations well worth a visit. Just north of Hanoi, Tam Doa is a former hill station now being developed into a 19,000 hectare national park. At an elevation of 900meters there is a lot of forest cover and birds like the Bar-backed Partridge, Grey Peacock-Pheasant, Pin-tailed Pigeon, Ratchet-tailed Treepie, several barbets, broadbills and babblers can be spotted. South of Hanoi, Cuc Phuong is Vietnam's first national park which is also well known for its birds. This 25,000 hectare park is mostly covered in lowland forest of 200 to 600 meters elevation. Look out for hornbills especially the Pied Hornbill (which is the most common) the Red-headed Trogon, Blue-rumped Pitta, Black-backed Kingfisher, White-winged Magpie, Rufous-throated Fulvetta, woodpeckers and other forest birds.

In Central Vietnam forest birds such as the Blyth's Kingfisher, Short-tailed Scimitar-Babbler, Bar-bellied Pitta, Red-vented Barbet, White-crowned Forktail and many other unusual birds have been found at Ky Anh and Cat Bin in South Nghe Tinh province. Further south the A Sau A Luoi area and the Buon Luoi area within the Kon Ha Nung Union Forestry Project in central Annan have been surveyed and many good forest birds found. Recently the Bach Ma National Park has also revealed interesting records of species spotted including the Silver Pheasant and Coral-billed Ground-Cuckoo.

In southern Vietnam, locations near Da Lat have been surveyed revealing many birds found along the Da Dung River and by the dam at Ho Tuyen Lam, including large numbers of the rare Pale-capped Pigeon. The Pale-footed Bush-Warbler, endemic Black-hooded Laughing Thrush and many other species have been found on the Da Lat and Di Linh Plateaus.

The Nam Bai Cat Tien National Park in Dong Nai province to the southwest of Da Lat is a forest habitat which is also famous for its populations of waterbirds including the Painted Stork, Wooly-necked Stork, White-shouldered Ibis and White-winged Duck.

Vietnam has been literally tormented by its many years of war followed by periods of severe underdevelopment. Rich forests were badly damaged by warfare through the deliberate spraying of herbicide and constant bombing which adversely affected the wildlife. Since then, a high population growth and agricultural development such as timber-production and the collection of firewood rapidly depleted the natural landscape. With a new era of better planning and guidance together with improved international coorperation, there is hope for the natural ecology and wildlife of Vietnam.

For more information on the birds of Vietnam and birdwatching opportunites, contact the Institute of Ecology and Biological Resource, NCSR, Hanoi, Vietnam. Dr Nguyen Cu, Professor Vo Quy and Truong Van La are some of the prominent ornithologists who can be of help. In England the Oriental Bird Club at The Lodge, Sandy, Bedfordshire, SG19 2DL, UK and the International Council for Bird Preservation at 32 Cambridge Road, Girton, Cambridge, CB3 0PJ, U.K. have experts on Vietnamese birding conditions. Field guides include *A Field Guide to the Birds of South-East Asia*, Ben Kemp et al, Collins, 1975 and *Birds of South Vietnam*, Philip Wildash, Charles E Tuttle, 1968.

~ *Morten Strange*

Water buffalos, faithful citizens of rural Vietnam.

said for most Asian nations. Among the 270 types of mammals found in Vietnam are extremely rare species like the Bengal tiger, Asian elephant, Sumatran rhino, Malay tapir, the douc langur monkey and a tree-dwelling primate called the gibbon. A giant forest ox called the kouprey was thought to be extinct until it was recently rediscovered in small numbers in secluded parts of the Central Highlands. However, you should not expect to see any of these animals on your next visit to Vietnam – unless you are willing to trek into remote areas, build a camouflaged hide and wait for weeks with your telephoto lens pointed at a salt lick.

Vietnam is equally rich in avian species, including the golden pheasant, cranes and several varieties of hornbill. Crocodiles and pythons survive in the U Minh Forest at the southern tip of the Indochina peninsula.

Natural Survival

Nature also survives in isolated pockets like the isolated Vu Quang Nature Reserve, where a Worldwide Fund for Nature expedition conducted in 1992 discovered some previously unknown species of birds, reptiles, fish and mammals. The expedition leader called Vu Quang a "lost world that modern science had never before looked at . . . like opening the door into a lost and neglected place". Their most surprising

Inspirational lotuses grow even from the muddiest waters.

find was a dagger-horned forest goat – one of the few new mammals recorded in the 20th century. Another recent find is Tram Chim in the Mekong Delta, where a remnant population of about a thousand rare Eastern Sarus cranes was discovered in 1986 – the first time in recent years that these birds have been found outside their Cambodian breeding grounds. A 9,000 hectare reserve has been established to protect them.

Woodland Cover

Today, only about a-fifth of Vietnam is covered in woodland –less than half of what it was in 1941. Under the banner of the National Conservation Strategy efforts are underway to promote ecology and replant as much of the forest and mangrove as possible. Unfortunately this herculean task is made even harder by the scarcity of resources and cash in post-war Vietnam.

This reforestation project strives towards several goals: the elimination of flooding and erosion on bare slopes; the cultivation of commercial trees for housing, furniture, medicine, fuel and other uses and a preservation of biodiversity.

The government is working towards a fifty percent forest cover. They are replanting about 1,600 square kilometers annually about 25 million trees which still falls short of the amount of forest being lost to cultivation, wildfire and logging operations.

National Parks & Wildlife

A less nervous deer.

Vietnam has a bounty of flora and fauna, but most of the wilderness areas are way off the beaten track and thus, beyond easy access and the imagination of the ordinary tourist. However, some areas are quite easy to reach.

Cat Ba National Park lies on an island of the same name in picturesque Ha Long Bay, about 23 kilometers east of Haiphong. The island is covered in thick subtropical vegetation and is largely composed of geological formations called *karst* (porous limestone hills) with sheer cliffs and extensive cave systems. Cat Ba offers a diverse range of ecosystems including beaches, mangrove, coral reefs and freshwater marshes.

in a single day's journey from Hanoi, although the last part of the road is extremely rough. The park comprises 22,000 square kilometers (8,500 square miles) of virgin forest including 1000-year-old trees that reach a height of 50 meters (150 feet).

The heart of Cuc Phuong is a heavily wooded valley – "The Yosemite of Vietnam" – that lies between steep limestone bluffs. Among the sites of the valley is the **Ancient People Cave** where the remains of prehistoric man have been discovered, dating back to c.8,000 BC. **May Bac** (Cloud View) offers an excellent panorama for those willing to hoof it all the way to the top and there is a modest guest house at the top end of the valley where visitors can stay overnight.

Local wildlife includes: tigers, spotted deer, squirrels and yellow macaque monkeys in addition to numerous species of birdlife.

About 2,000 Muong hilltribe people live inside the park boundaries in villages which are open to visitors. If you are lucky they might even consent to a blow-pipe demonstration.

The **U Minh Forest** is not protected within the boundaries of a national park, yet it remains an important refuge for flora and fauna. U Minh is not so much a traditional forest as it is a huge mangrove swamp (said to be the largest in the world outside the Amazon Basin).

You can arrange for a boat tour of the swamps from Cau Mau (which lies at the southern terminus of Highway Four).

The main attraction here is the mangrove, composed mainly of *nipah* palms, *melaleuca* and *cajeput* trees. If you are lucky – and have a good pair of binoculars – you might be able to spot crocodiles, snakes and monkeys. People visiting this area will be susceptible to malaria, so please take the necessary precautions.

Kon Ka King and **Kon Cha National Parks** are both situated in Binh Dinh province, offering a similar mix of *karst* scenery and thick tropical forest.

The only wilderness area in the Central Highlands that is readily accessible to tourists is **Cat Tien National Park** near Dalat, the home of several species of rare pine trees in addition to a smattering of cranes and rhinoceroses.

Among the wildlife in residence are: gibbons, spotted wildcats, deer, porcupines, wild pigs and about a hundred different bird species. There are also more than 600 different types of plants. Cat Ba Island can be reached via a regular ferry service from Haiphong.

Cuc Phuong National Park straddles the frontier between Ha Son Binh, Ha Nam Ninh and Thanh Hoa provinces beyond the southern fringe of the Red River Valley. It can be reached

From a distance it would seem that Vietnam is a fairly homogenous nation. But, like most of the countries of Southeast Asia, it is a great melting pot of people from around the Asia-Pacific region – the result of centuries of conquest and migration.

The lowlands and urban areas are dominated by a single group, the Viet or Kinh people who the French called Annamites. They comprise nearly 90 percent of the entire population. The countryside (especially the highland areas), plays host to a dramatic array of ethnic minorities (who to a large extent) have preserved their indigenous cultures. There are dozens of hilltribes – whom the French called *montagnards* (highlanders), while the Viets used the term *moi* (a derogatory term that means savages) – plus remnants of ancient civilizations like the Cham and the Khmer. Despite a dramatic decline in

Pearl of Vietnam – in her ao dai and tortoise shell fan.

Young girls from the coastal town of Vung Tau.

numbers (through post–war emigration) the largest minority group living in the cities is the ethnic Chinese. Overall there are 53 minority groups totalling under six million people.

Origins & Beginnings

Despite elaborate legends regarding their origins – and the modern Vietnamese animosity towards almost everything Chinese – the Viet people are actually thought to have come from Southern China. They were Stone Age migrants who first resided in limestone caves along the edge of the Red River Valley. They interbred with the Malayo-Polynesian tribes (who had occupied the valley ear-

lier) and Thai groups from the mountains, to create the Viet ethnic hybrid that we know today. Today, the Viet share many ancient religious and cultural traits with their cousins across the border in China's Guangdong province. Until the advent of French colonial rule, the Vietnamese wrote their language by employing Chinese characters and even now the Vietnamese language remains closely allied to Cantonese! In fact, Han Dynasty scholars in China used the term *Bach Viet* as a generic term for the various "barbarian" tribes living south of the Yangtze River. The southernmost of these tribes was the Lac Viet, from whom the modern Viet people are said to be descended.

By AD 1, the Viet were in firm con-

The faithful and the studious at QuanSo Pagoda, Hanoi.

trol of the Red River Valley and started to extend their influence both westwards and southwards in a slow cultural invasion that would eventually extend into the Mekong Delta. One of the first people they encountered were the Cham, a sophisticated Malayo-Polynesian group with close links to the Khmer culture. By the end of the 16th century, the Viets had overrun and largely destroyed the Cham civilization and by the 18th century, they had begun to settle on the fringes of the Khmer kingdom along the Mekong and Saigon Rivers.

Post–War Diaspora

The latest wave of Viet migration was overseas, a post-war diaspora that took millions of refugees to almost every corner of the globe. The largest *Viet Kieu* (overseas Vietnamese) communities are in Paris, Hong Kong, the San Francisco bay area and Orange County in Southern California, but you can find enclaves in places as diverse as Sydney, Montreal, New York and Berlin.

Although young *Viet Kieu* are gaining a reputation for bloody gang violence (mostly against their own people) many refugees have made a good life for themselves overseas as restaurateurs and shop owners. Their children are privy to educational opportunities that would never have been possible at home – in California especially, Vietnamese children are mostly at the top of their classes and attend the best universities in the USA.

Minority Matters

From a geographical point of view, Vietnam's minority groups can be divided into three areas: the Northwest Highlands, the Central Highlands and pockets along the southern coastal plain.

The Northwest Highlands are one of the most fascinating ethnographic regions in Asia, a patchwork quilt of various tribes who largely remain beyond the realm of 20th century life.

Many of the hilltribes are related to similar clans in Laos, Northern Thailand and Southern China. Despite the establishment of firm frontiers in modern times, the hilltribe people have managed to preserve some of their cross-border trade and exchange. Although there is no free-flowing commerce as in bygone days, the mountain people of this region have not lost touch with their cultural roots.

Thai (Zao)

The largest single group is the Thai (or Zao) with about 200,000 people divided into several distinct clans, the most prominent being the Black Thai and the White Thai.

As the name suggests, they are related to the major ethnic group of modern Thailand, although the cultural link is somewhat frayed after nearly two centuries of isolation from Bangkok.

Thais dominate the upland valleys and plateaus of Lai Chau, Son La and Thanh Hoa provinces. They are mostly rice farmers, with neat thatched-roof villages and a complex irrigation system used to water both fields and homes.

Thai women in colorful silk blouses with silver butterfly buttons are a common sight at markets throughout the Northwest Highlands; some of the men still wear black pajamas and French-style berets, but today most of them opt for military cast–offs or jeans.

Black Thai strongholds include the broad Dien Bien Phu Valley and the fertile plains on either side of Son La town; White Thais are the chief ethnic group in the beautiful Mai Chau district

Black Thai boys.

A Meo girl.

and the steep valleys that lead out from Lai Chau town.

Hmong (Meo)

Another major group in the northwest are the Hmong (or Meo) people, who speak a Sino-Tibetan language related to the Chinese dialect of Mandarin. Like the Thai, they are divided into sub-groups according to the predominant color or design of the womens' skirts. Among the clans are the Black, White, Red, Green, Flower and Motley Hmong – although the distinction in dress is gradually disappearing as the Hmong increasingly come into contact with Western-style culture and clothing.

The Hmong are among the most underprivileged people in Vietnam. Many are illiterate and infant mortality and health care remain pressing problems. They make a living off the marginal land on steep mountain slopes by growing dry rice, maize and vegetables in addition to raising pigs, chickens and horses. One of their "specialty" crops is opium, although their production is minuscule compared to the big–time drug production that goes on in Thailand and Burma. The Hmong are a very shy people and tend to avoid contact with outsiders. There are pockets of Hmong in the mountains between Dien Bien Phu and Lai Chau and on the isolated Sin Chai Plateau along the western banks of the Black River.

Hmong tribe in the Laichan Province.

Muong

Yet another prominent northern minority are the Muong, who live in the mountains and foothills of Ha Son Binh, Thanh Hoa and Ha Nam Ninh provinces. For the most part, the Muong have been integrated into the mainstream of society and there is little to distinguish them from the Viet people. However, in deep forest places like the Cuc Phuong National Park, the Muong still live in their traditional way, residing in wooden longhouses and hunting with blowpipes. Other ethnic groups in the north include the Giay, Nung and Tay tribes.

The Central Highlands play host to a wide variety of other hilltribes, al-
though most of them fall within the Malayo-Polynesian and Mon-Khmer linguistic groups. They were once prevalent in towns like Dalat, Pleiku and Ban Me Thuot, but they are now confined to isolated rural areas, many of them strictly off-limits to tourists for security reasons.

Perhaps the full story of the Central Highland *montagnards* (highlanders) will never be known, but initial reports seem to indicate that their numbers have steeply declined since the end of the Vietnam War. As they were ardent supporters of the American war effort in Vietnam they suffered post–war penalties after liberation. Several tribes survive in the high plateau country between Dalat and Ban Me Thuot includ-

War Orphans

The Vietnam War gave birth to a pair of artificial "ethnic groups" both of whom have struggled in the post-war era – the millions of *bo dai* (discharged soldiers) and thousands of Amerasian children, the progeny of American GIs and Vietnamese mothers.

Although almost every male above the age of thirty is a veteran of some sort, some did manage to find jobs and work their way back into the fabric of society after the American War and the Vietnamese withdrawal from Cambodia in 1989. But millions – especially the unskilled infantrymen – remain unemployed and on the margins of society. Thousands more are disabled or confined to wheelchairs and hospital beds.

Ameriasians, the new breed left behind after the Vietnam War.

Many of the most debilitated veterans live in "invalid camps" where they make transistor radios, garments and other goods which are then sold in local markets to support the camps. Yet, the government refuses to take responsibility for the vast majority of *bo dai*. In all honesty, it is a task that is way beyond the financial and social welfare resources of most third world countries. But, as a result, many of them have been forced into begging or a life of crime in order to survive. Most of the bandits who roam highland and jungle areas are ex-soldiers who fled into the hills after liberation. Armed with automatic weapons they created a *bo dai* problem which will continue to plague Vietnamese society for decades to come.

On the other hand the Amerasian issue, has largely resolved itself. As late as 1988, thousands of half–caste teenagers roamed the streets of Saigon, Danang and Hue begging in front of the tourist hotels, working at menial jobs and even sinking into prostitution. They found themselves at odds with both the government and the ordinary Vietnamese citizens who saw them as embarrassing reminders of traumatic war years.

Yet thousands of Amerasians have been able to migrate to the West thanks to a unique United Nations project called the Orderly Departure Program (ODP), in which it has become necessary for Amerasian children to identify or reveal their GI fathers in order to qualify for the program. All it takes is a face-to-face interview with an ODP official who determines whether or not the applicant has Caucasian or Negroid features. They spend six months at a special camp in the Philippines – learning everything from how to speak English to Western table manners – before boarding a plane to their new home (mostly in the US), where they spend time with a foster family before striking out on their own.

A cheerful Muong from Lac Son,
Son La Province.

ing the Ede, Ma and Mnong. Further
north, the secluded hills around Pleiku
and Kontum are home to various primitive groups including the Gia Rai, Bana,
Xo Dang, Brau and Ro Mam. Even further north, the Bru Van Kieu people live
in the valleys to the south of Highway
Nine in Quang Tri province, especially
in the area of Khe Sanh.

Bru Van Kieu

The Bru Van Kieu are a typical Central
Highland tribe. They live in wooden
longhouses with thatched roofs, in a
village set in a jungle clearing or along
a watercourse. They cultivate dry rice,
millet, cassava, bananas, coffee, pea-

nuts and tobacco on plots of land cleared
by means of "slash and burn" agriculture.

Bananas are the only cash drop in
addition to which they also raise chickens, pigs, cattle and water buffalo. They
also collect wood, rattan and other products from the forest. Villages have both
a headman and a *shaman* (medicine

In Quang Tri Province hilltribe settlements are common.

man) who oversees the rites of the tribe's ancient animistic faith.

Cham

The Cham people – progeny of the once great Kingdom of Champa – mostly live along the south-central coast between Phan Thiet and Nha Trang. There is also a small Cham community in Ho Chi Minh City.

Today, the Cham number about 100,000 people. Dark skin and round

Sporting something different.

faces reveal their Malayo-Polynesian ancestry. They are prosperous rice farmers, who also make pottery and textiles. Theirs is a very unique culture: a matrilineal society split into two distinct clans based on religion. About half the Cham are Muslims, the other half Balamon Hindus. The clans live side-by-side, respecting each other's faith yet they rarely inter-marry.

Lately the Cham have begun to revive many of their ancient songs and dances after four centuries of Viet cultural hegemony.

Khmer

Another great civilization is reflected in the Khmer people of the Mekong Delta. Altogether there are about 700,000 spread across Hau Giang, Cuu Long, Kien Giang, Minh Hai and Tay Ninh provinces.

As adherents of Theravada Buddhism, they have their own temples and monasteries as opposed to the majority of Vietnamese Buddhists who are more Taoist in orientation. Khmers are easy to distinguish from the Viet majority because of their dark, round faces and trademark red and white scarves.

Chinese (Hoa)

Ethnic Chinese (or Hoa) were once found throughout Vietnam but are now mainly concentrated in the Cholon district of Ho Chi Minh City.

Before liberation there were more than a million Chinese, but immigration has taken its toll and perhaps no more than half that number remain. Like residents of any Chinatown, the people of Cholon hold tight to their roots through the use of the Chinese language, Chinese writing, Chinese schools and publications and even Chinese cuisine. They are mostly merchants, traders and middlemen – shrewd businessmen who have transformed Cholon into a thriving entrepôt where almost anything can be purchased, for a price!

Many ethnic Chinese refugees are now returning to Vietnam armed with millions of dollars in investment funds.

Tamils

A tiny and almost forgotten minority group are the Tamils, whose ancestors came from tiny French enclaves like Pondicherry and Karikal along the south coast of India. Their small community in Ho Chi Minh City, now numbers only a few thousand.

Like small ethnic groups anywhere in the world, the minority peoples of Vietnam continue to struggle against absorption into mainstream society.

Meager economic opportunities in the countryside have drawn many minority people to urban areas where they must adapt to the ways of the late 20th century.

They return to their home villages with many of the vestiges of modern life: jeans, television sets and electric fans, continuing a gradual process of modernization that is as inevitable in Vietnam as in the Amazon rainforest or the savannahs of East Africa.

But, another force is also at work. Since the early 1960s, the communist regime in Hanoi has endeavoured to integrate minority groups into the dominant Viet population.

However, parents continue to teach native minority traditions at home as many of Vietnam's ethnic groups slowly reach the verge of extinction.

Religion

The government may adhere to the Marxist-Leninist faith, but the average Vietnamese still casts his lot with older religions. Like most other Asians, the Vietnamese are a deeply spiritual people who have not lost touch with their religious roots that sometimes stretch back for thousands of years.

71

Buddhism is the predominant faith. Although the exact number of devotees is not known, roughly 90 percent of the population (around 60 million people) were raised according to some sort of Buddhist tradition.

In serious devotion at the Caodai great temple in Tay Minh town.

Buddhism

Like elsewhere in the region, the Vietnamese brand of Buddhism is influenced by several strong factors. Most prominent are the teachings of Siddarta Gautama, a 6BC Indian prince who came to be known as Lord Buddha. The basic tenet of Buddha's philosophy is that anyone can reach *nirvana* (an eternal state of peace) by following the Eightfold Path. From its birth in India, Buddhism spread north

Big Buddha in Danang.

across the Himalayas into China and east through Burma and Thailand. As a result, two distinct forms developed – Mahayana and Theravada – both of which reached Vietnam. The Mahayana school of Buddhism crept into the country in AD 2, during the Han Chinese occupation of the Red River Valley.

Although the early history of the religion remains unclear, it is quite probable that Buddhism was introduced via direct trade connections with India and through early cultural contact with China.

ishing, with more and more young men and women choosing to shave their heads and don saffron robes. There are now more than 7,000 monks in Vietnam, with the largest concentration in Ho Chi Minh City and Hue. Meanwhile, contributions from the public have risen to the point where many monasteries and temples can now undertake badly needed renovation and restorations.

The Han Chinese were also responsible for the introduction of Confucian ideals. Confucius was a Chinese philosopher and scholar who lived at about the same time as Lord Buddha. But, rather than preaching individualism and equality among men, Confucius promoted duty and respect for authority as a means of preserving order in society. In effect, it was the perfect tool for the Chinese to impose their rule over the occupied Vietnamese.

Confucianism

Since the late 1980s, Buddhism has experienced something of a renaissance in Vietnam as the communist regime has relaxed its previously antagonistic attitude towards organized religion. Buddhist monasteries are once again flour-

Taoism

Two other factors influenced Buddhism as it is practised in Vietnam today. Taoism is a mystical religious ideology developed by Chinese philosopher Lao Tzu ("The Grand Old Master") who lived sometime between the 3-7 BC. It borrows from both Buddhism and ancient animist beliefs, with a large dose of faith in natural spirits and ghosts. Taoism has long been popular among the Cantonese people of Southern China, therefore it was inevitable that it spread southwards to the coastal dwellers of

Daily Life in a Buddhist Monastery

Buddhist nuns.

There are now dozens of monasteries and more than 7,000 active monks in Vietnam. One of the more famous cloisters is Linh Mu Pagoda in Hue. Thich Tri Tuu, long-time abbot of the monastery, gives us a rare insight into the dawn-to-dusk life of a Buddhist monk in Vietnam:

"We awake every day at 3 am. We sit on a bed and breathe very naturally. In that way we induce only natural thinking. We concern ourselves with thinking about Buddhism, what we call the best things in human life. There is another phase where we question who we are. [After meditating] we do some physical exercises that can help us regulate the blood and muscles — yoga and *t'ai chi* and oriental boxing. We do these individually, in the garden. It is still dark. Before breakfast, we read from a Buddhist book at the shrine.

The text is in Chinese characters, but we interpret the meaning and express the actions in a Vietnamese way ...

After sunrise we go about our daily affairs like cleaning the floor and taking care of all things in the pagoda. Some monks work in the garden producing food and fruit for us.

We do not eat any meat; we are vegetarians. At the moment we just grow flowers for decorations, but we have a plan in coming times to earn money for the pagoda by selling flowers outside.

The older monks teach general studies – language, science, literature and mathematics – to the young monks...

At noon we rest, but we do not sleep. According to the Buddhist point of view, a shorter time for sleep is better. If you sleep too much your mind becomes dull. And when you sleep you cannot control yourself. It leaves the mind free. I have many dreams when I sleep. The monks just study by themselves in the evening...

We train our monks how to avoid five things: money, power, women, rich foods and sleep. You see, our Buddhist monks usually live alone – a single life...

I entered service at this pagoda when I was 13. Now I am 43. I wanted to serve in the pagoda and my family also encouraged me because they are followers of Buddhism. A Buddhist family thinks that having someone serve in the pagoda it will bring happiness to the entire family. I see my family very rarely – just on special occasions like a marriage or sad ones like a death...

We are not involved in political activities, but we Buddhist people always have the anti-war spirit, support peace and demand freedom for the Buddhist religion. Back in 1966 we did demonstrations and one of our monks here (committed) suicide with fire (as a protest) against the war."

Monks from Soc Soai Pagoda, Kien Giang Province.

Indochina.

In some respects, Buddhism, Taoism and Confucianism are diametrically opposed. Yet in the cross-cultural millieu of Vietnam, they blend easily into a catch-all faith that forms a rock-solid foundation for society. Look behind the communist façade and you will quickly find that people still believe in reincarnation, they worship their ancestors as well as a pantheon of gods, they still believe in the solidarity of the family and respect for their elders as well as figures of authority.

Members of the Khmer ethnic group – most of the them in the Mekong Delta – continue to espouse Theravada Buddhism, which is the main religion of neighboring Thailand and Cambodia. They have their own temples and monasteries such as the Soc Trang Temple in Hau Giang province.

Christianity

Christianity, or more specifically Roman Catholicism as introduced by the French (see p 80), is the nation's second most important religion. There are currently about six million Catholics, the vast majority in the south, where church spires dot the landscape in both rural and urban areas.

More than any other faith, Catholicism and the Catholics suffered in the wake of liberation because of their traditional apathy toward communism and

Christian devotion enjoys a new freedom.

the strong Catholic support of the Americans in Southern Vietnam. After 1975, foreign priests and nuns were expelled, seminaries and parochial schools were shut down, church lands were confiscated and missionary work forbidden.

Authorities began to show a more relaxed attitude in the late 1980s, with a stipulation that priests and nuns refrain from political activity. Now, Catholics are flocking back to mass. Dalat, the old French hill station, has turned into something of a Catholic retreat with revitalized seminaries and convents.

Thanksgiving in a Catholic church.

But, the church labors under certain restrictions – Catholic schools are still forbidden (children can only attend catechism classes after they attend government school), foreign priests and nuns are still banned and there is restricted communication with the Vatican. The bulk of overseas donations for the Vietnamese church are received from Catholics in the United States and France.

Vietnam has hundreds of Catholic churches, ranging from tiny one-room chapels to huge Gothic cathedrals with turrets, vaults and flying buttresses. The most important shrines are **Notre Dame Cathedral** in Saigon, St **Josephs' Cathedral** in Hanoi and the **Church of Our Mother of Perpetual Help** in Hue.

Do not be surprised if you see Asian gongs and drums and even *joss* sticks in Catholic churches – as in many parts of the world, Catholicism has adopted certain local habits. All services are conducted in the Vietnamese language.

Muslims & Hindus

There are small groups of Muslims and Hindus in Vietnam. Most of them are Chams, one of the country's largest ethnic groups, who are almost equally divided between the two. The vast majority of Chams live along the coastal plain between Nha Trang and Phan Thiet or in Ho Chi Minh City which has both a mosque and a Hindu temple. Cham Hindus call themselves Balamons, a sect

Muslims have their place at Chau Giang Mosque, Chan Doc.

that traces it roots back to the ancient Kingdom of Champa which drew cultural and religious inspiration from the Khmer Hindus (who began the construction of Angkor Wat).

Muslim and Hindu Chams live in separate villages within the same communes; they rarely intermarry and they celebrate separate festivals. One of the emblems of their religious harmony is the fact that they produce "forbidden food" for one another: the Muslims do not eat pork but raise pigs for the Hindus, whilst the Hindus do not eat beef but they raise cattle for the Muslims!

Cao Dai

The Mekong Delta, a place of infinite mystery, has long been the breeding ground for bizarre religious sects. Two such groups are the Cao Dai and the Hoa Hao. In 1926, Ngo Minh Chieu started the Cao Dai movement and it quickly spread from its base in Tay Ninh province, northwest of Saigon.

The faith itself is a confusing mix of Buddhism, Islam, Hinduism, Christianity and Confucian teachings, and among the unusual pantheon of saints are Victor Hugo, Joan of Arc, Lenin and Shakespeare. But, the Cao Dai were also a major military force, with a private army and huge stores of arms. The Cao Dai reached the apex of their power (one million devotees) during the 1960s when they benefitted from the chaos created by the Vietnam War to increase their

Cao Dai devotees in Holy See Temple.

membership in isolated parts of the delta. The Vatican of the Cao Dai faith is the Holy See at Tay Ninh – one of the great oddities of Vietnamese architecture, a flamboyant building with thick columns, swirling designs and an "all-seeing" eye painted above the altar.

Hoa Hao

Although nominally Buddhist, the Hoa Hao were a militant spiritual sect founded by Huynh Phu So – the so-called "Mad Monk" of An Giang province – in 1939. The group was violently anti-French and as a result they became allies of the occupying Japanese. Later they became anti-American, and then anti-communist. As a military force after liberation in 1975, the Hoa Hao were forced to disband their private army.

Advent of Christianity

The first missionaries to set foot in Indochina were Portuguese priests from the Jesuit order who established their first mission in 1615. At that time, the Jesuits were the most active clerics in Asia, winning converts in places as diverse as Nagasaki, Malacca and Goa. They made little headway in Vietnam during the Le Dynasty and were expelled by the end of the century.

The first French missionaries appeared about a century later, at a time when the Trinh and Nguyen lords had divided Vietnam into two separate nations. But, once again the going was slow for the Christian cause. In fact, it was not until the end of the 18th century that the French Catholics made much progress and even then, their proselytization had more of a political than pious slant. The key event took place in 1787, when Nguyen Anh – the deposed leader of the Nguyen clan – asked Bishop Pigneau de Behaine (a French missionary), for assistance in regaining his crown. The bishop took one of Nguyen

Outside the Catholic church near Nha Trang.

Anh's sons to France to seek an audience with King Louis XVI. A treaty was forged which gave both the French government (and the Catholic church) its first foothold in Indochina.

By 1858, when France began its gradual annexation of Indochina, there were already more than 400,000 Catholics in Vietnam, mostly concentrated in the Red River Valley. They were considered loyal allies of the French during the colonial conquest. In fact, missionaries often used their converts to support French military operations and Vietnamese royalist forces.

Taken as a whole, Vietnam is a remarkable brew of all the great Asian faiths – remarkable in the sense that religion has survived and in many cases thrived despite more than three decades of atheistic Marxist dogma. And more so than any other channel, religion has helped to carry ancient Vietnamese culture into modern times.

Lunar **New Year** or **Tet** is Vietnam's most important annual event, a vibrant and heartwarming celebration that is both a public holiday and a major religious event (see box p 86). The period right after Tet (February and March) is packed with related festivals to usher in the new year and hail the advent of spring. The festival calendar is especially crowded in the Red River Valley and surrounding regions where nearly every town holds its own unique celebration in the month after Tet.

Preparing for an elaborate Tet.

Festivals

83

Start of the Celebrations

Dong Ky village in Ha Bac province stages an earthshaking event four days into the new year – the famous **Firecracker Festival** – during which millions of explosives are ignited. Sixteen local families spend the entire year making firework displays, with each of them

Letting go – Dong Ky Firecracker Festival, Ha Bac Province.

Lunar New Year (Tet)

Making merit on Tet Day at Quan Su Pagoda, Hanoi.

Vietnam's Lunar New Year is called **Tet Nguyen Dan** or merely Tet, the most joyous time of year throughout the country. It normally falls in late January or early February and also marks the arrival of spring when rice crops were traditionally planted in the north.

Hanoi, normally a drab and very somber city, is especially cheerful in the weeks before Tet. Homes and markets throb with excitement as families make their holiday preparations. People buy kumquat trees and plum blossoms to decorate their homes and they make *cay neu* poles from bamboo and betelnut to ward off evil spirits. One of the best Tet markets is along Dao Ngang Street in the old town, but there are stalls all the way around Hoan Kiem Lake which sell fireworks, flowers and tinsel.

Kitchens are filled with the aroma of *banh chung* (cakes made from meat, beans and sticky rice) – the Vietnamese equivalent of Christmas pudding. Another holiday favorite is *mut hot sen*

(lotus-seed candy) also made at home. Children and unmarried adults are the recipients of "lucky money" hidden in red-and-gold envelopes, similar to the *lai see* (red packets containing money) given away in China during the Lunar New Year.

The Day Before

Action reaches a frenzy on the day before Tet as two special ceremonies take place. **Le Tao Quan** – an ancient Taoist rite – involves a temple sacrifice to ward off evil spirits, while **Tat Nien** is a sort of spiritual invitation for deceased ancestors to join in the fun. Housewives and husbands pour into the streets in search of last-minute bargains.

That evening they don their best clothes and promenade around the shores of the lake. Young people cruise up and down the streets on motorbikes, trailing long strands of firecrackers

– yet another way to banish evil spirits. Then at the stroke of midnight, a massive fireworks display is held over Hoan Kiem Lake and everyone goes home exhausted but happy.

New Year's Day is a quiet time for family and temple visitations. People keep a close eye out for the first visitor of the day: if he or she is an evil person, then you can expect bad luck for the entire year. Every temple in the capital is packed, but one of the most popular places of worship is Quan Su Pagoda in downtown Hanoi.

While the actual public holiday may last for only a few days, Hanoi generally shuts down for over a fortnight either before or after Tet to make time for holiday preparation and recovery. It is a bad time to visit Vietnam on business, but a brilliant time to witness a celebration that remains at the very heart of Vietnamese culture. If you intend to visit Hanoi during Tet, make sure that you book your flight and hotel accomodation in advance.

Pre-Tet street scene.

spending the equivalent of US$500 on gunpowder, fuses and wrappings. Those judged to have made the best displays get a prize. The highlight of the festival is a grand procession which culminates in the explosion of the firecrackers in a field outside the village. The more macho male inhabitants stand as close as they can to the blasts even though serious injuries and fatalities have occurred at festivals in the past. Yet, the Dong Ky celebration gets bigger every year.

Another Ha Bac province highlight is the **Hoi Lim Song Festival**. Teams of singers compete against one another in a musical format that dates back hundreds of years. The contest was originally a courtship ritual in which youngsters could meet potential mates from other villages, but nowadays even older (married) people compete. The lyrics tend to reflect romantic themes and mirror the daily lives of rice farmers. The winners split donations obtained from the audience. Held two weeks after Tet, the festival also includes an indoor circus, gambling tents, wrestling and chess competitions.

The **Co Loa Festival**, staged amid the ruined capital of the Lac Viet Dynasty is in closer proximity to Hanoi. During this festival local villagers stage a colorful procession to the old royal pagoda to honor the memory of King An Duong (who built Co Loa in 3 BC) and his daughter Mi Chau, who betrayed her father and the secret of the city's defense after she fell in love with the son of an enemy general.

Singing Festival in Ha Bac Province – loud, crowded and colourful.

At this time of the year, pagoda festivals are popular all over the Red River Valley. One of the best known is the **Huong Tich Pagoda Festival** held in Ha Son Binh Province, which attracts Buddhist devotees from all over Vietnam. Pilgrims follow a sacred route along the Yen River while intermittently stopping to worship at various caves and temples until they reach Huong Tich Pagoda where they can have their fortunes told and purchase good luck charms. Although the festival reaches its climax on the full moon of the second lunar month, the pilgrimage lasts for a fortnight before and after the festival. You can hire boats to take you up the Yen River and along the way you can stop at scenic and religious spots.

One of the lesser known but more spectacular celebrations of the post-New Year period is the **Da Sy Festival** which takes place two weeks after Tet in Da Sy village about 10 kilometers outside of Hanoi. The celebration takes place over five days and is centered on the 17th-century village temple. The festival starts with a brilliant procession: the temples' gods are carried through the village on golden palanquins escorted by young virgins dressed in white, shaggy lion dancers, people dressed in costumes from bygone days and silk dragons that measure up to 50 meters long! After three days of eating, drinking, talking and relaxation, the festival ends with another parade in which the gods are taken back to the temple to the accom-

Having a swinging time at the Lim Festival.

paniment of drums, gongs and firecrackers.

The fifth day of the third lunar month (normally in mid-April) is reserved for honoring the dead. **Thanh Minh** is similar in both origin and practice to the Ching Ming Festival observed by the Chinese. Families trek to graveyards by the thousands to clean the graves of their ancestors and families, leaving offerings of food, paper money and *joss* (incense) sticks. Most families then take a picnic on the same spot.

Later in the month comes **Liberation Day** (April 30) which marks the fall of Saigon in 1975, as the North Vietnamese Army (NVA) destroyed the last remnants of the US-backed Republic of South Vietnam. A Soviet-style military parade is usually held in Hanoi. Wake up the following morning to **May Day** (May 1), the international socialist holiday which Vietnam celebrates with various labor union, factory and school events. May 19 is **Ho Chi Minh's Birthday** which is also marked by special events related to the man who is universally hailed as the father of his country. All three days are public holidays; government offices and schools are closed.

Phat Dan Day marks the birth of Siddarta Gautama, Lord Buddha, born in India c. 563 BC. It falls in early May, on the eighth day of the fourth lunar month. Buddhist devotees flock to give offerings at their local temples.

Tet Doan Ngo falls on the fifth day of the fifth lunar month (late May or

A wrestling match in the sand is part of the Festival agenda.

early June). This summer solstice festival is of minor importance in Vietnam, but elsewhere in Asia this auspicious date is the time for dragon boat races.

Hungry ghosts are said to roam the earth in the month prior to **Vu Lan Day** (full moon of the seventh lunar month,

sometime in August). Restless souls are placated by burning paper offerings in temples and on the streets. This is yet another time when Vietnamese trek to the cemetery to spruce up the graves of their departed kinsfolk. This celebration is also called **Trung Nguyen** or Wan-

A special **Cham Festival** is now held at the Po Klong Garai Temple complex near Phang Rang each September in which the dances, customs and music of old Champa are revived. Several distinct dances are featured including a graceful fan dance performed by half a dozen women, a swaying pottery dance performed in baggy white pants and colored tunics and a very sensual Balinese-type dance that features two men and a woman. Cham music sounds like a cross between traditional Hindu songs and African drum beats.

Tet Trung Thu goes by several pseudonyms: **Children's Festival**, **Harvest Festival** and **Lantern Festival** (the name by which it is known in Asia). Falling on the full moon of the eighth lunar month (late September), this holiday originally celebrated the harvest.

Nowadays, it is for youngsters who gather in temples and parks with paper lanterns made in the shapes of tigers, lions, dragons and more modern creatures like cars and airplanes! Vietnamese like the Chinese devour *banh trung thu* (moon cakes) on this day.

Year-end Festivities

The end of the year is punctuated by two Western holidays: **Christmas** and **New Year's Eve**. Hanoi and the north remain fairly quiet, but there is a lot of festive spirit in Ho Chi Minh City and in the south where most of Vietnam's Catholics live.

dering Souls Day.

National Day is on September 2, the date that the Japanese surrendered to American forces in Tokyo Bay and the day that Ho Chi Minh declared the formation of the Democratic Republic of Vietnam in 1945. The following day (September 3) is the **Anniversary of Ho Chi Minh's Death**, another holiday.

Most Asian nations have a strong theatrical tradition, and Vietnam is no exception. *Tuong* (classical Vietnamese opera), is a fusion of song, dance, mime and somber oration in which the players don flamboyant historical costumes on stage. Most of the stories are historic tales from the past that highlight the deeds of great men and women who have shaped the Vietnamese nation; these people include the Trung Sisters and "Uncle" Ho Chi Minh. You do not need to be fluent in Vietnamese to follow the action: the good guys sport red faces and the villains flash white.

Ceiling mural at the tomb of Khai Dinh in Hue.

Theatrical Tradition

Tuong is thought to be derived from rural dramas that have been popular in Vietnam for several thousand years and the traditional dramas of ancient India and Cambodia. But, the music, dance steps and costumes are heavily influenced by traditional Chinese opera which filtered south-

93

Culture

Water puppets, a typical Vietnamese folk culture entertainment.

wards over several millennia.

The 14th century ushered in the "golden age" of *tuong* , during the later stages of the Tran Dynasty, when opera enjoyed royal patronage. The plots remained largely static until the French and American war periods when mod-ern revolutionary elements were combined into the story lines. But, opera has declined in popularity in recent times as young people flock to less formal drama.

One last bastion of *tuong* is the city of Quy Nhon on the central coast, base of the nation's top professional opera

amateur opera companies. Once every five years *tuong* troupes from around Vietnam gather for a national competition, the next one scheduled for 1995 is to be held in Nha Trang.

Roi Nuoc

Roi nuoc (water puppets) are another ancient dramatic style, although they have become increasingly rare in modern times. Water puppets are thought to be a Vietnamese invention. Legend holds that medieval puppeteers refused to abort their shows despite floods in the Red River Valley and that after many years of inundation, a "liquid stage" became part of this art form. Like *tuong*, most of the water puppet plays are based on historic events and heroes. Water puppet performances are sometimes staged at venues in Hanoi and Ho Chi Minh City, but the best place to witness this vanishing art is at the Water Puppet Festival at Thay Pagoda in Ha Son Binh province in the Red River Valley which takes place on the seventh day of the third lunar month (normally in April).

company: the Dao Tan Theater Troupe, named after a famous 19th century opera director. Dao Tan presents four productions each year, ranging from three-hour "modern" performances to marathon historical dramas that can last up to one month – a different act is presented each evening. In addition, Binh Dinh province has more than 60

Popular Theater

Another drama form that traces its roots to ancient days is *cheo* (popular theater). The name means "song of oars" and is thought to be derived from the ballads sung by peasants and fishermen in the Red River Delta more than 2,000 years

Dr Le Van Khor, historian and man of letters.

ago. Although the original themes were rustic, in the later days *cheo* became a form of peasant protest against brutal feudal overlords and then later against the French – the Vietnamese equivalent of Negro slave chants in the American South. Other forms of Vietnamese drama have modern roots. The 19th century royal court in Hue gave birth to *ca hue* (traditional folk music performed in a formal setting that includes costumes and stylized dance steps borrowed from *tuong*). *Cai luong* (renovated theater) also dates from the days of the Nguyen Dynasty, when it evolved from the simple peasant entertainment popular in Southern Vietnam into a nationwide protest movement against the French. French colonial censors once banned *cai*

luong performances with seditious themes. *Kich noi*, another form of drama was introduced to urban Vietnam in the 1920s, as a local equivalent to Western-style stage drama. After the 1954 independence, communist authorities used *kich noi* as a tool to convey socialist themes to a mass audience and to render foreign (mostly Eastern bloc) plays in Vietnamese.

Music & Dance

Bronze drums and lithophones discovered at archaeological digs testify to the fact that music has been popular since prehistoric times. It can be assumed that song and dance gained royal patronage from the very first dynasty onwards. But, it became especially vital in feudal times when the Ly and Tran rulers sponsored orchestras and dance troupes to accompany royal protocol, religious rites and palace entertainment. At the same time, folk music and dance has always been popular among the peasant class, creating a separate genre of amusement.

Folk music is still popular among the rural populace, especially at Tet and during the many village festivals that follow the Lunar New Year. Traditional courtship tunes are very popular, including songs with impromptu (often suggestive) lyrics in which teams of boys and girls croon to one another.

Vietnamese classical music – which dates from dynastic times – is most often heard at formal concerts held in urban areas. Similar in style and content to a classic Chinese orchestra, a full Vietnamese ensemble includes about 40 musicians playing traditional instruments like the *dan bau* (zither), lithophones, bamboo flutes and bronze gongs. Western classical music is also popular, with the Hanoi Conservatory being the best school for pianists and violinists.

Revolutionary music dates back to the 1940s when communist party cadres began composing protest songs against the French, Japanese and Americans. They are still popular in movies and on the radio, but like elsewhere in Asia, mass-produced pop and rock has found a ready ear among young Vietnamese.

Music and dance at Hue City.

Colonial facade of the Art Museum, in Ho Chi Minh City.

Unpleasant memories of the bombing of Hanoi captured vigourously on canvas.

Painting & Sculpture

The oldest "art" in Vietnam are Neolithic cave paintings and ornamental pottery found in grottos on the edge of the Red River Valley. By AD 13, elegant artistic calligraphy and silk painting had been introduced from China with a range of subjects including peasant scenes, moral themes and mythological and fabled animals like dragons and tigers. The Western-style of painting was introduced by the French, as seen by the Impressionist and Cubist styles that dominated Vietnamese urban art during the first half of the 20th century.

However, the advent of communism in the 1950s ushered in a period of bold, stylized Soviet painting in North Vietnam – art with a distinct social message. It is only in recent years that Vietnamese painters have been able to depict more esoteric and abstract themes.

Sculpture, on the other hand, has a long and rich tradition. The Kingdom of Champa produced a dazzling array of Hindu-inspired stonework between AD 7-14, including the depiction of gods, mythological animals, warriors and dancing girls. The world's largest collection of Cham artifacts is housed in Danang's excellent Cham Museum; for *en situ* sculpture visit the ruined Cham city of My Son.

The Viet people of the Red River Valley – lacking a ready supply of suitable stone – largely confined themselves

Museum of Revolution in Ho Chi Minh City.

to wooden sculpture, primarily for use in Buddhist temples and monasteries with gods, Buddhas and dragons being the favorite subjects.

The **Temple of King Dinh Tien Hoang** at Hoa Lu, the 10th century capital of Vietnam, has a superb collection of wooden effigies. Among other masterpieces that have survived the centuries are "The Buddhas With One Thousand Eyes and Arms" which can be enjoyed at But Thap Pagoda outside Hanoi and "The Sixteen Arhats" (Buddhist holy men) at the Fine Arts Museum in the capital. The best examples of northern stone sculpture are the dozens of stelae (15th-18th century) at the Temple of Literature in Hanoi.

A new sculptural era evolved during the 19th century reign of the Nguyen Dynasty in Hue. The nine dynastic urns in the courtyard of Phung Tien Palace are priceless masterpieces that were somehow involved in the destruction of the Citadel in 1968. The royal mausoleums along the Perfume River are flush with various friezes and statues, the most flamboyant being the Tomb of Khai Dinh which holds an army of stone warriors and a golden effigy of the emperor himself.

Architecture

A number of distinct architectural epochs took root in Vietnam. The most noticeable being French colonial archi-

Cao Dai Temple in Tay Ninh.

tecture, which still dominates the older parts of Hanoi and Saigon. But, this is by no means the oldest or most important.

The Kingdom of Champa – a contemporary and cultural ally of the people who built Angkor Wat – flourished along the central coast for more than seven centuries, until the Chams fell to Vietnamese aggression in AD 14. However, they left many of their ancient buildings behind which showcase superb examples of Cham stone and brickwork architecture, such as those at My Son near Danang, Po Klong Garai outside Phan Rang and at Po Nagar on the river at Nha Trang.

The ruins at My Son have a mystical, romantic quality, although many have been encroached by the jungle.

Religious Architecture

Despite numerous wars, some classic examples of ancient religious architecture survive in the north. The 11th century Temple of Literature in Hanoi and Tay Phuong Pagoda in the Red River Valley are the country's best examples of the brick-and-wood style that marked the high point of architectural design practiced during the Ly Dynasty. The ancient capital of Hoa Lu in Ha Nam Ninh province has several superb Ly Dynasty temples.

Hue is the nation's architectural showcase; although almost all the buildings look a thousand years old, most structures only date back to the 19th

Western Films on Indochina

Vietnam and to some extent Cambodia have proved fertile ground for Western filmmakers over the last 40 years. Most of them reflect the American war experience, but some of the best films draw their inspiration from French colonial times. A brief filmography:

The Quiet American: (US 1957) Director: Joseph L Mankiewicz. Cast: Michael Redgrave, Audie Murphy and Claude Dauphin. Film version of the Graham Greene classic about a naive young American trying to come to terms with *amour* and intrigue in old Saigon and a cynical English journalist who loves the same woman. An amazingly accurate prophesy of the American era in Indochina.

The Green Berets: (US 1968) Directors: John Wayne and Ray Kellogg. Cast: John Wayne and David Janssen. The first Vietnam War movie, and perhaps the only one with an avid gung-ho theme. One critic called the film "crude propaganda" upon its original release.

The Deer Hunter: (US 1978) Director: Michael Cimino. Cast: Robert De Nero, Meryl Streep, Christopher Walken, Jon Savage and John Cazale. A modern American classic in every sense of the term. The first half is a portrait of insipid steel-town life in Pennsylvania, an essential precursor to the horror of three buddies going off to fight in Vietnam. Won Oscars for Best Picture, Director and Supporting Actor (Walken).

Coming Home: (US 1978) Director: Hal Ashby. Cast: Jane Fonda, Jon Voight and Bruce Dern. The Vietnam War as seen from a different angle – the home front. Fonda is a naive and patriotic Marine Corps wife who volunteers at a local veteran's hospital while hubby (Dern) is away in Indochina.

Her world is turned upside down when she meets and falls in love with a paraplegic veteran played by Voight. Best Actor Oscars for both Fonda and Voight.

Apocalypse Now: (US 1979) Director: Francis Ford Coppola. Cast: Marlon Brando, Martin Sheen, Robert Duvall, Harrison Ford. A modern resurrection of Joseph Conrad's *Heart of Darkness*, about an ill-fated journey up–river to find a renegade US Army colonel. This will always be the ultimate Vietnam War film, not so much because the combat scenes are realistic (they

are not) but because it is an accurate metaphor for the American nightmare in Vietnam. The soundtrack is an all-time classic and the famous helicopter sequence is one of Hollywood's greatest scenes.

The Killing Fields: (UK 1984) Director: Roland Joffe. Cast: Sam Waterston, Haing S Ngor, John Malkovich, Julian Sands, Craig T Nelson and Spaulding Gray. A marvelous cast and superb acting highlight this true story about *New York Times* reporter Sidney Schanberg and his friendship with Cambodian journalist Dith Pran who gets left behind when the Khmer Rouge take Phnom Penh. Haing Ngor, a Cambodian refugee himself, won an Oscar for his portrayal of Dith Pran.

Rambo: *First Blood II*: (US 1985) Director: George Pan Cosmatos. Cast: Sylvester Stallone and Richard Crenna. Rambo goes back to Vietnam on a secret mission to find missing–in–action soldiers (MIAs). The highly successful sequel to the first *Rambo* movie reflects what many Americans wish they had actually been able to do during the war: annihilate the enemy. The irony is that Rambo became a hero to many Asian kids and a box office champ across the entire Far East.

Platoon: (US 1986) Director: Oliver Stone. Cast: Tom Berenger, Willem Dafoe and Charlie Sheen. The first in Oliver Stone's trilogy of Vietnam War films, this movie won the 1986 Oscar for Best Picture.

The movie works on two levels: on the surface it is the story of a young man who volunteers for military service in order to prove himself; on a deeper level the film is a metaphor for the good and evil sides of America during the war.

Full Metal Jacket: (US 1987) Director: Stanley Kubrick. Cast: Matthew Modine, Adam Baldwin and Vincent D'Onofrio. A lot of American veterans say that this is the most realistic of all combat Vietnam films. An utterly frightening portrayal of the Tet Offensive of 1968, this is the story of young GIs trying to retake the demolished Citadel in Hue.

Good Morning Vietnam: (US 1987) Director: Barry Levinson. Cast: Robin Williams, Forest Whitaker, Tung Thanh Tran and Chintara

Sukapatana. People said that it could not be done: a comedy on Vietnam.

But Robin Williams pulls it off in brilliant style, the true life story of disc jockey Adrian Cronauer who dares to defy the rules of both musical and military decorum on Saigon's Armed Forces Radio in 1965. Williams was nominated for an Academy Award.

Hamburger Hill: (US 1987) Director: John Irvin. Cast: Anthony Barrile, Michael Patrick Boatman, Don Cheadle and Michael Dolan. Another brutally realistic film, made in the style of a documentary about one of the bloodiest clashes of the Vietnam conflict: a 1969 battle in the A Shau Valley. The Americans lost 241 men trying to take the hill from NVA troops and then abandoned the ridge just a few weeks later.

Born on the Fourth of July: (US 1990) Director: Oliver Stone. Cast: Tom Cruise. The second in the Oliver Stone trilogy won Oscars for both the director and the leading man, as well as the Best Picture of 1990.

Based on a true story, this is the tale of a high school football star from Long Island who gets drafted into the army and sent to Vietnam. One day he is an innocent teenager, the next a bitter trooper soldier who eventually goes home in a wheelchair. One of the most compelling anti-war films ever made.

L'Amant (The Lover): (France, 1992) Director: Jean-Jacques Annaud. Cast: Tony Leung and Jane March. The most of successful of a spate of new French films on Vietnam.

Based on the Marguerite Duras novel, this is the story of a steamy love affair between a young French woman and her Chinese lover. Even in Paris, the realistic bedroom scenes caused blushes, but beneath the lip service this film exposes the brutality of plantation life in 1920s Indochina.

Dien Bien Phu: (France, 1992) Director: Pierre Schoendoerffer. Epic re-make of the bloody 1954 battle that rocked the French colonial empire and brought North Vietnam its independence.

This is a highly autobiographical tale, because director Schoendoerffer was there – at the real Dien Bien Phu – as a young combat photographer.

century when the Nguyen kings transformed Hue into one of the most fabulous cities in Asia. Much of the royal Citadel (started in 1804) was destroyed during the French and American wars, but since liberation urban authorities have done their best to rebuild and restore many of the ancient buildings. Among the architectural high points are the Ngo Mon or Noon Gate, Thai Hoa Palace, the Royal Library and Hien Lam Cac with its famous bronze urns. Further up the Perfume River are Thien Mu Pagoda – an archetypal Buddhist monastery – and the ornate royal tombs with their various temples, shrines and pavilions.

French Architecture

Most of the great French structures of Vietnam date from the *belle epoch* and thus reflect the romance of turn-of-the-century Paris. Saigon possesses the lion's share of French marvels including the Hotel de Ville (1908) and Notre Dame Cathedral (1883). In Hanoi you will find St Joseph's Cathedral (1886) and the Opera (1911). Another edifice that dates back from the French period is the Holy See at Tay Ninh, an unusual building that meshes several styles in the tabernacle of the Cao Dai faith.

Prose & Poetry

Vietnam has always considered itself a

Costumed girl at Niet Ban Tinh Xa Sleeping Buddha Temple in Vung Tau.

nation of prose and poetry, a tradition that goes back several thousand years, to the Han Dynasty occupation, when scholars began recording her oral stories in Chinese characters. Although the Chinese invaders were expelled by the 10th century, Vietnamese scholars continued to write in Chinese characters for another 800 years. At the same time, a folksy national literature written in the indigenous *Nom* script came into being in the 14th century – a movement which eventually give birth to modern Vietnamese literature.

Most of the works that have survived from the times of the Ly Dynasty (11th-12th century) are Buddhist scripts which contain deep philosophical dissertations that have little to do with everyday life or the common man. But the Tran Dynasty (13th to 14th century) gave birth to a diverse national literature that included spiritual works, military treatises, patriotic poems and romantic verse which paid homage to nature and country life. One of the great bards of this period was Tran Nhan Tong, a king who abdicated from power in 1293 to become a Buddhist monk.

But, the greatest period of national literature was in the 15th century, when writers flourished under the patronage of kings from the Le Dynasty. Nguyen Trai (1380-1442) dominated Vietnamese writing to the same extent that Shakespeare would a century later in England. His most famous work was an epic poem called **Proclamation of Victory**

A Night at the Opera : Quy Nhon Style

Vietnam's premier *tuong* (traditional opera) company is the Dao Tan Troupe in Quy Nhon, a city on the southern coast, halfway between Danang and Nha Trang.

The troupe was founded in 1952 as part of the growing anti-French movement in Binh Dinh province. In 1954, after the United Nations partition of Vietnam, the company fled north, to the communist zone, where as the Fifth Zone Theatre Troupe, it performed in exile for more than twenty years.

After liberation in 1975, the company returned to its original home base in Quy Nhon and eventually changed its name to honor the memory of Dao Tan (1845–1907), a *tuong* master who is generally credited with keeping this art alive during the early years of the French occupation.

The troupe is currently under the direction of Vo So Thua, a director and writer, who works from a small office above the famous Tuong Theater situated on the south side of Quy Nhon. Vo has taken his Dao Tan players on more than half a dozen foreign tours, including performances in Germany, France, Italy and Spain. They also tour extensively within Vietnam and present several new productions each year in Quy Nhon.

Tuong theatre is able to embrace any number of plots, but there are three traditional subjects: Classic plots which are drawn from the middle ages, the early days of *tuong* many of which relate to ancient Vietnamese myth and legends; historical plots which portray the lives of national heros and modern plots which deal with the lives of famous communist leaders or socialist doctrine.

The play *Song Hau* is a good example of the classical format. The story concerns two men, Khung Ling Ta and Dong Kim Lan, who become friends and combine forces against a bad *mandarin* (high court official). The complete enactment of the play takes an entire month, with a different act performed each night, a grand total of more than a hundred hours of theater!

Historical and modern formats are much shorter and can last for up to two to three hours on a single evening. One of the most popular historical plays is *Mat Troi Dem the Ky* ("Son of the Sun in the world of Dark") by playwright Le Duy Hanh, about the life of the late 18th century peasant leader Nguyen Hue, who also came from Binh Ding province.

Modern plots often feature some aspect extracted from the life of Ho Chi Minh. But other communist leaders are also featured. For instance, *We Believe in Moscow* tells the story of the early days of the Communist party in Vietnam.

The main protagonist is a woman called Nguyen Thi Minh Khai, the first Communist Party Secretary for Saigon, who was executed by the French in 1941.

over the Ngo, but he also wrote about nature, geography and history. Nguyen Trai also broke new ground in the sense that he composed his poetry in both Chinese characters and in *Nom* – which started to emerge as a popular written form among writers.

Revolutionary Writing

By the 18th century, most new works were being penned in *Nom* with a corresponding decline in Chinese writing. At the same time, literature became a revolutionary tool, a way for critics to chide the feudal system through metaphorical short stories, novels and verse. The great literary masterpiece of this era was *The Tale of Kieu* by Nguyen Du (1765-1820), an epic poem with more than 3,000 verses that relates the trials and tribulations of a young woman named Kieu.

Students practising traditional dance at the Hanoi School of Dance.

Nguyen Du & *The Tale of Kieu*

Vietnam's imperial tombs, temples, pagodas and palaces are often her most beautifully decorated architecture, with sculpture and intricate woodcarvings. However, many ancient Vietnamese buildings were destroyed during the Chinese occupation during the 10th century. Subsequently, Vietnamese architecture became inspired by Chinese and Buddhist influence.

Vietnamese poetry like architecture is also a dominant art form in Vietnam. The language is well suited to poetry, as there are six tonal pronunciations for every syllable, which conveys six different meanings. Thus, Vietnamese sentences are modified into verses or songs by combining these tones to create specific moods in poetry.

The poetry is usually in the form of folk songs, *Ca Dao*, or literary poetry, *Tho Van*. Written by kings, scholars, monks and *mandarins* (high court officials), poetry has developed into an important way of communication, used by political dissidents, feminists, revolutionaries and even children. The most famous Vietnamese poem is **The Tale of Kieu**.

The Tale of Kieu was written by the renowned poet Nguyen Du, 1785-1820. He was also known as To Nhu, Thanh Hien, Hong Son, Liep Ho, Nam Hai and Dieu Do. He was born in Tien Dien, a village of the Nghi Xuan district in Nghe Tinh. He belonged to a family of scholars and *mandarins*. Having served Le Canh Hung as a military *mandarin*, he refused to serve the Tay Son. He was later made a Deputy Minister of Rites.

He was part of several conspiracies and was detained. When he was set free, he returned to his village in the North of the country. There his poetry matured amongst the sufferings of the people. He also wrote in classical Chinese. Later, he returned reluctantly to serve the new leader, Gia Long. Nguyen Du was sent to China on a diplomatic mission in 1813.

The Tale of Kieu is a highly evocative adaptation of a 16th century Chinese work, telling the story of a beautiful girl, Kieu, fated to endure much suffering as a courtesan before being reunited with her lover.

The poem is a narrative in 3,254 verses, and its humanism and realism captured the hearts of

the Vietnamese with verses of remarkable resonant beauty. Until today, every Vietnamese in his joy and suffering is well familiar with the **Tale of Kieu**.

Some extracts...

"The Blue Pavilion"
A prisoner now she must remain,
Locked in the Blue Pavilion and alone
In her young beauty. Only the distant mountains,
Though so far, she felt as friends, and the near moon
Watched at her window. All about, below around
The sand dunes, ochre-tinged and barren, spread afar;
Dust from the roads blew a red restless mist.
Morning in the heavens piled bright clouds,
At night the lamp's lone fluttering flame danced in her eyes.

Music and dance, colour and vigour at Thai Hor Palace.

All that she saw, all that she thought and felt
Turned in confusion in her troubled heart.
Where is he now who drank love's cup with me?
Day after day he waits for news of me
In vain, in that lost country, under the skies of home
Love fresh, red and living in my heart still waits ...."

"Oath of Eternal Love"
The flowers grew richer, their perfume more insistent,
The ardour of their eyes lit in one flame,
Kirn's passion surged within him, a strong flood
And now some licence pierced his tenderness.

She warned him... Let us not treat lightly this great love
Now let me speak to you one simple word.
Tender is the blossom of the peach and to the blue bird's coming
Never would I unlock the garden gate,
But we have sworn to marry and for that
She who must wear the wife's plain smock her body must keep pure,
If like wantons in the mulberry-groves I fail,
And all unworthy prove you I merit your contempt
Should we the passing flower of a day thus seize
To stain henceforth the wholeness of our love?

~ *Laure Lau*

The theater in regal French architecutral style presides over the busy boulevard.

Cinema

To some extent, Vietnamese cinema is still in its infancy. Movies had barely broken ground in Indochina when war broke out in 1941. Fifty years of almost continuous fighting – and depravation in the North – stunted the development of an indigenous movie industry. Nevertheless, film has become an important cultural style for both art and entertainment in modern times.

The first Vietnamese "film" was a 16-mm newsreel of Ho Chi Minh reading the nation's declaration of independence in 1945. Black-and-white documentary films were popular in the North during the 1950s as a means of propagating national liberation and then reunification.

However, it was not until 1959 that Vietnam produced its first full-length feature drama: *On The Banks of the Same River*.

The film industry in Hanoi continued to produce films throughout the American War period. Naturally, most of them reflected war themes such as *The Second Line of Fire*, *A Young Combatant*, *The Little Girl from Hanoi* and so on. Even as bombs fell on Hanoi, North Vietnam continued to stage its first national film festival in 1970 at which Golden Lotus awards were presented in various categories.

Today, the film festival takes place every three years and alternates between Hanoi and Ho Chi Minh City.

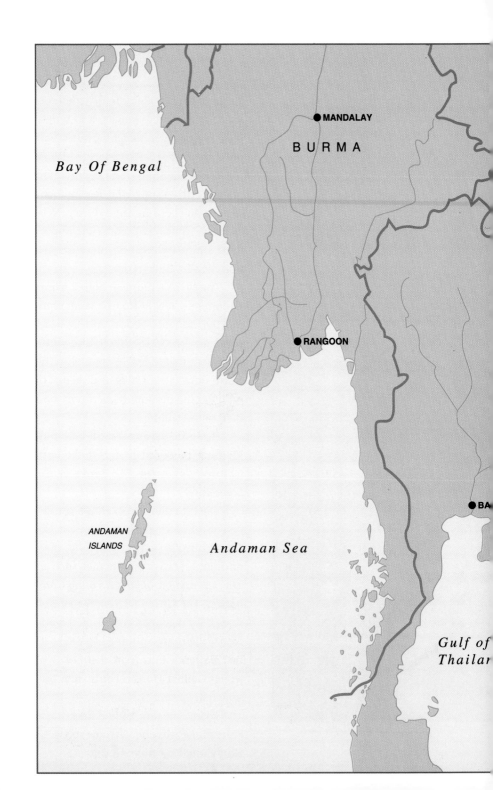

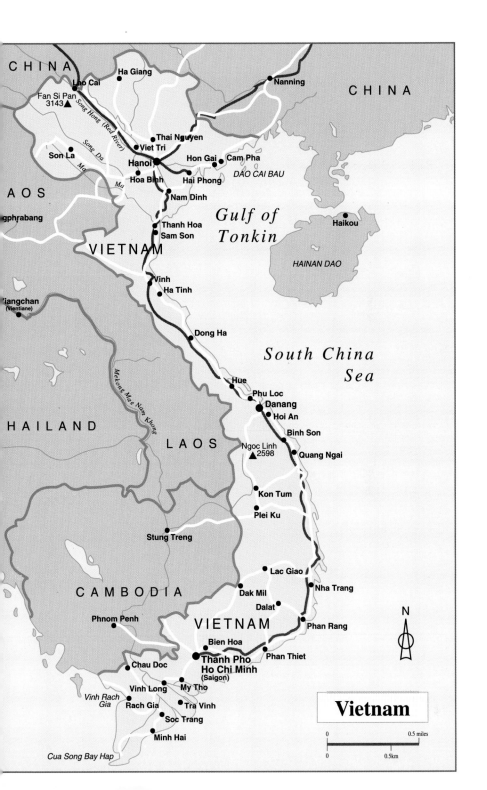

Hanoi & The North

Hanoi is the mother city of Vietnam and is at the hub of government, education and culture. It may not have the bright lights and flashy appeal of its vaunted rival to the south, but Hanoi retains a bygone charm that is difficult to find in modern Asia.

Hanoi moves to the beat of a much slower drummer than most cities her size. Private vehicles are still a rarity (although this will surely change in the years to come) and most people still get around on foot or on bicycles. Hanoi's residents always seem to have time for a smile and a chat – even if they do not always speak in your language. And despite their socialist façade, the people of Hanoi seem more in touch with ancient traditions than their modern cousins to the south. Many still practice the "old time" religion while maintaining a healthy respect for family values.

Watching the world go by in Hanoi.

Heart of Hanoi

The heart of Hanoi, in both a spiritual and geo-

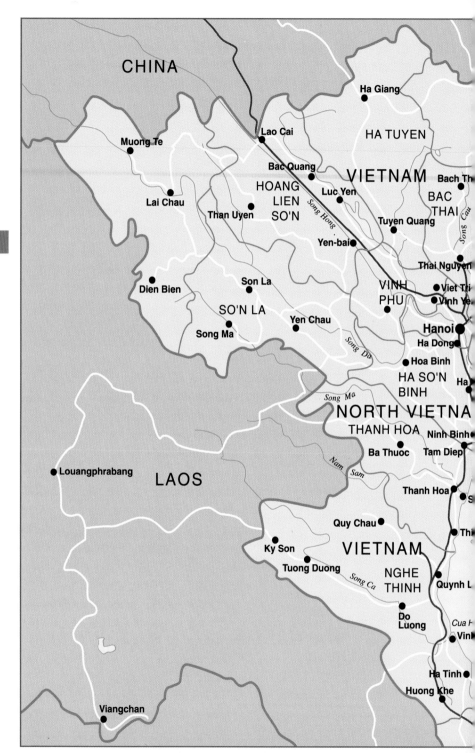

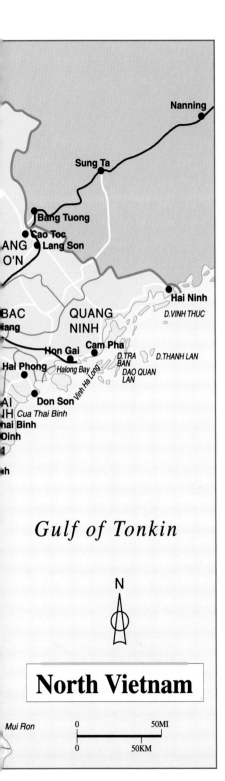

graphical sense, is a body of water called Hoan Kiem – the Lake of Restored Sword. Hoan Kiem does not impress by girth or depth, but by myth, a story that is sometimes called the Vietnamese version of Camelot. Legend holds that Emperor Le Loi came to pray at the edge of this lake in the early 15th century, asking the gods for good fortune in his struggle against the invading Chinese.

A sage turtle who lived in the lake heard his prayers and presented him with a magic sword forged from lightning not steel, which Le Loi used to vanquish the invaders. After the Chinese fled, the magic sword flew from the emperor's hands and sank back into the lake, where it was later reclaimed by the turtle.

Turtle Pagoda, now ruined and overgrown with weeds, sits on a tiny island located at the center of the lake, which you can only reach by boat. But, on the eastern shore is a much more impressive sight, **Huc Bridge**, a 19th century wooden span that connects **Jade Mountain (Ngoc Son) Temple** with two smaller religious structures called the **Penbrush** and the **Inkslab**.

The bridge offers a splendid view of the lake and surrounding shore, which is best explored immediately after dawn when residents flock to the waterfront to perform *tai chi* (a Chinese system of exercise and self-discipline) and play cards.

In the late afternoon, down a beer or sip a cup of tea at one of the outdoor cafés on the lake's northwest shore.

The old quarter in Hanoi.

Old Hanoi

The older parts of Hanoi flow around the banks of the Hoan Kiem. Beyond the north bank is the Old Town with its narrow streets and dark alleys and an ambience that harks back to medieval times. Along the southern shores is the old French business and government district, with its *belle époque* villas and tree-lined avenues.

Drive into the **Old Town** by way of Hang Dao Street which (under various names) runs clear across the medieval quarter. Each street is named after commodities sold in bygone times – Hang Gai was the street of hemp vendors, Hang Quat was the street of the paper fan makers, Hang Bo the street of the basketweavers and so on. But, do not expect to find many ancient products being sold today. Most of the Old Town shops sell contemporary clothing, kitchen and electronic items. But, wedged between the clutter of modern capitalism, you can stumble into traditional medicine shops, bamboo vendors and ancient guild temples that were originally financed by the masters of a specific craft. There are five guild temples located along Hang Bong Street, although years of wear and tear have left them somewhat dilapidated.

Another place where the spirit of the middle ages survives is **Dong Xuan Market**, located deep in the heart of the Old Town. Here, fruit, vegetables and

The Ho Chi Minh Mausoleum.

live animals are sold by weather–beaten old ladies with betelnut–stained teeth. Just beyond the market, the eastern edge of the old quarter is drawn by Tran Nhat Quat Street, which runs along the banks of the Red River. To the left is the famous **Long Bien (Doumer) Bridge** (1902), which still wears much of its war-time damage and to the right is the modern **Chuong Duong Bridge** (1985) which leads to the airport and the northern reaches of the Red River Valley. Another sight in the old quarter is the small **Ho Chi Minh Museum** at 48 Hang Ngang Street, where Ho Chi Minh wrote the Vietnamese Declaration of Independence.

Hang Khai Street runs along the south shore, and this is perhaps the best place in Hanoi to hunt for artwork, handicrafts and other souvenirs. At the intersection of Hang Khai and Hang Bai is a large government department store and further down the street (in the direction of the Opera) is a foreign language bookshop (maps of Hanoi can be bought on the street outside) and popular ice cream stalls.

Operas & Museums

The **Opera** (or Municipal Theater as it is now called) is the most flamboyant of Hanoi's wealth of old French buildings. Built in 1911, it was meant to be an exact (albeit smaller) replica of the famous Paris Opera House. While it does

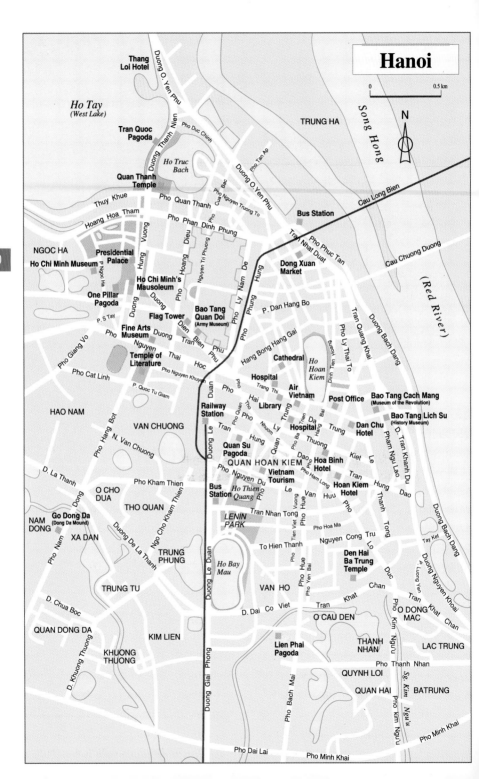

Hanoi

0   0.5 km

N

Ho Tay
(West Lake)

Song Hong

TRUNG HA

Thang
Loi Hotel

Duong O. Yen Phu

Tran Quoc
Pagoda

Duong Thanh Nien

Pho Duc Chinh

Pho Tan Ap

Duong O. Yen Phu

Cau Long Bien

Ho Truc
Bach

Quan Thanh
Temple

Thuy Khue

Pho Quan Thanh

Cua Bac

Pho Nguyen Truong To

Bus Station

Pho Phuc Tan

Hoang Hoa Tham

Pho Phan Dinh Phung

Tran Nhat Duat

Cau Chuong Duong

(Red River)

NGOC HA

Presidential
Palace

Ho Chi Minh Museum

Pho Ngoc Ha

Duong

Hung

Vuong

Dieu

Hoang

Nguyen Tri Phuong

De

Ly Nam

Hung

Dong Xuan
Market

Ho Chi Minh's
Mausoleum

One Pillar
Pagoda

P. S Tay

Duong

Flag Tower

Bao Tang
Quan Doi
(Army Museum)

Phung

P. Dan Hang Bo

Tran Quang Khai

Duong Bach Dang

Fine Arts
Museum

Dien

Tran

Bien

Phu

Hang Bong Hang Gai

Cathedral

Ho
Hoan
Kiem

Pho Giang Vo

Nguyen

Thai

Hoc

Pho Ly Thai To

Dinh Tien Hoang

Temple of
Literature

Pho Cat Linh

Pho Nguyen Khuyen

Hospital

Trang Thi

Post Office

Bao Tang Cach Mang
(Museum of the Revolution)

P. Quoc Tu Giam

HAO NAM

Railway
Station

Duan

Pho

Hai
Ba

Air
Vietnam

Library

Tho

Pho Quan

Nhuom

Trung

Da

Bai

Thien

Dan Chu
Hotel

Bao Tang Lich Su
(History Museum)

D. Tran Khanh Du

Pham Ngu Lao

Pho Hang Bot

N. Van Chuong

VAN CHUONG

Tran

Hung

Ly

Quan

Dao

Thuong

Hospital

Hoa Binh
Hotel

Kiet

Le

Tran

Hung

Dao

Duong Nguyen Khoai

D. La Thanh

Dong

Quan Su
Pagoda

QUAN HOAN KIEM

Pho Nguyen Du

Vietnam
Tourism

Pho Ham Long

Hoan Kiem
Hotel

Thanh

Duong Bach Dang

O CHO
DUA

Pho Kham Thien

Bus
Station

Ho Thien
Quang

Le

Van

Huu

Pho

Tay Ket

NAM
DONG

Go Dong Da
(Dong Da Mound)

Duong De La Thanh

Ngo Cho Kham Thien

Tran Nhan Tong

Pho Hue

Vuong

LENIN
PARK

Pho Hoa Ma

Nguyen Cong Tru

Lo

P. Luong Yen

Duong Nguyen Khoai

Pho Nam

XA DAN

THO QUAN

TRUNG
PHUNG

Ho Bay
Mau

To Hien Thanh

Pho Hue

Pho Yen Bai

Den Hai
Ba Trung
Temple

Duc

Tran

Khat

Chan

O DONG
MAC

LAC TRUNG

D. Chua Boc

TRUNG TU

D. Dai Co Viet

VAN HO

Tran

Khat

Chan

Pho Kim Ngu'u

Sg. Kim

BATRUNG

QUAN DONG DA

KIM LIEN

O CAU DEN

THANH
NHAN

Pho Thanh Nhan

Ngu'u

D. Khuong Thuong

KHUONG
THUONG

Lien Phai
Pagoda

QUYNH LOI

QUAN HAI

Pho Kim Ngu'u

Duong Giai Phong

Duong Le Duan

Pho Bach Mai

Pho Dai Lai

Pho Minh Khai

Pho Minh Khai

White-washed façade of the Musuem of Revolution.

not achieve the majesty of its Parisian archetype, the building does exude a certain grace and charm that is sadly lacking in most of the capital's modern structures. This is especially so at night when the *baroque* façade is lit and you can imagine the days of the French occupation of Vietnam when Gaelic merchants and military men flocked to the Opera to see productions of Victor Hugo or Moliére. Crowds still descend on the opera, but nowadays they are more likely to be entertained by a visiting Hungarian folk dance troupe or by a flamenco guitarist from Cuba. But, without a doubt the Opera's most famous performance was in 1945 when Ho Chi Minh stood on the balcony before an exuberant crowd cheering from the square below declare Vietnam's independence from France.

Just beyond the Opera are two small museums, well worth a short visit. The **Revolutionary Museum** tells the story of Vietnam's various struggles against foreign repression (not just against the French and Americans), stretching as far back as China's Han Dynasty. Down the street is the **History Museum**, housed in an unusual red structure that was once the French School of the Far East. The displays inside relate the non-revolutionary aspects of local history, from prehistoric through dynastic times. The treasures displayed have been culled from old temples, citadels and archeological sites throughout Vietnam.

Yet, another grandiloquent struc-

The old grand style of the Governor General's House.

ture, is the **Hotel Metropole**, which sprawls for an entire block along Ngo Quyen Street near the Opera. After recent renovations, the Metropole is once again the most elegant (and most expensive) place to stay in Hanoi. Opposite it is the **Government Guest House**, a 19th-century palace that was once home to the French Governor of Tonkin. It is an almost perfect specimen of *belle epoque* architecture with plaster curlicues and wrought-iron metalwork, reminiscent of the original Paris metro stations. Just beyond the Metropole is a huge square dominated by the **Foreign Trade Bank** and a huge portrait of Ho Chi Minh that has become the symbol of modern Hanoi.

More French influence is found in the area east of Hoan Kiem Lake. **St Joseph's Cathedral** (1886) is a fine gothic structure and the seat of Hanoi's Roman Catholic diocese. The soaring nave, stone buttresses and stained-glass windows were inspired by the Cathedrals of Notre Dame and Chartres. St Joseph's has remained a functioning church throughout the communist era, with its own retinue of priests and nuns.

One of the city's most important Buddhist shrines is situated just a few blocks from the cathedral. **Quan Su Pagoda** on the street of the same name was founded in the 17th century as a hospice for visiting Buddhist scholars (hence its other name: **Ambassadors Pagoda),** but it has evolved in modern times into the centre for Buddhism in

An awesome war souvenir at the Army Museum.

the north. The area immediately to the west of the pagoda is Hanoi's main embassy district, where foreign missions are comfortably located in old French villas. A block to the north is one of the city's more notorious sights – **Hao Lo Prison** – dubbed the **Hanoi Hilton** by American POWs who were interned there during the war. The prison is not open to the public and may not be much longer in this world as plans call for its demolition to make way for Hanoi's first modern hotel and shopping complex.

Dien Bien Phu Street leads west in the direction of Ho Chi Minh's Tomb, a district called Ba Dinh which suffered heavy bomb damage during the American War. Along the way is a huge fortress called the **Citadel**, built during the early part of the Nguyen Dynasty and fashioned after the Napoleonic bastions of Europe. Little of the original structure remains, except for a 60-meter-high hexagonal tower which flies a vast Vietnamese flag.

The Citadel is still the headquarters of the nation's armed forces and is off limits to civilians (and tourists) except for one small portion that houses the **Army Museum**. This is probably the most fascinating of the half dozen museums in Hanoi because so much of the history displayed here is still fresh in our minds. The twisted hulk of metal in the forecourt was once an American B-52 bomber, but there are also lots of intact weapons on display, including airplanes, tanks and artillery. Do not

The Dating Game, Hanoi Style

For thousands of years, Vietnamese parents fixed their children's marriages in much the same way that they would embark on a livestock or property deal. The sage Confucius dictated respect for authority, and this meant tying the knot to whomever your parents thought was best, a decision normally related to social or monetary factors.

But, things began to change in the 1950s, as communism ushered in a less stringent social era. Arranged marriages are still common, but these days young people are likely to choose their own mates. As in the west, the best place to meet the opposite sex is at school, at work or at a gathering of friends.

One of the most common first dates in Hanoi is a group outing to a soccer game at the national stadium. But, once you get to a more intimate level, a more secluded place is desirable. As in elsewhere in Asia, absolute privacy is an alien concept, especially in working class homes which are often shared by three generations of the same family. Thus, young lovers head for more leafy confines...

Although many lovers rendezvous at night in the small park opposite the Opera House in downtown Hanoi, the most popular spots are in the suburbs, in places like Lenin Park, the banks of West Lake and the zoo, where you can almost get lost amidst the undergrowth. They may not be totally private, but at least the only other people around are other loving couples!

get the notion that this museum is only about the American War as evidence of Vietnam's numerous conflicts are enumerated within its walls. One may forget what the last struggle was about – a statue of Vladimir Lenin stands in the small park across the street.

Only a few blocks away, on Nguyen Thai Hoc Street, is the **Fine Arts Museum**. However, do not expect the Louvre. Most of the exhibits dislayed here only date over the last 40 years – paintings, sculpture and handicrafts executed by northern artists, many of which espouse revolutionary or socialist themes.

Across the street from the museum is the famous **Temple of Literature (Van Mieu)**, but you have to go all the way around the block (to Quoc Tu Giam Street) to gain admittance. This is really Hanoi's most precious sight. Founded in AD 1070 as Vietnam's first institution for higher learning and one of the few remaining examples of Ly Dynasty architecture, the temple served as the national university for more than 700 years. During this time it was almost singlehandedly responsible for perpetuating the rule of the upper class by educating new *mandarins* (high court officials) in the teachings of Confucius. From the years 1442 to 1778, pupils sat for doctoral exams every three years and those who passed had their names inscribed on stone stelae in the temple garden. Eighty-two of the stelae remain, priceless relics of Vietnam's scholarly culture and structure.

Ho Chi Minh's Tomb is a large, stark edifice that looks down on Ba Ding Square, a rather cheerless building that offers a sharp contrast to the warm and humble nature of the person interned within. Although Ho Chi Minh himself wished to be cremated when he died in 1969, his will was ignored by high-rank-

The famed garden of literature.

ing Communist Party officials, who wanted to preserve his body for posterity as a symbol of the revolution. There is always a long queue of people – mostly school children and peasants – waiting to get inside, but foreign visitors are politely shown to the front of the line. Whether you were friend or foe during the war years, shuffling along in the dark with hundreds of emotion-choked Vietnamese is a moving experience. Ho Chi Minh lies entombed inside a glass sarcophagus, attired in a simple cotton shirt, with his hands folded across his chest in a posture of eternal serenity. Please observe the rules: no photos, no hats, no shorts, no hands in your pockets, remain quiet at all times and do not tap on the glass.

The area around the mausoleum is filled with interesting sights. On the north side of Ba Dinh Square is the **Presidential Palace**, constructed in 1906 for the colonial governor of Indochina. Indochina was the French base in Asia from which the French ruled over their dominions of Vietnam, Cambodia and Laos. Today, it is a government reception hall. In the lush gardens situated behind the palace is **Ho Chi Minh's House**, a modest dwelling where the father of modern Vietnam lived for the last eleven years of his life. The house is built in the style of a hilltribe dwelling and is made from native wood and bamboo. On the eastern fringe of the square, directly opposite the tomb, is the **National Assembly Hall**, which houses

One Pillar Pagoda rises above the lotus plants.

both the Communist Party headquarters and the national legislature.

On the south side of the square, obscured by huge trees and set in the middle of a lily pond, is a petite wooden structure called the **One Pillar Pagoda**. This is actually a reconstruction of the original pagoda, built in the 11th century and then destroyed by the retreating French in 1954. Emperor Ly Thai To, the founder of the Ly Dynasty, commissioned this tiny temple after he moved his capital from Hoa Lu to Thang Long (Hanoi) in 1010. The successive emper-

Tran Quoc Temple.

ors of the Ly Dynasty continued to pray at this shrine twice a month. Situated directly behind the pagoda is a huge new building with a golden façade – the **Ho Chi Minh Museum** – where books, videos and personal artifacts culled from the life of the great man are exhibited. Near the museum, at the busy crossroads of Ngoc Ha and Le Hong Phong streets, are a number of shops that sell flower arrangements for reverent people to leave outside Ho Chi Minh's Tomb.

The Ba Dinh district also contains **West Lake (Ho Tay)**, a large body of water that delineates Hanoi's northern boundary. The **Thang Loi Hotel** sits on a narrow isthmus between West Lake and the Red River, and there is a new floating restaurant which offers roman-

tic views of the water. A 13-kilometer trail winds around the edge of the lake, but most of the interesting sights are down in the southeast corner, along Tran Nien Street. **Tran Quoc Pagoda** is the city's oldest place of worship, built in AD 6 before Hanoi was designated the capital. A stone stelae relates the history of the temple. Further south is **Quan Thanh Pagoda**, a Ly Dynasty shrine famous for its 17th-century bronze bell and Buddha. The temple is dedicated to Tran Vo, God of the North and just outside are the ruins of one of the original gates of Thang Long.

Between the pagodas, on the banks of a small lake called **Ho Truc Bach**, is a monument dedicated to the anti-aircraft gunners who protected Hanoi dur-

Tribespeople of Hanoi

It is often difficult for foreigners to distinguish one tribe from another, even when they exist in close proximity to one another. The following guide may help:

Black Thai

Found mostly in the Son La and Dien Bien Phu areas, the Black Thai people are one of the largest of Vietnam's ethnic groups. They live in the large valleys between mountains, farming rice in neat little paddies which often reach up the hillsides in a series of emerald green terraces. Their secondary trades include silk weaving and gold mining.

Most of them still live in traditional longhouse dwellings, with wooden sides and thatched roofs, and their religious beliefs (like most of the hilltribes) are still firmly rooted in ancient animist beliefs.

Black Thai women wear ankle-length black skirts, topped by silk blouses woven in a number of bright colors. The blouses have solid silver buttons, often fashioned in the shape of butterflies and after marriage the women place old silver coins (minted in French Indochina or Siam) in front of their hair. Their headscarves are also distinctive: black base edged with multi-colored embroidery. One sure way to tell them apart from other minority groups is a quick glace at the women's collars: Black Thai ladies have a round collar which they button tightly against the neck, right up to the top.

Among the best places to see (and photograph) Black Thai, are in the Dien Bien Phu market, various villages in the Dien Bien Phu Valley, Tong Nho village on the outskirts of Son La, and a market town called Bon Phang on the highway between Son La and Tuan Giao.

White Thai

The White Thai are closely related to the Black Thai in terms of language, religion, lifestyle and clothing. But, they speak a slightly different dialect and tend to lead less traditional lives. Many tribesmen in the Lai Chau and Mai Chau areas are now abandoning their traditional turtle-shaped thatched and wooden longhouses, in favor of slate roofs.

Women of the White Thai tribe originally wore white skirts, but convention has given way to more practical colors, even denim skirts! They sport slightly different hairstyles, headscarves and silver buttons similar to the Black Thai, but their blouses have an open collar, that is not so tight around the neck.

White Thais comprise about 60 percent of the population of Mai Chau District in Son La province. But the best place to see the more traditional White Thai villages is the high plateau country between Lai Chau and Tuan Giao, which, in spite of the miserable road, is fascinating all the same.

Muong

Most members of the Muong are assimilated into mainstream Vietnamese society, but many in the more remote regions of Ha Son Binh province still live in villages with longhouses perched on stilts. The men once wore green or brown pajama-type outfits, but nowadays they dress in military uniforms or store-bought city clothes. However, Muong women still favor traditional garb: long black skirts, pastel-colored blouses with a deep V-shaped neckline and conical hats.

The Muong are also rice growers, but among their other agrarian pursuits are sugarcane and tea farming. Some experiment with coffee, which they hope to turn into another cash crop. Silk production and weaving is a common village industry. About 90 percent of the people in Lac Son District are Muong, but they can also be seen in Cuc Phuong National Park.

Hmong (Meo)

The Hmong people – also called the Meo – are closely related to a tribe of the same name living across the border in Laos. In Vietnam, they are divided into several clans according to the traditional hue of the women's skirts: black, white, red, green and flowered. They cling to their ancient ways, living high on the mountainsides and shunning contact with outsiders, even members of other minority groups. They are among the poorest people in Vietnam, with almost no access to modern education, health care or utilities.

The Hmong survive by cultivating dry rice and maize on steep slopes, raising chickens, pigs and buffalo, and tending small vegetable plots. Hmong men continue to wear black pajama outfits, and many of them carry old flintlock rifles.

Hmong women, for the most part, wear skirts that match their tribal name. Among the most distinctive are the Red Hmong ladies with their flowing red dresses and Victorian hairstyles.

Their villages are found in the mountain passes between Dien Bien Phu and Lai Chau, and in the high plateau country between Lai Chau and Tuan Giao.

Quan Thanh Pagoda at West Lake, Hanoi.

ing the American War.

Hanoi's southern precinct is called Hai Ba Trung after the famous Trung Sisters, military heroines from the first century who temporarily rid the country of the dreaded Chinese. In keeping with that theme, the major place of interest is the **Trung Sisters Temple**, a 12th-century shrine where the sisters are still worshipped. Nearby is **Lenin Park**, one of the city's most popular green spaces, which boasts a large lake at the center, called **Bay Mau**.

There are a number of interesting sights scattered throughout the countryside around the capital, embraced by the more rural parts of the Hanoi municipality. They can easily be reached in half-day tours from the city.

Meo lady.

The slow pace of the Red River.

North of the river and just off the airport highway are the ruins of **Co Loa**, the ancient Bronze Age capital of Vietnam, built in 3 BC by the Lac Viet kings. The city was once protected by a series of ramparts and moats built in a spiral with the royal citadel sitting at the very center. In fact, the name Co Loa means "snail" as the immense fortress was said to resemble the inside of a snail's shell. Only three of the earthen bulwarks remain, but within the ruined citadel are temples dedicated to King An Duong (who founded Co Loa in 257 BC) and his daughter Princess Mi Chau, who betrayed her father to the Chinese invaders in the greatest act of love-inspired treachery in Vietnamese history.

Tay Phuong Pagoda is 44 kilo-meters due west of Hanoi, near Thach That village. The pagoda features three wooden temples set amidst reflecting ponds and is famous for its wooden bas-reliefs and sculptures, including replicas of the *sixteen Arhats* (sixteen saints) a masterpiece of Vietnamese Buddhist art (the originals are housed in Hanoi's Fine Arts Museum). Although construction began in 3 AD, over the years various additions and embellishments have eclipsed the original design. Thus, most of what you see today dates from the 18th century.

Ha Son Binh province, south of Hanoi, has two lovely pagodas set against the backdrop of the lush Red River Valley. **Tay Pagoda** is 35 kilo-meters south of the city, built during the

Black River Gold Rush

There is still lots of gold on the northwest frontier, especially along the watershed of the Black River where hilltribe people utilizing unique methods extract this alluvial treasure.

Black Thai groups start by building a stone dyke about halfway across the stream, creating a small bay in which the silt comes to rest. Then two or three of the strongest men, standing waist-deep in water, push a metal sled along the bottom with the aid of sturdy bamboo poles. At the other end are two women pushing the arms of a wooden capstan with a rope attached to the sled. As the sled reaches the dyke, one of the women dumps its muddy contents onto a washboard contraption, where a man rinses it with buckets of water, whilst looking out for flecks of gold.

Teams can "pan" as much as a tenth of an ounce of gold each day, which they can sell to local assayers or in the gold shops of Hanoi for about US$40. It does not sound like much – especially after it has been split six ways – until you consider that the average wage in Vietnam is only a few hundred dollars. There is nothing romantic about this sort of work, but like fortune seekers everywhere else in the world the miners of the Black River basin see gold at the end of their rainbow!

Ly Dynasty and dedicated to both Lord Buddha and the aforementioned *arhats* (Buddhist saints). Water puppet shows are sometimes staged in a shallow pond at the temple, while the hill standing behind the temple affords a good view of the surrounding farmland.

Huong (Perfume) Pagoda is even further out of Hanoi, roughly 60 kilometers from the city center along the banks of the River Yen. Thousands of Buddhists flock here during the second and third months of the lunar calendar on a pilgrimage that takes them to various holy grottos and shrines set along the river and adjacent limestone outcrops called Huong Son – the "Mountain of Perfumes". At the very end of the trail is **Huong Tich Grotto** which many people claim is the most beautiful spot in Vietnam.

Red River Valley

Hanoi sits at the heart of a giant natural fan called the **Red River Valley**, a classic V-shaped delta formed by millions of years of silt pouring down from the Himalayas and the rugged hills of southern China. There are a number of other large cities in the valley region including Haiphong, Thai Nguyen, Nam Dinh and Thanh Hoa. But, for the most part they are drab industrial towns which have little to offer the foreign visitor. The valley's greatest charms are its picturesque farmlands that spread all the way up to the horizon, divided by earthen dykes they add up to a million separate rice paddies punctuated with thatched-roof villages. Peasant life is readily apparent along major routes like Highway One that runs between Hanoi and Nam Dinh. But, to really experience country life, drive along the narrow backroads that link rural districts (where new photo opportunities abound around every bend)!

Haiphong is a shadow of its former self, a broken down and somewhat depressing city that has definitely seen better times. Most of the ethnic Chinese have left, and many of the boat people

A farm house outside Hanoi.

who have fled to Hong Kong and other "free" ports, are from villages in the Haiphong region. This port city at the northwest corner of the delta was developed by the French into a thriving export gateway through which all the great products and commodities of Indochina – rice, rubber and coal – once moved. The advent of communism shut the export door, and a decade later the city was almost destroyed by the American bombardment.

Most travelers bypass Haiphong on their way to Ha Long Bay. But, there are

wharves and river is along Ben Bach Dang Street, which boasts a small ferry that crosses to the north bank. The city's Buddhist temples including the 17th century **Du Hang Pagoda** in the Lam Tuong Quarter were largely spared the ravages of war. The ancient **Hang Kenh Communal House**, famous for its wooden friezes and sculptures is also located nearby.

Just east of Haiphong is gorgeous **Ha Long Bay**, almost universally acclaimed as the most photogenic spot in Vietnam. This would be just another indentation in the Indochina coast if not for the presence of roughly 3,000 limestone islands, many of which rise straight from the sea as sheer cliffs and bizarre eroded formations. According to local legend, the contorted landscape was carved by the tail of a giant dragon making its way into the sea. In fact, Ha Long means "Sea Dragon," in Vietnamese. But, in geological terms, the *karst* (porous limestone hills) formations resulted from millions of years of wind and water action against limestone rock. Keep in mind that the view depends on the weather: do not visit in winter, when thick clouds and drizzle will obscure most of the scenery.

The jumping off point for Ha Long Bay is a small waterfront town called **Bai Chay**, near the large coastal coal-mining center of Hon Gai. Bai Chay has a provincial tourist office, numerous small hotels and a dock area where junks and other boats can be hired. The nearest excursion is to **Hang Dau Go –**

a few sights for those who choose to linger in the bygone port. The old French **Opera House** (Thanh Phoi Theater) looks down on Tran Hung Dao Street. The **Tourist Office, Roman Catholic Cathedral** and **Haiphong Museum** are all located on Dien Bien Phu Street, the main street which runs through the downtown district. The best view of the a grotto that the French dubbed the "Cave of Marvels" – which boasts stalactites, stalagmites and other geological oddities. The southern fringe of the bay is protected by mighty **Cat Ba Island**, which boasts of abundant wildlife and virgin forest, protected within the bounds of a national park. At the eastern edge of the bay is the **Fai Tsi Long Archipelago** which contains numerous larger islands yet to be discovered by tourists.

Northern Highlands

One side of the Red River Valley is flanked by the Gulf of Tonkin, but the other sides of the triangle are delineated by rugged mountain ranges, mostly populated by ethnic hilltribe people.

The northern frontier region – Hoang Lien Son, Ha Tuyen, Cao Bang and Lang Son provinces – was the scene of fierce fighting during Vietnam's 1979 war with China. Despite rampant smuggling, the border was officially closed for many years. However, in 1992, Hanoi and Beijing agreed to re-open the border, paving the way for a revival of both trade and tourism in the region. Anyone who travels in the northern border areas should take note that tourist facilities are minimal or nonexistent.

Lang Son, the easternmost of the big border towns, is expected to boom once the railway reopens between Vietnam and China (probably sometime in the next few years). You can see hilltribe

A black Thai girl at rice harvest time.

groups in the market, but otherwise Lang Son does not hold much aesthetic appeal. **Cao Bang** presents a similarly dull façade, but at least it has some intriguing scenery in the surrounding countryside. Of particular interest is the **Ba Be Lake** area with its many waterfalls, streams and traditional villages of the Zao tribe.

Lao Cai sits at a strategic junction where both the Red River and the old railway line between Hanoi and Kunming cross from China into Vietnam. This is another town that is expected to thrive once Sino-Vietnamese trade gets back on its feet. The mountain areas around Lao Cai are gorgeous and are some of the most beautiful parts of Vietnam. **Sa Pa** is an old French hill

Paddy field mosaic in rural Vietnam.

station that snuggles between forest and fruit orchards on a high plateau above the Red River Gorge. Many hilltribe people live in the surrounding woods. Vietnam's highest peak, **Fan Si Pan**, which towers to more than 3,100 meters (10,300 feet) is also located nearby.

The northwest highlands along the border with Laos are one of the most spectacular parts of Indochina in terms of both human and natural landscapes. The Lai Chau and Son La provinces are the best places in the whole of Vietnam to meet hilltribe people, including members of the Thai, Muong and Hmong groups, who continue to live in traditional longhouses and go about their daily lives in much the same manner as their ancient ancestors. Like other parts of the highlands, tourism is still in its infancy, with little more than basic food or lodging being offered. But, with its abundant resources, the region will probably blossom into something equivalent to the Chiang Mai area of northern Thailand which offers hilltribe treks, whitewater rafting and other adventure travel pursuits.

Provinces & Valleys

Highway Six shoots straight across the Red River Valley from Hanoi to **Hoa Binh** (with its big Russian-built hydroelectric project) and then straight into the foothills of Ha Son Binh province. Almost immediately you will be in

A farmer threshing grain outside his home in the country side.

hilltribe country. The air is crisp, the people look different and the road becomes progressively tougher. The luxuriant **Mai Chau Valley** shimmers like a silver pool, with tiny villages that cower beneath the towering *karst* cliffs.

Son La is a small but bustling provincial capital and is something of a metropolis for all the northwest highlands. Its dusty lanes are filled with Black Thai people from the surrounding villages and recent Viet immigrants who run most of the shops. Of special interest is **Son La Prison**, which was built by the French in 1908 as a brig for leaders of the local Black Thai rebellion, but which was later reserved for political prisoners from around the country.

The prison museum tells the story of those who were once interned here, but even more gripping is a walk through the old prison yard, which has mostly been destroyed by American bombardment. Below the kitchen is a notorious dungeon where according to the prison guide, wardens were known to keep the more difficult prisoners, often filling the cells with water. In May 1941, wardens shoved 156 political prisoners into the underground cells, turned on the taps and kept them drenched up to their necks for 12 days. Many died.

Highway Six continues in a northwesterly direction beyond Son La, threading deep tropical valleys and high plateaus where the Black Thai people plant rice. **Tuan Giao** is just over the border in Lai Chau province. From here the road splits into two – the northern fork heading for Lai Chau and the western fork to the spacious Dien Bien Phu Valley.

Dien Bien Phu was virtually unknown to the outside world until the spring of 1954 when the large French army under General Navarre was besieged by the Viet Minh under General Giap, a legendary military strategist who also left his mark during the American War. The French hoped to draw the enemy into a conventional battle in which they could use their superior air cover and weaponry. But Giap responded with twice as many soldiers as the French reconnaissance had predicted and new artillery from China, which the Viet Minh dug into the surrounding hills.

The siege lasted for 55 days, with heavy casualties on both sides, until the French – cut off from their supply base and completely demoralized – surrendered on May 7 signifying the end of French rule in Indochina.

Some of the bloodiest fighting during the Dien Bien Phu campaign took place on **Hill A1**, west of the government guest house, a one-time French stronghold that has now been turned into a memorial park with old French bunkers and the rusting hulk of a tank in its grounds. At the base of the hill is a small museum with relics of the fighting, and just across the street is a military cemetery with the graves of many of those who died in 1954.

Prior to the 19th century, the Dien Bien Phu Valley was a thriving crossroads of trade between the Red River Valley, southern China and Thailand, but few traces of that period linger. Near **Phu Village** are the remains of an 18th century citadel including earthen walls and a small temple dedicated to General Hoang Cong Chat, who liberated the valley from Laotian invaders in 1758. The temple lies beneath the limbs of a great banyan tree.

Near the southern edge of the valley is **Pom Lot Citadel**, an 11th century bastion that today is little more than a mound of dirt. The summit offers a panoramic view of the encircling farmland and mountains.

Heading South

Highway One runs the entire length of Vietnam, from Hanoi to Ho Chi Minh City and into the Mekong Delta. From the capital, the route cuts due south across the Red River Valley through the typical rice-paddy terrain of Ha Son Binh and Nam Ninh provinces. There is water everywhere: canals, ponds, lakes, rivers and puddles, and plenty of livestock too, from stark white ducks that seem to be fresh from the cleaners to lumbering water buffalo with their ever-present cloak of mud.

Slightly off the highway is **Hoa Lu**, one of the ancient capitals of Vietnam and a highly scenic area with a gentle river running through *karst* hills. Hoa Lu was the capital of Vietnam from AD 968 to 1010, when the royal court moved to Thang Long (Hanoi). The palace and

Birthplace of Ho Chi Minh near Vinh.

citadel have vanished, but several important 11th century temples remain, although they are now badly in need of renovation and protection from both the elements and smugglers of antiques. Despite the coat of dust and chipped paint, the **Temple of Dinh Tien Hoang** is a magnificent building and is one of the finest examples of medieval architecture in Vietnam. Inside are massive wooden statues, panels and an altar where local people still come to worship. Nearby is the smaller but equally ornate **Le Hoan Temple**. Boats can be hired at **Truong Yen** village – many of the oars-

men solicit their trade from the front of the temples. The journey takes you on a winding route through rice paddies and into sunken limestone caverns, a marvelous way to spend an afternoon.

Cuc Phuong National Park lies at the junction of three provinces. The reserve embraces 22,000 square kilometers of virgin forest and many rare and endangered animal species. Some of the trees are a thousand years old and tower to more than 50 meters (150 feet). At the heart of the park is a narrow valley that lies between two parallel limestone mountains – "the Yosemite of Vietnam"

dawn, but then strangely head for the shade shortly after the sun peeks over the Gulf of Tonkin. Vietnam narrows below Ninh Binh into a fragile isthmus of land between Laos and the South China Sea. This is one of the nation's poorest regions, afflicted with sandy soil, gross erosion and frequent typhoons. Bomb craters litter the side of Highway One – although some have been turned into fish ponds – and many bridges and buildings still bear the scars of war.

Vinh

Prosperity will not show its face again until you reach **Vinh**, the capital of Ngee Tinh province and the last of the big cities of the north. Vinh was decimated during the American War and is still being rebuilt. But, the surrounding farmlands have fully recovered, a panorama of paddy fields and hamlets that seems little changed since ancient times. **Cua Lo Beach** with its long white strand and pine forest is 20 kilometers north of the city center. But, the main reason to stop in Vinh is to go to **Ho Chi Minh's home town**, located at Kim Lien commune west of town. The house where Ho was born is preserved in Chua village, a modest compound that includes three thatched-roof dwellings and a small family temple. Nearby is **Sen village**, where Ho lived with his father until he went away to school. Behind his father's house is a museum detailing the life of Ho Chi Minh.

– with forest paths that lead to famous local attractions such as the **Ancient People Cave** (where the remains of prehistoric man have been found) and **Half Moon Cave**.

Beach Retreat

The only proper beach retreat along the entire coast of north Vietnam is **Sam Son**, in Thanh Hoa province, a spartan resort frequented by farmers, factory groups and soldiers. Lodging is in tents, bungalows and cement-block motels, with food stalls arranged along the strand. Vietnamese bathers swim before

Street life in Trang Tien Street, Hanoi.

Hanoi Hana, happier today.

The beret, an old French habit has never gone out of style.

A happy school girl.

T he central region of Vietnam successfully links the Mekong Delta in the south with the Red River Delta in the north. **Hue** is like no other place in Southeast Asia, an alluring city resting on the banks of the Perfume River, that combines imperial majesty with old world charm in a breezy ambience that recalls another age. In fact, Hue is from another age and the reason to visit it is for its history. The city was founded in the late 17th century but it did not blossom into a full-blown metropolis until the early 19th century when Gia Long, founder of the Nguyen Dynasty, chose Hue as the site for his royal court. The Nguyens may not have been the most benevolent rulers, but under their guidance Hue developed into the cultural capital of Vietnam – a city of artists, architects and writers who found both inspiration from the natural surroundings and royal patronage to support their pursuits.

Although it suffered during the

■ ■ ■ ■ ■ ■

The Red River Valley in Ha Nam Ninh Province.

Hue & The Central Coast

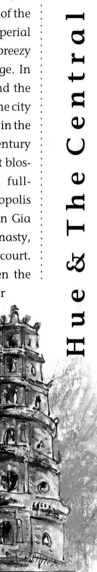

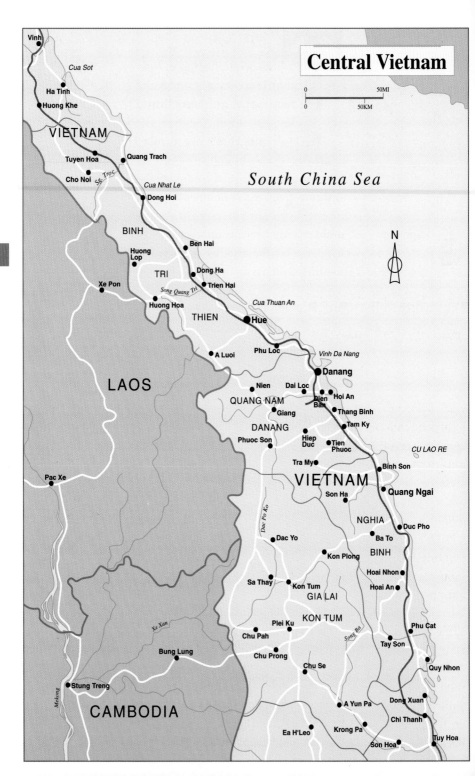

Binh Tri Thien, the Perfume River, Hue.

wars of liberation, Hue retains much of its bygone charm. But, at the same time Hue has a certain youthful charisma, a university town with a population of students, artists and intellectuals who are not afraid to share their thoughts and ideas with outsiders.

The Citadel on the banks of the Perfume River in Hue, is the most famous structure in Vietnam, due to both its imperial legacy and wartime history. This huge fortress-palace complex was started by Gia Long, the first king of the Nguyen Dynasty, in 1804 after the French had helped him seize control of the country from the Tay Son rebels. Subsequent rulers added to the Citadel's girth and intricacy until it was one of the most magnificent royal courts in all of

Asia, amounting to more than five square kilometers (two square miles) in size, complete with a labyrinth of inner courtyards and passages.

Fashioned after the Imperial City in Beijing, the Citadel is protected by several distinct fortifications. The outermost wall (Kinh Thanh) has ten gates and was built in the style of a Napoleonic fortress. It runs along the banks of the Perfume River and adjacent canals, but the only part worth scaling is the **King's Tower** (Ky Dai) with a huge flag pole that overlooks the river and Highway One. Inside which is the Imperial City (Dai Noi), a heavily fortified cube embraced by a moat and thick stone walls that have defied destruction through two separate wars. Sitting at

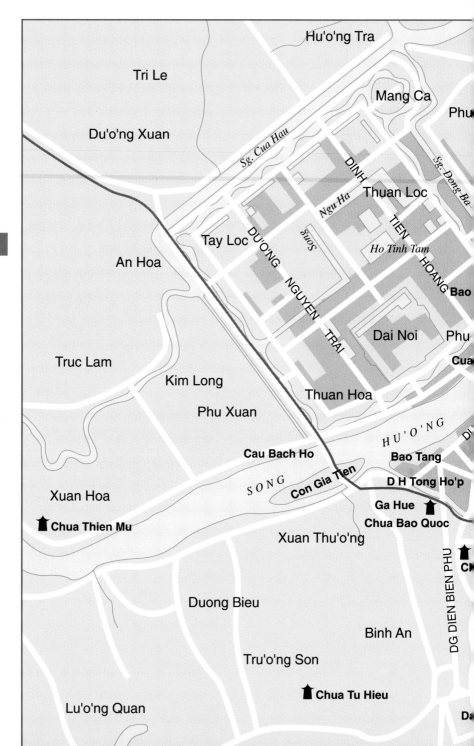

Hu'o'ng Tra

Tri Le

Mang Ca

Phu

Du'o'ng Xuan

Sg. Cua Hau

DINH

Thuan Loc

Sg. Dong Ba

Ngu Ha

Tay Loc

DU'O'NG

Song

TIEN

An Hoa

Ho Tinh Tam

HOANG

Bao

NGUYEN

Truc Lam

TRAI

Dai Noi

Phu

Cua

Kim Long

Thuan Hoa

Phu Xuan

HU'O'NG

D

Cau Bach Ho

Bao Tang

Con Gia Tien

D H Tong Ho'p

SONG

Xuan Hoa

Ga Hue

🏯 **Chua Thien Mu**

Chua Bao Quoc

Xuan Thu'o'ng

DG DIEN BIEN PHU

Duong Bieu

🏯 **C**

Binh An

Tru'o'ng Son

🏯 **Chua Tu Hieu**

Lu'o'ng Quan

Da

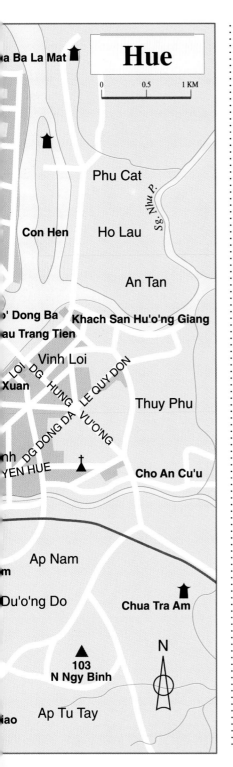

the very heart of the Citadel is the **Purple Palace** – where only members of the royal family and their servants could tread. Arrayed around the palace are the homes of other members of the royal household, imperial offices and servants' quarters. The outer parts of the Citadel are open to the general public, but the Imperial City is now a national monument. Entrance is through the **Noon Gate** (Ngo Mon), where you can purchase a ticket with coupons to enter various parts of the city. The gate is beautifully restored to its former glory and offers a good view of the royal precinct. Beyond the gate is a courtyard with brilliant white frangipani trees and a stone pond crossed by the **Golden Water Bridge** (Cau Trung Dao) which was solely reserved for the use of the king (other people had to walk around the outside of the pond).

The **Court of Major Rituals** (Dai Trieu Nghi) spreads out before your eyes, it boasts a restored audience hall called the **Palace of Supreme Peace** (Dien Thai Hoa) on the north flank. The "great rites" were religious ceremonies and royal audiences overseen by the king, some involving hundreds of *mandarins* (high court officials) and other government officials dressed in splendid silk gowns and peaked caps, who were forced to *kowtow* (to abase or prostrate oneself) before the king on the stone pavement.

In dynastic days commoners were not allowed beyond this point, but today you can step right into the Vietnamese version of the Forbidden City, or at

The fearsome Dragon on Hien Nhon gate in Hue.

least its remains. The Purple Palace (Tu Cam Thanh) was bombarded during both the French and American wars; by the end of the Tet Offensive in 1968 there was nothing left but broken mortar and charred wooden beams. Two small *mandarin* palaces (the **Huu Vu** and **Ta Vu**) have been restored and now contain art galleries, but the former royal quarters is now a cassava field tended by elderly ladies. Standing amidst the ruins are a few bronze cannons and huge urns. To one side of the cassava patch, shielded by a grove of trees, is the **Read-**

of the royal temples and households on the west side. The most precious of these is the **Pavilion of Splendor** (Hien Lam Cac), a three-story wooden palace fronted by nine dynastic urns called the Cuu Dinh. Weighing close to 2,000 kilograms and etched with highly detailed images, the bronze urns were cast in the 1830s during the reign of Emperor Ming Mang as a pictorial tribute to the accomplishments of the Nguyen Dynasty. Today, they are considered a priceless national treasure. Across the courtyard is the **Generations Temple** (The Mieu), a shrine to the Nguyen kings which contains many of their personal belongings. Nearby are other places of imperial worship – the **Thai Mieu Hung Mieu** and **Dien Phung** temples, all badly in need of restoration.

The king's mother once lived in the **Everlasting Longevity Palace** (Dien Tho) in the northwest corner of the Imperial City, while his grandmother resided in the adjacent **Truong Sanh Palace**, both of which have been taken over by squatters, including homeless students who attend the various colleges on the south bank of the Perfume River. The palace gardens are now filled with banana trees and maize plants.

Outside the Imperial City

Outside the Imperial City, but still within the grounds of the Citadel, is the **Museum of Antique Objects** which is filled with royal mementoes. The building

ing Book Palace (Thai Binh Lau), a restored royal library. At the rear of the field is a stone rostrum with interesting dragon stairs and beyond is the weed-covered **North Gate** (Hoa Binh).

Government offices ran down the western edge of the Imperial City, but most of these were destroyed during the Tet Offensive. However, much remains

Quiet charm of Linh Mu pagoda in Hue.

was constructed in 1845 as a pavilion for royal relaxation, and also served as a place where the body of the dead emperor was kept for eight months prior to his burial. Emperor Khai Dinh turned it into a museum in 1923, but it was not open to the public until after 1975. Among the hundreds of objects on display are Khai Dinh's imperial robes and bed, an ornate bureau once used by Tu Duc and the golden palanquin of Bao Dai, the last emperor of Vietnam. Also exhibited are ivory chopsticks in the shape of a dragon, a silver betelnut case, a tree made from glass, an ivory whisky decanter and court poetry incased in goldleaf frames. Across the street are the **Military Museum** and **Natural History** collection.

West of the Citadel

West of the Citadel, on the same side of the river, is **Thien (Linh) Mu Pagoda**, the most important Buddhist shrine in Hue. There has been a place of worship on this site from the 17th century, but the current complex, a seven-story octagonal pagoda with a square bell tower and three wooden halls, dates from 1844. You have to ask the monks for permission to climb the pagoda, but the view from the top is spectacular, looking straight down on the Perfume River and across the vast expanse of the valley towards the imperial necropolis. Ceremonies are held inside the temple three times daily (3.30 am, 10.30 am and 5

Hawkers at the Fish Market in Dong Ha, Quang Tri Province.

pm) – a retinue of saffron-clad monks and novices chant before a huge Laughing Buddha. A huge bell housed in a tower next to the entrance gate was cast in 1710 for the original pagoda. The bell is rung daily at 7 am and 4 pm by means of a thick wooden battering ram; the monks testify that one can hear the toll from as far as ten kilometers away. On the grounds is also a garage, which has an old Austin sedan that was used to drive one of Thien Mu's monks to his self-immolation in Saigon in 1963 to protest against the policies of the cor-

The DMZ: Relics of War

Collecting ordnance off Route Nine.

blockhouse, surrounded by rusted American tanks. But, the best place to get a view of the actual DMZ is from the top-floor restaurant of the Dong Truong Son Hotel, west of town along Highway Nine.

Start your tour at **Hien Luong Bridge**

The Geneva Peace Conference of 1954 divided Vietnam into separate halves along the 17th parallel and the Ben Hai River. The area to the north was handed over to Ho Chi Minh and the communists, while the region to the south came under the aegis of the Republic of Vietnam and its western backers. A five-kilometre strip on either side of the border was designated the Demilitarized Zone (DMZ), a temporary no-man's-land that was meant to keep opposing forces at bay until free elections could be held to reunify the country. The elections were never held, and so the DMZ continued for more than 20 years, until liberation in 1975.

The war was over long ago, but the DMZ endures as both a psychological and physical divide between north and south. Those who continue to clamour for southern independence, see this imaginary line as their future frontier. Meanwhile, the five-kilometre strip on either side of the DMZ continues to bear the scars of war – an anguished landscape of bomb craters, twisted bits of metal and vast desert-like areas created by chemical defoliants.

Quang Tri province to the south of the Ben Hai River has more battle sites and war relics than any other part of Vietnam. A bustling market town called **Dong Ha** on Highway One is the best place to base your exploration of this region. Standing in the middle of a traffic circle in the middle of Dong Ha is an old French

across the Ben Hai River, which was built in 1973 on the site of an earlier French bridge that linked north and south. All is quiet now along the former front, a pastoral scene that often includes elderly fishermen and children leading buffalo to the edge of the water. A wooden structure on the south bank was once a reception house for distinguished visitors including Jane Fonda and her ex-husband Tom Hayden who came south to view the front. South of Dong Ha is the old provincial capital, **Quang Tri Town**, which boasted a miniature version of the Hue Citadel until it was destroyed by communist shelling and American bombing in 1972. You can still see the bullet-riddled remains of a Catholic church and the old French prison.

American forces built a supposedly impregnable barrier called the McNamara Line across the southern flank of the DMZ between the coast and the Laotian border. The line was actually a string of powerful "firebases" surrounded by "free fire zones" where anything that moved was shot at. The ruins of famous firebases like **Con Thien** and **Doc Mieu** can still be seen, although little remains except for trenches, bunkers, rusted ammunition boxes, shell fragments and tattered bits of camouflage netting and military clothing.

Camp Carroll, west of Dong Ha along Highway Nine, was once the supply base and headquarters of US operations in the region, but nowadays it is a ghost town, decrepit and overgrown with weeds. Part of the camp has been turned into a pepper plantation worked by immigrants from the north, while **Hill 241** (once a platform for 175 millimeter howitzers) affords another good view of the DMZ, looking straight across to **The Rockpile**, a former Marine Corps observation post which sits on top of a sheer pinnacle.

Highway Nine takes to the south at The Rockpile through a broad valley populated by the Bru Van Kieu hilltribe people, into the upper reaches of the Han River. **Dakrong Bridge** was opened in 1976; the valley of the Dakrong River was once a Viet Cong sanctuary and carried part of the **Ho Chi Minh Trail**, although the actual trail is now overgrown with jungle.

The main road continues west to **Khe Sanh**, a lofty plateau that witnessed some of the bloodiest fighting since the inception of the Vietnam War. Khe Sanh was the scene of a famous 75-day seige in 1968 that coincided with the Tet Offensive, as 6,000 Marines and South Vietnamese Rangers (ARVN) held their ground against the much greater North Vietnamese Army (NVA) forces dug into the surrounding hillsides.

The similarities to the seige of Dien Bien Phu were uncanny, and there was a widespread fear that US-forces would meet the same fate as the French had 14 years earlier, especially after the Special Forces Base at Lang Vei were overrun by huge losses of life. The siege was broken on April 7th, after more than 100,000 tons of bombs had been dropped on the NVA positions. But, in one of the great ironies of the war, the US high command decided to order a withdrawal from Khe Sanh a few months after the siege, claiming that the area was no longer of strategic value.

Today's Khe Sanh is a big disappointment for war buffs. American forces destroyed most of the combat bases so that they would not fall into the hands of the communists.

The Vietnamese military now controls whatever is left of the old Marine air field – which means that it remains off-limits to tourists. A few old bunkers still remain at Lang Vei, and you can still see the shaved-off summits of Hill 881 and Hill 1015 north of this valley.

rupt American-backed Diem regime.

Dong Ba Market and Hue's commercial district lie just outside the Citadel gates, with Tran Hung Dao as the main thoroughfare. The old French quarter spreads along the south banks of the Perfume River, with villas and administrative buildings set along shady avenues. From the south bank wafts the air of higher learning. Here are the numerous educational institutes which boast of having educated the previous and present generation of national leaders.

Most of them are situated on Le Loi Avenue, which runs along the river. Among the illustrious alumni of **Quoc Hoc Boys School** are Ho Chi Minh, General Vo Nguyen Giap (the hero of Dien Bien Phu) and former South Vietnamese president Ngo Dinh Diem. Next door is **Trung Trac Girls School**, which in bygone days was said to school the loveliest girls in Vietnam. Further west is the campus of **Hue University** and the **Ho Chi Minh Museum**.

Of Churches & Towers

Of the half dozen churches on the south bank, the most interesting is the **Cathedral of Our Lady of Perpetual Help** (Notre Dame). Christened in 1962, this is like no other church in Vietnam, a bizarre combination of French gothic, modern American and Buddhist styles have been blended into a surrealist fantasy worthy of Dali. The nave towers 53

Tu Duc's Tomb in Hue.

meters above the marble floor, with a cast-iron bell tower (made by the Eiffel company in Paris) that reaches 70 meters at its highest point. Ask one of the priests for permission before you climb to the top of the tower.

The imperial necropolis is situated further up the Perfume River, on the outskirts of modern Hue. The seven rulers of the Nguyen Dynasty are buried in this area, which is the Vietnamese equivalent of Egypt's Valley of the Kings. Opinions vary on the architectural merit of the various graves. But three graves should not be missed: the tombs of Tu Duc, Khai Dinh and Ming Manh. The royal mausoleums were normally constructed before the king died, so that he could have the privilege of designing his own final resting place and the pleasure of using its tranquil gardens and lakes. In effect, the tombs doubled as country palaces where royalty indulged in frivolous pursuits like writing poetry or frolicking with their concubines.

Tombs & Pavillions

Tu Duc's Tomb is the first tomb encountered as you travel upriver. It is an absolute masterpiece that showpieces the design acumen of the Nguyen Dynasty, and is set against a pleasant grove of trees near the river. Tu Duc ruled from 1848 to 1883, and was the longest serving and most cultured Nguyen king. His wooden palace (**Hoa**

Restoring Imperial Majesty

Vietnamese archaeologists and architects have spent much of the last two decades trying to restore the Imperial City in Hue, which was destroyed during the Tet Offensive of 1968. It has been a painstaking task, because the damage was so extensive and because poverty-stricken Vietnam lacks both the cash and expertise to embark on a repair job.

Still, the work that has already been carried out is quite impressive. An initial survey identified more than 300 historic structures covering a total area of 4.5 million square meters, most of them were either completely destroyed or at least partially-damaged during the war.

The first phase called for the reconstruction of ten of the most important buildings within the Imperial City at a cost of 500 million dong. Among the structures that were saved were the **Noon Gate** (Ngo Mon), **Palace of Supreme Peace** (Dien Thai Hoa), **Pavilion of Splendor** (Hien Lam Cac), **Generations Temple** (The Mieu) and the two small *mandarin* (high court officials) palaces. At the same time, funds were set aside for the renovation and continued upkeep of 51 other structures that were largely spared war damage, including the seven imperial tombs situated on the outskirts of Hue.

Although most of the funding came from the national treasury, UNESCO gave a grant of US$100,000 as well as valuable material aid that included aluminum roofing to protect historic sites from the elements, vehicles, tools and office equipment. UNESCO also helped sponsor Vietnamese restoration experts to study abroad at famous archaeological sites in Thailand, Indonesia and India. Meanwhile, Vietnamese scholars traveled to the Oriental Museum in Paris to trace the original plans and documents relating to the construction of these imperial buildings.

Phase two, which is currently underway, includes the renovation of the Royal Library (Thai Binh Lau), Everlasting Longevity Palace (Dien Tho) and the Museum of Antique Objects. But, the ultimate goal of local conservationists is the total reconstruction of the Purple Palace, which includes a number of buildings such as the Heaven's Law Palace (Dien Can Chanh). They would like to start work in 1995, but a severe lack of funds could put the project on permanent hold. According to UNESCO estimates the restoration of Dien Can Chanh alone will cost US$1.3 million.

The end of the American-led embargo will allow conservation experts from America and Europe to participate in Hue's resurrection, and at the same time even open up new avenues of funding.

Khiem) perches on a stone platform, overlooking a small lake filled with lily pads.

There are a number of interesting sights inside the palace, including a room that was set aside exclusively as a cinema and another for the royal harem. Built out over the lake is gorgeously restored **Xung Khiem Pavilion**, where Tu Duc rested on hot afternoons, while writing poems, fishing or watching plays performed by his concubines. The actual tomb is around the corner, at the far end of a courtyard, decorated with stone elephants and soldiers, and a massive stone stelae which bears a final autobiographical message from Tu Duc to all his subjects.

The **Tomb of Khai Dinh** is a stark contrast. It is a cement edifice that rises above the river as a series of dark gray terraces. There is nothing even remotely tranquil about the setting. If anything, the design exudes the cool aloofness of dynastic rule, especially in the later years when Khai Dinh (1916-1925) and his son Bao Dai (1925-1945) ruled. Sinister wrought iron gates guard the entrance

Fishing in the gardens of Minh Mang Tomb.

to the tomb, beyond which is an army of life-sized stone soldiers who are said to guard the emperor on his journey to the afterlife. But the crowning glory is the tomb itself, dark and foreboding on the outside, but an explosion of color within. Purple and black dragons are painted on the ceiling of the entrance hall, with doors that lead into an inner chamber with a bronze effigy of Khai Dinh sitting on his throne. The walls are covered in mosaic tiles, and at the very back of the room is a huge solar image. It would be difficult to find anything more flamboyant in the whole of Indochina.

Minh Mang's Tomb is the only mausoleum on the left bank, and the easiest way to reach it is by boat from a landing not far from Khai Dinh's Tomb.

A short path leading from the shore to the tomb entrance is marked by a graceful gateway.

Minh Mang ruled from 1820 to 1840, but his magnificent tomb was not built until after his death. The lavish gardens are laid out in the shape of the Chinese character for eternity, with a butterfly-shaped lake and several ponds along which the royal pavilions are arranged. This is the sort of place where you could linger for hours, lounging beneath the trees or reading a book on the steps leading up to the **Minh Lau Temple**. The place is an intriguing blend of nature and humanity, a symmetry rarely reached in modern architecture. And in that respect, Minh Mang's Tomb reflects the prevailing mood of Hue.

Pass of Clouds in Danang.

Danang & The Central Coast

South of Hue the coastal highway traverses some of the most spectacular scenery in Vietnam, before culminating in the Pass of Clouds, the traditional geographic divide between north and south Vietnam. The road first passes through typical rice paddy country, then around the edge of an elongated body of water called the Dam Cau lagoon, which is separated from the open ocean by a narrow sand spit. At the very tip of the spit is a picturesque fishing village called **Lang Co**, where you can spot the stark white steeple of a Catholic church poking through the palms. The beach here is one of the best in Indochina, with fine white sand fringed with towering coconut trees and warm turquoise water, against a backdrop of emerald green mountains that dramatically plunge straight down to the sea.

Next comes the laborious ascent of the famous **Pass of Clouds** (Doi Hai Van). Stop and take your photographs on the lower switchbacks (notice the railway tracks below) because true to its name the summit is often choked in thick mist. There is a small truck stop at the top, where you can park and explore the various fortifications that have protected the pass over the years, including the remains of Nguyen, French, Japanese and American bunkers. But do not wander too far out into the footpaths because a good deal of live artillery still

Bao Dai: The Last Emperor of Vietnam

Bao Dai ascended the throne in 1925 as the thirteenth emperor of the powerful Nguyen Dynasty. But, the number thirteen was definitely unlucky in his case as Bao Dai was forced to abdicate his crown in 1945. He stayed in Vietnam for another nine years, a king without a court, a powerless figurehead caught in the middle of a rapidly-escalating domestic crisis that would soon explode into a full-scale war.

Depending on your politics, Bao Dai is sometimes viewed as a brazen playboy who was only interested in fast cars and hunting, or he is sometimes viewed as a tragic victim of events that moved far beyond his control. He was only twelve years old when his father, Emperor Khai Dinh, passed away. Rather than assume his imperial duties at this young age, Bao Dai was sent away to boarding school in France where he remained for nine years.

He did not return until 1935, a period when anti-colonial hatred was steadily escalating in Indochina and the first seeds of the communist revolution were being sown. The horrible legacy of Vichy France and the Japanese occupation hung over the last five years of his reign, and just as he was about to assume his full powers the communists forced him to abdicate once again.

Not that life without imperial duties was insufferable! Bao Dai and his family still continued to live a life of unabashed luxury (some say decadence) within the walls of the Imperial City in Hue and their summer palace in Dalat. He had a fondness for hunting, fishing, horseback riding, tennis and sports cars. One of his favorite pastimes was long and involved hunting expeditions in the Central Highlands that sometimes included as many as 20 elephants which were used to encircle the prey. His mother – Khai Dinh's queen – refused repeated requests to go into exile. She lived in a private villa in south Hue until her death in 1980. The house is still occupied by former royal servants who look after photographs, relics and shrines dedicated to various members of the royal family.

Bao Dai fled Vietnam in 1954 to seek permanent exile in France where he still lives today, and where he remains active though in his 80s. He never returned to Vietnam, and once he dies it is highly unlikely that the communist authorities will allow his body to be entombed with the rest of the Nguyen emperors in the royal necropolis at Hue. Bao Dai's son – first in line for the throne – served in the French armed forces and now works in a Parisian bank.

---

remains hidden in the undergrowth. A rapid descent brings you back into the sunlight again and out among the secluded coves on the northern fringe of **Danang Bay**. The city basks in the hazy distance, at the foot of a rugged 2,200-meter hill called **Monkey Mountain** (Nui Son Tra) which juts out into the South China Sea. On the western edge of the bay are small villages famous for their huge production of firecrackers.

Danang is famous as the place where both French and American forces first set foot in Vietnam. Napoleon III's troops landed in 1858 and gave the

place a French name – Tourane which is still found on some maps. The American marines hit the shore at Red Beach in 1965. Even more so than Saigon, the city was the major American gateway to Indochina. Between 1965 and 1973 it was like a little slice of America on the coast of Asia, with American GI bars and restaurants, military hospitals, strategic air fields and a stretch of sand – China Beach – that was packed with GIs taking a break from the fighting.

After the Americans left, Danang passed back into its previous tropical slumber and to a great extent the local

The fine sands of China Beach, Danang.

economy has never recovered from the loss of military contacts and GI revelers. Today, Danang has the broken-down, depressing air of a city that has seen better days, rusty ships are moored along the wharf, piles of garbage dot downtown streets and French villas beg for renovation. Local authorities hope to revive the economy by turning Danang Airport – at one time the longest runway in Southeast Asia – into an international gateway for charter flights.

Cham Museum

Essentially there are two reasons to spend a couple of days in Danang: a museum and the beach. The excellent **Cham Museum** contains one of the finest collections of ancient art in Southeast Asia. The building itself needs major renovation as most of the works are still exposed to the elements. However, the statues and friezes contained within are northing short of astounding. The items date from the 8th through the 14th centuries when the Kingdom of Champa flourished along the central coast of Indochina between present-day Hue and Phan Thiet.

The Chams were greatly influenced by their Khmer neighbors (the builders of Angkor Wat) and as a result their artwork contains the same exotic blend of Hindu, Buddhist and Javanese influence, scenes that depict voluptuous dancing girls, chariots with fierce warriors,

The Japanese Bridge at Hoi An.

prancing lions and elephants, the mythical *garuda* (the celestial vehicle for the Vishnu) birds and images of Hindu gods like Shiva, Vishnu, Brahma and Ganesh.

China Beach

China Beach is a long, curving strand that runs between Monkey Mountain and Marble Mountain. The major tourist facilities are set at the foot of the mountain: a new resort hotel and several waterfront cafés set in a grove of pines. In the village behind the beach is the rusted skeleton of an old US army tank and a vast number of marble cutters who are hard at work fashioning statues and tombstones.

The caves of **Marble Mountain** (Ngu Hanh Son) were a Viet Cong sanctuary during the war, a place from where they could easily strike the nearby US Marine air base. Today, the peak is a pleasant park, with several trails leading to the summit and various natural grottos that have been transformed into religious sites and shrines.

Hoi An

An hour's drive south of Danang is a much older city, **Hoi An**, with a colorful history that stretches back for several hundred years. Hoi An thrived as a trading port in the 16th and 17th centuries, with a large community of foreign merchants including many Chinese and

Japanese. Both left their permanent architectural mark on the city.

Many of the old shophouses and clan temples along **Tran Phu Street** bear a distinctly Chinese mien, while a Japanese style is depicted in the design of the **Lai Van Kieu**, a 16th-century wooden bridge that once connected the Japanese and Chinese quarters. A number of 16th-century Japanese tombs were discovered on the outskirts of town by a Japanese television crew in 1990.

Hoi An's star began to fade in the late 17th century when the river silted up, blocking direct access to the sea. But, the city was spared major damage during both the French and American wars. Today, the town has a cheerful feel to it. The lush coastal scenery continues south of Danang, but the pleasant vistas are often interrupted by memories of war. **Truong Lagoon** stretches for more than 60 kilometers (37 miles) along the shore of Quang Nam province south of the Hoi An estuary.

There was once a big American base at **Chu Lai**, a sight that remains barren due to the use of chemical defoliants. Just outside **Quang Ngai** is a rural district which was the site of the My Lai Massacre in 1968. The horrendous massacre is marked by a stark monument dedicated to those who died. **Sa Huynh** is one of the few towns along this stretch of coast that boasts some tourist facilities: a fairly new beach hotel and a few seafront restaurants.

The coastal plain in Binh Dinh province widens to embrace the flood plains

The Waterfront at Nha Trang.

of the Lai Giang and Ha Giao rivers, before reaching a wide indentation in the coast called Quy Nhon Bay.

Quy Nhon is still a bustling port, with a big fishing fleet and seafood restaurants. The downtown district opens onto a wide, palm-shaded strand, but this is actually one of the few unclean beaches along Vietnam's coast – soiled by maritime pollution and raw sewage. Fortunately, the bay still looks attractive with its wooden boats bobbing up and down in the swell and huge fishing nets mounted on stakes that are lowered into the water at high tide.

Towards the southern end of the waterfront is the **Tuong Theater** (854 Nguyen Thai Hoc Street), base of the Dao Tan Troupe, regarded as the best traditional opera company in Vietnam.

Much more interesting is **Tay Son District**, about 50 kilometers (31 miles) inland along Highway 19, which was the cradle of an 18th century peasant uprising called the Tay Son Rebellion and is home to a unique form of martial arts called *Tay Son Von Si* (Tay Son Boxing) only found in Vietnam.

Nha Trang

Of all the towns situated along the south-central coast, **Nha Trang** is perhaps the only one that retains an atmosphere that recalls the French colonial era. Translated, the name means "white house", after the modest dwelling where

Cham Sites: Vietnam's "Lost" Civilization

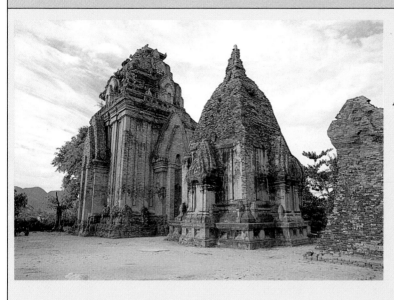

Towers of Cham history at Nha Trang.

The Kingdom of Champa flourished along the central coast of Indochina between AD 8–14, when it was finally overrun by Vietnamese invaders who descended from the north. The Chams were a highly sophisticated people who drew much of their cultural and religious inspiration from the adjoining Khmer Empire, centered in Angkor Wat. Like the early Khmers, the Chams were Hindus. As such, their temples and religious art were heavily influenced by ancient Indian design. However, Buddhist and Javanese inspiration are also evident. Little remains of their cities and palaces, but a number of interesting temples – called Cham towers – survive at various places along the central coast. The following is a guide to the best Cham relics:

Cham Museum: This collection housed in Danang contains more than 300 pieces of Cham sculpture and is the world's most comprehensive collection. It is also the best place in Vietnam to learn about ancient Cham culture.

My Son: Stunning remains of a huge Cham religious complex, set amidst the jungle 60 kilometers (37 miles) southwest of Danang in the upper reaches of the Thu Bon River basin. The ruins are divided into ten distinct groups, most of them separated by bush and small watercourses. The main sanctuary area contains a number of splendid red-brick buildings with stone statues and friezes, erected between the 8th and 10th centuries. Polish archaeologists restored much of My Son in the late 1980s. People call My Son the "Angkor Wat of Vietnam" although it actually pales in comparison to the great Cambodian relic.

Thap Doi: These are twin temples located on a hill overlooking the Ha Giao Valley in Binh Dinh province, about 15 minutes north of Quy Nhon. Made of brick, these towers with massive granite doorways resemble forts more than places of worship. Some of the stone sculpture remains *en situ*, but most has been carted away.

Po Nagar: A temple complex situated on the banks of the Cai River in Nha Trang. The three towers were erected between the 7th and 12th centuries. The North Tower is still an active place of worship. A small museum stands here.

Po Klong Garai: Restored tower complex on a cactus-covered hill overlooking the Thap Cham railway yard in Thuan Hai province. Four separate buildings crown the summit, including a beautifully restored *kalan* (main temple) that dates from the 13th century (which is the end of the Cham epoch). Chams living in nearby Phan Rang and around the province hold a big cultural and religious festival here annually.

Bao Dai's villa overlooking Nha Trang.

Dr Alexandre Yersin, one of the first medical missionaries to Indochina, lived when he arrived in Vietnam in 1895. Yersin, a former protegé of Louis Pasteur, is still fondly remembered by the locals for the introduction of anti-malarial drugs, vaccinations and the arrival of the rubber tree to Indochina. In fact, he is one of the few Frenchmen whose name continues to adorn streets and buildings in Vietnam. Yersin's office is preserved as a small museum on the grounds of the **Pasteur Institute** on the waterfront.

Nha Trang Bay is protected by a

Most people come to Nha Trang just to relax and catch some rays. But, there are plenty of attractions away from the beach. **Po Nagar Temple** on the north bank of the Cay River is one of the country's most important Cham sites, which boasts of three separate brick shrines sheltered by a grove of trees on a rocky ledge overlooking the river. They were built between the 7th and 12th centuries by Cham Hindus, but at least one of the shrines (North Tower) has been taken over by local Buddhists, who worship within its murky, smoke-stained confines.

At the south end of the beach, perched on a small hill, is **Bao Dai's Villa**, the former residence of the last emperor of Vietnam, who exiled himself to France in 1954. The villa served as a secluded retreat for government officials until the early 1990s when it was renovated and transformed into a tourist hotel, and is now one of the more romantic places to stay in while visiting Vietnam. On the far side of the villa is the **Oceanographic Institute**, once a leading academy of marine study but now little more than an assemblage of bottled and petrified specimens. Still, anyone who enjoys bizarre collections should pay the institute a visit. Further south is a small industrial port called **Cau Da**, from where you can catch ferries to the outer islands, including a small marine park on **Mieu Island** that is a popular venue for the locals.

About an hour's drive north of Nha Trang is a highly scenic area lying on

chain of barrier islands and the main beach which has a long curving strand with fine white sand and a mellow surf. French villas sprawl along the waterfront, although most of them have been turned into hotels, schools and government buildings. Pleasant residential streets spread behind the coast giving the town a soothing, sunny disposition.

either side of the **Hon Gom Peninsula,** including the wide **Ben Goi Bay** and a picturesque fishing village called **Dai Lanh** which boasts of red-tiled roofs and lanky palms. The rice paddies in this part of Khanh Hoa province are often punctuated by stands of coconut trees and nipah palms.

Dalat & The Central Highlands

Dalat is an old French hill station that lies snuggled among the highlands of Lam Dong province, one of the most delightful spots in Indochina and a perfect place to escape the sweltering coastal climate. The town can be reached via two routes: Highway 11 from Phan Rang or Highway 20 from Ho Chi Minh City.

Lovers and honeymooning couples flock to Dalat, not just for the crisp mountain air, but for the various resort activities that are not normally available in urban Vietnam. They hire small sailboats and go horseback riding on stout mountain ponies through the aptly named **Valley of Love,** or merely curl up on a blanket in the pine forest that covers much of the hinterland.

Except for a secret communications center, Dalat was strictly off-limits to American military personnel during the Vietnam War and as a result it escaped serious damage. Most of the old French villas remain and the **Palace Hotel** (opened in 1922) still graces the shores of Xuan Huong Lake in the center of town. Dalat's central market is a frenzy of color, with stalls selling fruits and vegetables from all over the highlands, while **Hoa Binh Square** nearby is a good place from where one can glimpse old Citroen and Peugeot taxis. South of Dalat, off Highway 20, are a number of scenic spots including the **Prenn** and **Datania Waterfalls.**

Dalat was the only part of the Central Highlands that was open to tourists at the time of writing. The rest of the region is generally off-limits to foreigners, although travelers with a little gumption can make their way to a number of closed cities by using public transport. The highlands are of particular interest to war buffs; many of the famous battles of the American War were fought in this region including Kontum, Pleiku, La Drang and Hamburger Hill.

Government authorities normally cite "security precautions" as the reason for keeping tourists out of the Central Highlands. An anti-communist guerrilla group called FULRO (United Front for the Struggle of the Oppressed Races) continues to operate from sanctuaries across the border in Cambodia, sometimes striking at economic and military targets in the region.

Yet, it is an interesting region as the government has moved many ethnic Viet settlers into the Central Highlands since the late 1970s as part of a transmigration exercise to relieve overcrowding in the Red River Valley and to dilute the ratio of ethnic minorities in Dak Lak and Kontum.

Dantula Falls, Dalat.

The rich interiors of Thai Hoa Palace in Hue.

Outside Quan Cong Temple in Hoi An.

A wood-carved lantern fit for emperors at the Imperial Museum in Hue.

Stress-free school children visit the Purple City in Hue.

I
ts official title is Ho Chi Minh City, but tourists and residents alike still like to call the place Saigon. By whatever name it is called, this is one of the most vibrant cities in Southeast Asia, a throbbing metropolis of nearly four million people. It sprawls along the banks of the Saigon River on the northern edge of the Mekong Delta. Despite the Marxist-Leninist façade, Saigon is an intensely commercial city with more than a million self-employed entrepreneurs (from street corner salesmen to black market tycoons) and a long history of trade with the outside world. Nearly two decades of communist rule have failed to dampen the essential mercantile drive of the local populous, and with the end of the American embargo, Saigon will no doubt take her place alongside other modern boom towns like Bangkok and Jakarta.

■ ■ ■ ■ ■ ■ ■

The Rex Hotel and Central Saigon at night.

175

Old Saigon

Saigon was born in the 14th century as a Cambodian fishing village called Prey Nokor,

Ho Chi Minh City

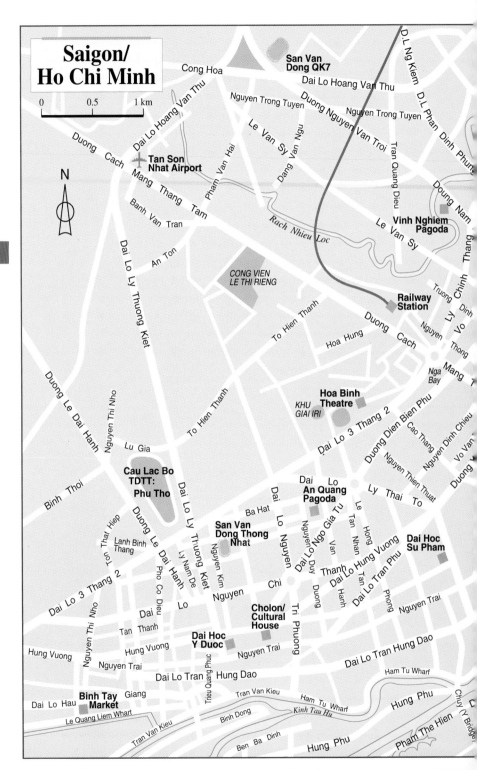

Saigon/
Ho Chi Minh

0   0.5   1 km

N

Cong Hoa

San Van
Dong QK7

Dai Lo Hoang Van Thu

D.L Ng Kiem

D.L Phan Dinh Phung

Duong   Cach

Dai Lo Hoang Van Thu

Nguyen Trong Tuyen

Duong Nguyen Van Troi

Nguyen Trong Tuyen

Le Van Sy

Tan Son
Nhat Airport

Mang   Thang   Tam

Pham Van Hai

Dang Van Ngu

Tran Quang Dieu

Doung Nam

Banh Van Tran

Rach Nhieu Loc

Le Van Sy

Vinh Nghiem
Pagoda

An Ton

Thang

Dai Lo Ly Thuong Kiet

CONG VIEN
LE THI RIENG

Truong   Chinh   Dinh

Railway
Station

Ly   Vo

Nguyen   Thong

To Hien Thanh

Duong   Cach

Nga
Bay

Mang

Hoa Hung

Duong Le Dai Hanh

Nguyen Thi Nho

To Hien Thanh

Hoa Binh
Theatre

KHU
GIAI IRI

Duong Dien Bien Phu

Cao Thang

Nguyen Dinh Chieu

Lu Gia

Dai Lo 3 Thang 2

Nguyen Thien Thuat

Vo Van

Duong

Binh Thoi

Cau Lac Bo
TDTT:
Phu Tho

Dai Lo Ly Thuong Kiet

Dai
Lo
An Quang
Pagoda

Ly   Thai   To

Ton That Hiep

Lanh Binh
Thang

Duong Le Dai Hanh

Pho Co Dieu

Ba Hat

Dai   Lo

Nguyen

Le

Tan Nhan

Hong

Dai Hoc
Su Pham

Dai Lo 3 Thang 2

Nguyen Kim

San Van
Dong Thong
Nhat

Nguyen Gia Tu

Van

Duong Tan Hanh

Dai Lo Hung Vuong

Phong

Nguyen Trai

Ly Nam De

Lo

Chi

Dai Lo Duy

Thanh

Dai Lo Tran Phu

Nguyen Thi Nho

Dai

Nguyen

Cholon/
Cultural
House

Tri   Phuong

Hung Vuong

Tan   Thanh

Dai Hoc
Y Duoc

Nguyen Trai

Nguyen Trai

Dai Lo Tran Hung Dao

Hung Vuong

Nguyen Trai

Dai Lo Tran   Hung Dao

Ham Tu Wharf

Dai Lo Hau

Binh Tay
Market

Giang

Tran Van Kieu

Ham Tu Wharf

Hung Phu

Chuy (Y Bridge)

Le Quang Liem Wharf

Trieu Quang Phuc

Binh Dong

Kinh Tau Hu

Tran Van Kieu

Ben   Ba   Dinh

Hung Phu

Pham The Hien

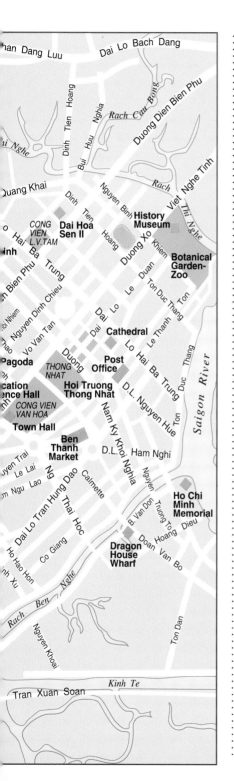

but it soon developed into a thriving market town with a Khmer garrison and a merchants' quarter situated along the river. It was a perfect site: the last dry land before the start of the delta, slightly elevated above the surrounding plains and protected on three sides by water. By the end of the 17th century there was a large community of Vietnamese traders who represented the interests of the Nguyen Lords of Hue. With the imminent collapse of the Kingdom of Champa to Vietnamese aggression, there was nothing to prevent the Nguyen rulers from also snatching Saigon. By the middle of the 18th century, the city was under firm Vietnamese control. Although it may seem unbelievable today, late-18th century Saigon was an imperial city of the same stature as Hue or Hanoi, with a royal palace protected within the confines of a sturdy fortress called the **Citadel of Eight Trigrams**. Between 1789 and 1802, it was the capital of Nguyen Anh, a deposed lord who (with French help) led a counter-revolt against the Tay Son rebels. He eventually triumphed, moved the royal court back to Hue and changed his name to Gia Long. But, Saigon continued as the commercial fulcrum of southern Indochina. The first French arrived in the 1850s, when they were granted permission to establish a trading post between the Citadel and the river, an area which now comprises downtown Saigon. Today's city has several important hubs, including the old French quarter (District 1) and a bustling Chinatown

Ho Chi Minh City on a red-flagged day.

area called **Cholon** (District 5) which started its life in the late 18th century and eventually merged with colonial Saigon.

Dong Khoi Street

Dong Khoi Street sits at the heart of the city's tourism and nightlife zone. It encompasses an area that stretches from the Notre Dame Cathedral to the Saigon River. Prior to independence the street was a chic tree-lined avenue called the Rue Catinat which boasted boutiques and cafés frequented by the movers and shakers of French society and famous visitors like Somerset Maugham and Graham Greene who wrote about local colonial life. During the American period it was called Tu Do Street – a sleazy forerunner to Bangkok's Patpong district – with possibly more pubs and red light areas per square inch than many other places in Asia!

Dong Khoi was a ghost town through most of the 1980s, but now the local action is fast catching up. Many of the city's best hotels, bars and restaurants are sited along this stretch and the adjoining streets. The area is also packed with souvenir shops selling Vietnamese arts and crafts, antiques, books, clothing and mementoes of the American period such as dogtags, watches and coins. At the same time, Dong Khoi has also retained some of its former sleaze including pushers and pickpockets!

At one end of Dong Khoi is an imposing red brick building – **Notre Dame Cathedral**, the single most important example of French architecture in Vietnam. Consecrated in 1880 on what had been the Citadel Arsenal, the twin spires soar 40 meters (120 feet) high and remain the most imposing landmark dotting the Saigon skyline. The square outside the cathedral where the statue of the Virgin Mary stands was once called the Place Pigneau de Behaine, after the French missionary and mercenary who conspired with Nguyen Anh to overthrow the Tay Son regime in 1802. The compound at the southeast corner of the square was reputed to be used by the French *Surete* (secret service) to interrogate and torture leaders of the opposition to French rule in Indochina. On the eastern edge is the old **General Post Office** (1883) – even if you do not have a letter to post, take a look inside the glass dome and the long vaulted ceiling with a giant portrait of Ho Chi Minh at the far end.

Three blocks down Dong Khoi in the direction of the river is **Lam Lom Square**, dominated by the flaxen façade of the **Municipal Theater** (1899) – a building with various reincarnations. After independence from France it became the Lower House of the Vietnamese Assembly. Then in 1975 the new communist regime turned the building back into a theater where performances by domestic and foreign troupes are staged on a regular basis. Sit on the front steps reading *The Quiet Ameri-*

The Post and Telegraph Building.

can, if you want to get an idea of what Lam Lom Square was like in the rowdy 1950s.

On the north side of the square is the famous **Continental Hotel** (1885) which features in so many literary accounts of Saigon. During the American War years the rooftop bar was a famous foreign correspondent hangout dubbed the "Continental Shelf". The hotel was nicely refurbished in the early 1990s and is once again the city's most elegant abode. A rather different sort of lodge sits on the opposite side of the square: the **Caravelle (Doc Lap) Hotel**. The rooftop bar is still emblazoned in classic 1960s decor, with a stunning view of the downtown area.

The next section of Dong Khoi is

The new happy generation of post-war Vietnam.

chock-a-block with cafés, bars and souvenir shops. About the only establishment that remains from pre-liberation days is **Maxim's** with its plush interior and famous floor show. **Saigon Central Mosque** with its four minarets (1935) is half a block down Dong Du Street and is

the main place of worship for the city's 3,000 Muslims. Dong Khoi ends at the Saigon River, with the **Majestic (Cuu Long) Hotel** to your right. The hotel's **Cyclo Bar** is a good place to down a cold drink, while the windows in the hallway leading to the penthouse restaurant of-

ney in Tay Ninh province, flowing into the South China Sea near Vung Tau. The river bustles with all sorts of sea craft: fishing boats, ferries, tugs and big cargo ships that ply the ocean. The French built a pleasant promenade along the waterfront, a place where hundreds of people perform their *tai chi* (a Chinese system of exercise and self-discipline) exercises at dawn, and where thousands of others gather to gossip while the evening breeze blows at dusk. Floating restaurants anchor opposite the Majestic Hotel, while further upstream is the **Saigon Floating Hotel** and **Hero (Me Linh) Square** where a statue of General Trang Hung Dao (the hero of the "Glorious Resistance" against the invading Mongols in the late 13th century) now stands.

The junction near the Saigon River and Ben Nghe Canal was once called the **Pointe des Blageurs**. It was the notorious place where French colonial authorities executed capital criminals by decapitation. Today, there are ferry piers for the Mekong Delta and the opposite shore. Across the canal is a large oriental-style building with a red-tiled roof, which was built in 1863 as the headquarters of the **Messageries Maritimes**, the French transport company. A young Ho Chi Minh departed from the Dragon Wharf outside this building in 1911 on a 30-year journey that would bring him into contact with various concepts of freedom and revolution. After liberation the building was converted into the **Ho Chi Minh Memo-**

fer a sweeping panorama of the waterfront.

Life Along the River

People often mistake the **Saigon River** for the Mekong, but it is actually a separate waterway that starts its jour-

rial Hall with mementoes and displays from his life.

Further downstream are the **Newport Docks**, the hardcore harbor area where giant cranes work night and day shifting bulk cargoes of rice and timber. Ships of up to 10,000 tonnage can dock here. During the days of the Vietnam War, the port area (District 4) was called Soul City because most of the bars catered to black GIs.

The financial district once ran along the north bank of **Ben Nghe Canal**. The **State Bank** building used to be the Bank of Indochina and a neighboring structure was the Hong Kong and Shanghai Bank. Parked across the street are dozens of vintage American cars from the 1950s and early 1960s, most of them painted candy apple red, with lots of chrome and big fins. These are "**wedding taxis**" rented out for the day to transport both the bride and groom. Further along the street are vehicles hired out for funerals. Ton That Dam Street has a **Thieves' Market** that survives from pre-communist days. During the war it mostly sold pilfered US military supplies. Today, the outdoor stalls sell goods from overseas.

Boulevards & Thoroughfares

Nguyen Hue Boulevard runs parallel to Dong Khoi, a spacious thoroughfare that was meant to be the Champs Elysee of colonial Saigon. The lower end of the street looks rather rundown and shabby,

Hotel de Villa, in true French colonial style.

A Day At The Races

The Vietnamese, like many other fellow Asians, can be passionate gamblers.

It may not have been as elegant as Longchamp, but the Hippodrome at Phu Tho was a paragon of culture for the French residents of old Saigon. There was a time when gentleman in stove-pipe hats and ladies in Victorian frocks gathered to gossip and gamble on Sunday afternoons.

With independence in 1954, ethnic Chinese from nearby Cholon began to dominate both the betting and the horses at Phu Tho. Then came the fall of Saigon in 1975 – communist authorities banned racing as a decadent bourgeois pursuit and both the bookies and horse owners were literally and figuratively put out to pasture.

The track may have remained closed forever if not for an overseas Vietnamese named Philip Chow, who was born and raised in Cholon into a family of Chinese entrepreneurs who ran

horses on the side. The family fled to Hong Kong in the 1960s, where Chow built a small business empire of his own based on restaurants and the import and export trade. Despite his success in the British colony, Chow had a yearning to return to his homeland.

When he stepped off a plane at Tan Son Nhut in 1987 with the idea of restarting the races at Phu Tho, officials at first thought him crazy – until he explained how much money the municipal authorities could make by taxing the winnings. Chow pumped US$200,000 of his own money into getting the track back into shape and organizing a group of horse owners and jockeys. Within two years, the newly christened Saigon Turf Club was a reality. The writer was a guest of Chow and visited the club.

Meets are held every Saturday and Sunday,

but the upper reaches of Nguyen Hue still bear a certain majesty. Dominating the northern end of the street is the lovely **Hotel de Ville** – a flamboyant building built in the neo-renaissance style and unveiled in 1908 as Saigon's city hall. Now it is used to headquarter the new municipal government – the HCMC People's Committee.

The bronzed Ho Chi Minh sits in the plaza beneath the towering bulk of the **Rex (Ben Thanh) Hotel**, *the* place to have fun in the 1960s when the building functioned as the US Army's Bachelor Officers' Quarters (BOQ) and the scene of afternoon press briefings fondly called the "Five O'clock Follies". Naturally, things are not quite as lively as they were back then, but the Rex still has a pleasant rooftop bar (another good

with seven races around the two-kilometer oval. The first race starts at noon. The old cement grandstand has hosted crowds of nearly 30,000 spectators, although many of them are gawkers rather than serious gamblers. A picnic atmosphere prevails as people crowd into food stalls and kids play games in the infield.

Wagers are strictly controlled so that nobody makes a killing at the club's expense and so that the house gets a guaranteed percentage of the stake. Bets are limited to no more than a few American dollars and bettors must choose the win and place horses in a given race.

There are no odds; payout is based on a percentage of the total amount wagered, divided by the number of punters who pick the winning one-two combination, which functions like a lottery. The track rakes in US$80,000 a day. But purses are rather modest with only about US$150 going to the winners, and ten percent of the win going to the teenage jockeys.

The Museum of Revolution, Saigon.

Grounded at the Revolution Museum.

view), an excellent Vietnamese restaurant and a lively nightclub complete with lava lamps and a live band.

Le Loi Boulevard runs between the Municipal Theater and a large traffic circle which was in colonial days was called the Place Eugene Cuniac. In the middle is an equestrian statue of Tran Hung Dao. **Ben Thanh Market** (1914) with its trademark clock tower is on the north side of the circle. This is Saigon's equivalent of a modern shopping mall, with more than a hundred stalls located beneath the same roof selling goods from all around the world: clothes, shoes, kitchen products, jewelry, watches, toys, games, television sets and boom boxes. The narrow lanes around the market are filled with even more stalls, many of

them selling food and drinks. Two blocks further west, on Truong Cong Dinh Street, is the **Mariamman Hindu Temple**, erected in the late 19th century by Tamil immigrants from the French colonies of Southern India.

The area north of the city hall and the cathedral was the heart of the 18th-century Citadel, although few traces remain. After 1859 when the imperial fortress was destroyed, it became a fashionable French residential area with lovely villas and tree-lined streets. Since independence, this area developed into the presidential and diplomatic quarter. Today it is a district of government offices, hospitals and museums.

The **Museum of the Revolution** is housed in the former Gia Long Palace

The Saigon Floating Hotel

Saigon Floating Hotel.

The Saigon Floating Hotel is a strange beast indeed. It floats, but it is definitely not a cruise ship. It has eight floors, but neither is it a building. And for the time being, the hotel is the only one of its breed in the world.

Constructed in Singapore in the mid 1980s, the 200-room Floating Hotel was originally deployed as a scuba diving resort along Australia's Great Barrier Reef. But business was not so good, so the management group – Southern Pacific Hotels, based in Sydney but owned by the same people who run the Hyatt chain – decided to make a change. They had a brilliant idea: since Southern Pacific wanted to expand its presence in Southeast Asia and Saigon was badly in need of more guest beds, they moved the Floating Hotel to Vietnam.

The transfer took place in 1989, in a slow float through the Indonesian archipelago and across the South China Sea. The boat was towed into place on the Saigon waterfront before thousands of local residents, who must have wondered at this bizarre sight. With limited deck space, recreation amenities were developed on the adjacent quay, including a swimming pool and the only grand prix approved tennis courts in Indochina. The Floating Hotel established a number of national "firsts," including Vietnam's first in-house video and satellite television channels, the first facility that accepted credit card payments, the first international direct dial telephones, the first rooms catering to handicapped people and the first modern business center equipped with computers, fax and modem. In addition, the hotel has its own water purification system and back-up generator.

Southern Pacific says that it eventually wants to build a permanent onshore hotel in Saigon, which means the Floating Hotel may some day sail off into the sunset on its way to another destination.

Entrance porch of Reunification Palace.

(1886), the one-time home of the French governor of Cochinchina, but now telling a comprehensive tale of the nation's struggle against various oppressors including the French, Americans and Chinese. Among the larger items on display are an American helicopter and a Russian tank. Across the street is the old **National Library**, housing a collection of scientific and technical books.

Presidential Memories

The former Presidential Palace (1966) remains a symbol of the decadent American-backed dictators who ruled South Vietnam between 1954 and 1975 and stands as a classic statement of modern cement slab architecture.

After liberation the building was renamed **Reunification Hall**, but rather than demolish the structure and transform it into something more functional, communist authorities commanded that every chair, rug and painting be left in place as a permanent reminder of what the revolution accomplished. A guided tour of the hall is one of the highlights of a stay in Saigon and represents a journey into a past of molded plastic furniture and plush red carpets.

American Memories

The **Museum of American War Crimes**, is located one block north of the old presidential gardens. It is a highly disturbing sight because of its gruesome detail. Many of the photos featured have been taken directly from US press reports. Reunification Hall faces a wide tree-lined street called Le Duan Boulevard. Four blocks east are the offices of the State Petroleum Authority, and the former **US Embassy** building which was immortalized in photographs of people fleeing by helicopter from the roof in 1975 as North Vietnamese troops poured into Saigon. The French and British compounds are located nearby.

At the eastern end of Le Duan is the **Saigon Zoo** which also contains an amusement park, museum and the oldest botanical garden in Indochina (1864). The zoo is the closest thing Saigon has to a central park and is especially crowded on weekends when entire families flock here to enjoy the various attractions. The **History Museum** (1929) boasts a superb collection of artifacts from the Bronze Age through dynastic times, as well as an excellent research library.

Cholon & The Outlying Districts

Cholon is the city's ethnic Chinese district, a warren of crowded streets and tightly packed shops that has not lost its vigour in the post-war years. Its name means "Big Market" and that is exactly what Cholon is. You can buy anything here, legal or illegal, and it is a place where money talks and the black market answers. **Binh Tay Market** is a huge wholesale food and commodities market where sundry products from the countryside are displayed. Number **3 Thang 2 Boulevard** is the great white way, a consumer electronics playground that dispenses the latest in Japanese televisions, music systems and refrigerators. Each shop is illuminated at night by naked neon tubes and in keeping with the Chinese penchant for gambling, Cholon is also home to the **Phu Tho Racetrack**, where the ponies run every weekend.

But Cholon also has its quiet side – venerable temples and churches that successfully deflect the street noise. There are four Buddhist temples located within a one-block radius of Nguyen Trai and

Courtyard of Thien Hau Pagoda.

Trieu Quang Phuc Streets in central Cholon. The most impressive being the **Thein Hau Temple** which underwent extensive renovation in the late 1980s. Dedicated to Tin Hau, the Chinese goddess of the sea and protector of sailors, the temple contains elaborate ceramic friezes brought from southern China in the late 18th century, shortly after the first Cantonese immigrants came to Cholon.

Nearby shrines include the 19th-century **Tam Son Hoi Quan Temple**, dedicated to the goddess of fertility, which is especially popular among women of childbearing age; the **Nghia An Hoi Quan Temple** which is dedicated to a fierce war god depicted on horseback wearing a black beard and the **Quan Am Temple**, dedicated to the goddess of mercy. The **Phung Son Pagoda** (1820), on the outskirts of Cholon is one of the largest and most elaborate in Saigon. The temple houses an abundance of wood, metal and ceramic sculpture, as well as numerous drums, gongs, urns and other Buddhist relics.

The **Sacred Heart (Cha Tam) Church** is the most famous place for Catholic worship in Cholon, not so much for its architecture but for the fact that President Diem and his brother were captured and murdered here in November 1963 – three weeks before the assassination of John F Kennedy in Dallas. The **Cho Quan Church** at the opposite end of Cholon has a statue of Jesus hallowed within a neon structure.

Most of the city's great Buddhist shrines are situated in the outlying districts, places that were essentially in the countryside during early Nguyen Dynasty times and the first years of the French occupation. **Giac Lam Pagoda** lies in the Tan Binh district in the northwest part of the city. This is Saigon's oldest Buddhist temple, which was founded in 1744 during the latter part of the Le Dynasty. The pagoda is noted for its thick hardwood columns, carved with ancient *nom* (inscriptions) and filled with numerous gilded statues.

The **Giac Vien Pagoda** is in the same general area, sited on the banks of tranquil Dam Sen Lake. Emperor Gia Long was especially fond of this temple and visited it often to give thanks for his victory over the Tay Son forces. The interior contains more than 150 statues, many of them carved out of jackwood. Two important temples are located off the main road to Tan Son Nhut Airport. **Vinh Nghiem Pagoda** is a modern edifice, which was opened in 1973 after nearly a decade of Japanese-funded construction.

In the forecourt is a seven-storey tower with a peaked roof, while the main hall contains a huge golden Buddha and a bronze bell cast in Japan. The temple stands as a thriving center for modern Buddhism and hosts an annual gathering of monks who make the journey from the most far-reaching places in Vietnam.

The last of the old suburban shrines is the **Emperor of Jade Pagoda** (1909) off Dien Bien Phu Street, near the Thi Nghe Canal. Get ready for a full-scale assault on the senses: this typical Cantonese temple is an explosion of unique colors and designs, filled with leaping dragons and numerous gods.

Vung Tau

The French founded a custom's post on a stout peninsula near the mouth of the Saigon River, a place they called Cap Saint Jacques. By the 1890s it had become a prosperous little seaside resort for the bureaucrats and businessmen of Saigon who built holiday villas and cafés along Front Beach, in an attempt to recreate the ambience of the French Riviera. They almost succeeded, as mod-

Sealed baskets which make the most amusing-looking boats at Vung Tau.

ern **Vung Tau** is Asia's closest answer to St Tropez or Nice.

The Asian Riviera

Vung Tau, 125 kilometers (80 miles) east of Saigon, is noteworthy for a number of reasons. The peninsula and the offshore Cong Dau Islands are Vietnam's only special economic zone, which basically means that capitalism is allowed to flourish at any cost. It has its sleaze and the primary moneymaker is oil. Vung Tau is a staging area for oil and gas exploration in the South China Sea, an industry on the verge of a major boom as European energy companies carve the seabed into competing blocks.

A number of offshore rigs are already pumping, and the Vietnam Oil Services Company runs Vung Tau like a company town.

At the same time, Vung Tau has resurrected its appeal to Saigon's elite – this time including Communist Party officials and *nouvelle* capitalists. Vung Tau taps to the rhythm of "Saigon cowboys" on their speedy Honda scooters and young ladies clad in tight jeans or skimpy bikinis and exists as the nation's great snub against the basic tenets of socialism. One historical footnote: along with China Beach at Danang, Vung Tau was the only other spot within Vietnam sanctioned for US military R&R (rest and recreation).

The peninsula harbors at least a

dozen strands, but the most popular are **Front Beach** (Bai Truoc or Thuy Duong) and **Back Beach** (Bai Sau or Thuy Van), with the urban area sprawling between. Front Beach is the more picturesque of the two, especially around dawn when the local fishermen land their catch along the sand.

Hundreds of tiny craft bob up and down in the swell – in fact, Vung Tau is often called the "Bay of Boats". Later in the day numerous stalls are set up along the shore selling refreshments and souvenirs. Back Beach is the haunt of serious sunseekers, a seven-kilometer (four-mile) stretch of white sand with relatively clean water. Cabanas and cafés line the beachfront, with motels and campsites situated across the road. Two other nice strands are the palm-shaded **Bai Dau Beach** and the rocky **Roches Noires Beach**, which is located just beneath the giant figure of Jesus looking out to sea.

Temples & Shrines

Despite its *laissez faire* morals, Vung Tau with over a hundred shrines is also a place for Buddhist and Catholic pilgrimage.

The most famous place of worship is **Small Mountain** (Nui Nho) at the southern end of the peninsula. Dominating the summit is a stark white **Statue of Jesus**, 30 meters (90 feet) tall with outstretched arms, similar to the infamous one in Rio. A French lighthouse

School girls in the city.

(1910) crowns another ridge, offering a panoramic view of the entire peninsula.

Housed within the shadow of the mountain are three temples: **Niet Ban Tinh Xa** (1971) is considered the most important local pagoda, with a famous Reclining Buddha and a huge bronze bell.

On the inland side of the mountain is **Linh Son Tu**, which was built in 1911 and is Vung Tau's oldest place of worship. At the tip of the peninsula is an old French fort and a rocky islet with a small pagoda.

Dong Nai province lies due east of Saigon, beyond a wide river of the same name. This is rubber country, with plantations lining both sides of Highway One as it crosses the province. **Bien Hoa**

Everyone on wheels in Dinh Tien Hoang Street, Ho Chi Minh City.

is the provincial capital and former home to the world's largest military base. For many years the town was known for its porcelain and pottery workshops.

But in 1966, the American high command decided to move its major base of operations away from Saigon. They chose Bien Hoa, 32 kilometers (20 miles) away which became a home base for the US Army's III Corps, the 1st Aviation Brigade (the globe's largest helicopter force), an air force fighter squadron and the huge Long Binh logistics and supply depot.

Another huge US military base was located 30 kilometers (20 miles) northwest of Saigon in the Cu Chi district (formerly Hau Ngia province), a major area of communist infiltration from Cambodia by way of the Ho Chi Minh Trail. From the very start, American troops were under siege – but they could not find the enemy! Eventually it became evident that the Viet Cong forces were right beneath them, attacking from a labyrinth of earthen tunnels which dated from French times.

Today, the **Tunnels of Cu Chi** are a major tourist attraction, with a visitor center and a chance for war buffs to get their hands and feet dirty. Several of the tunnels have been widened to accommodate bulky western tourists, including a section located beneath a roadway that quakes whenever a vehicle passes overhead! Nearby is the rusted corpse of an American M48 tank.

The stunning lines of the Vinh Pagoda.

Vietnamese grace and charm.

You can easily combine a trip to the tunnels with a visit to **Tay Ninh**, 96 kilometers (60 miles) from Saigon via Highway 22, the same road where Graham Greene's characters get stranded in *The Quiet American*. Tay Ninh was the birthplace of Cao Dai, an unusual sect founded in 1926 by Ngo Minh Chieu, a local mystic. This religion combines various aspects of Buddhism, Christianity, Confucianism and Taoism with a pantheon of saints that includes Victor Hugo, V I Lenin, Jesus Christ and Joan of Arc.

All geared up for a ride around town.

The **Holy See** in Tay Ninh is the Cao Dai equivalent of Vatican City. It is housed in a structure that resembles a cross between a Catholic church and a Buddhist temple.

The exterior is of a pale yellow color, with a red-tile roof and four pagoda-like steeples. The long, vaulted nave features pink columns entwined in the bodies of green dragons with an "all seeing" eye painted on a huge blue globe at the front of the room. There is nothing else like it in Vietnam, and perhaps in the world!

Southwest of Saigon, the Mekong Delta is the most southern segment of Vietnam. This soggy land mass was formed by sediment from the Mekong River and it continues to grow due to the continued accumulation of silt. Before passing through Vietnam, the Mekong flows from its source in the upper reaches of Tibet, through China, Burma, Laos and Cambodia picking up tons of silt along the way.

The delta is largely an agricultural region with rice being its most important crop. Other products grown in the delta's rich alluvial soil include coconuts, sugarcane, longans, bananas, mangoes, oranges, maize, soya beans and a variety of vegetables.

The Vietnamese name for the delta is Cuu Long ("Nine Dragons") because the river splits into

Delta ducks and their herder.

Mekong Delta

199

nine separate channels before entering the South China Sea, although some people say that the name might have been chosen quite coincidently.

Along the Tien Giang

My Tho is home to about 100,000 people and the capital of Tien Giang Province. It is an easy day trip from Saigon, just 70 kilometers (43 miles) south. The city is situated along the left bank of the Tien Giang (Upper River), the northernmost branch of the Mekong, and is largely a fishing and farming community, famous for its orchids and fruit. My Tho was founded in the late 17th century by refugees from Formosa.

My Tho Church is situated along the main thoroughfare at 32 Hung Vuong Boulevard and serves the city's 7,000 Roman Catholics. Mass is held daily at 5 am and 5 pm and on Sundays there is an additional service at 7 am. Tourists can visit the 100-year-old building every day from 4:30 am to 6:30 am and 2:30 to 6:30 pm.

Due East of Hung Vuong Boulevard is Trung Trac Street which houses the **My Tho Central Market**. The area surrounding the market is closed to traffic, so you are free to wander around and savor the bustling atmosphere. Just about everything the town needs is on sale here – rice, peanuts, sweet potatoes, melons, pumpkins, durians, tobacco, fresh fish, live animals including chickens and pigs, machinery, electronics and clothing.

Across the Bao Dinh Channel, on Phan Thanh Gian Street, is the old **Chinese District**, and about one kilometer further east is **Vinh Trang Pagoda**. Built in 1848, this is the oldest Buddhist temple in My Tho and was a "safe house" for Viet Cong guerrillas during the war years.

About 12 kilometers (eight miles) out of town is a **snake farm**. Owned by a pharmaceutical company, the snakes are raised for their medicinal properties – for use in general tonics, as a remedy for coughs, migraines, rheumatism and even mental disorders.

A twenty-minute boat ride downriver from My Tho will take you to **Phung Island**, the one-time headquarters of the Tinh Do Cu Si religious sect led by the famous Coconut Monk (so named because he ate nothing but coconuts for three years). The sect was a synthesis of Buddhism and Christianity, with equal respect accorded to both Jesus and Buddha. The congregation was disbanded by the communists after 1975 and its devotees dispersed. The main hall of worship is now ruined and faded, but you can imagine how grand it must have been in the 1940s with its ornate, imposing columns and grand tower topped with the huge globe.

Several other islands in the My Tho area are of special interest. **Tan Long Island** with its longan plantations is a quick boat ride from the docks at the bottom of Le Loi Boulevard. But it takes at least 40 minutes to reach **Thai Son**

The Mekong at Can Tho.

Island where you can see typical farmhouses and sample the local produce.

Along the Hau Giang

On the Hau Giang (Lower River), the southern branch of the Mekong, about 170 kilometers (105 miles) south of Saigon, is **Can Tho**, the political and cultural hub of the delta and the capital of Hau Giang province. With 150,000 inhabitants, Can Tho is by Vietnamese standards a modern city with wide streets and tall buildings. It is also an important river port, especially for the export of rice.

Can Tho University has a teacher training unit and a medical faculty, but the facility is famous for its agronomy department, which specializes in rice research – developing new strains of grain and training students to lead rice-related campaigns around the country.

The waterfront is dominated by a towering silver statue of Ho Chi Minh and the sprawling **Central Market** which is situated at the section of Hai Ba Trung Street now closed to vehicular traffic. Take time out for a river cruise to discover life on the myriad waterways around Can Tho. Boats can be hired from the wooden docks in front of the Quoc Te Hotel.

A river trip is best at sunrise, when the waterways are most active. You can cruise up the Can Tho River to a floating market at the junction of seven canals

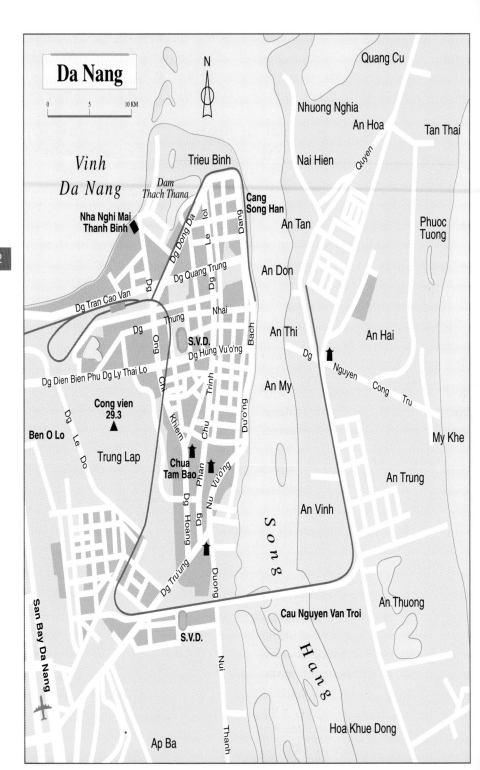

where trade in fish, fruit and vegetables is fresh and brisk. Or you can head for the Mekong proper (which was called the Bassac River during French colonial days).

Can Tho has a number of handicraft cooperatives and visitors are also welcome at various factories around the city including the pineapple cannery in the Tra Noc industrial complex and a frozen food factory.

The 2,000-strong Khmer community worships at the **Munirangsyaram Pagoda** at 32 Hoa Binh Boulevard. Built in 1946, there is a statue of Siddhartha Gautama Buddha in the upstairs sanctuary. Prayers are held daily at 5 am and 6 pm. In the nearby Soc Trang town, now considered part of Can Tho, there is an ancient **Cham temple** with ornate carvings of animals and dancing females. Some very colorful festivals are also held here.

For after-dark entertainment, check to see if there is anything interesting playing at the **Ha Giang Theater**, or you could perhaps watch a Vietnamese film at the **Lao Dong Cinema**.

Heading upriver in the direction of Cambodia, the next big port is **Long Xuyen**, the capital of An Giang province. The city sees very few tourists due to its proximity to the border, so do not expect much in the way of tourist activities or amenities. The population is about 100,000 strong.

The city was once the center of the Hoa Hao sect, which was started in 1939 by a local prophet named Huynh Phu

So. Born into a prosperous rural family, Huynh learned magic, spiritualism and hypnosis while being treated for an unknown illness at the Tran Son Pagoda. All of the above became key components of his religion. The sect became so popular that French authorities feared it would become uncontrollable and they imprisoned Huynh in 1941. After his release in 1945, the Hoa Hao became a nationalist, anti-Marxist political organization with its own army. It continued to gain power even after the prophet's death in 1947. When he came to power in 1954, President Diem tried to wipe out the sect and ordered the execution of its leaders and the destruction of their altars. There was a revival following Diem's overthrow. After 1975, the communists were able to significantly reduce the influence of the Hoa Hao.

Today, the sect balances political opportunism with their puritan, mystical façade. The remnants of the sect can still be found in Long Xuyen, especially at the Hoa Hao University and secondary school. Male devotees are easily identified by their long beards and long hair which is tied into a bun.

The **Tong Duc Thang Museum** in Long Xuyen displays archaeological artifacts from the ancient Oc Eo civilization that prospered in the delta before the arrival of the Vietnamese.

Quan Thanh De is a small Chinese temple built in the 1920s on Le Minh Ngu On Street. Effigies of Quan Cong, a general named Chau Xuong and the

Temple architecture at Chan Doc.

administrative *mandarin* Quan Binh are displayed on the main altar. The temple is open daily from 5 am to 8 pm. The **Dinh Than Long Xuyen Temple** is also located nearby on Le Minh Ngu On Street.

Long Xuyen Catholic Church is situated on the triangle formed by the intersection of Tran Hung Dao, Hung Vuong and Nguyen Hue streets. It is absolutely difficult to miss with its 50-metre high bell tower. Completed about 20 years ago, the church accomodates 1,000 people and is open to the general public from dawn to 8 pm. Mass is held daily at 4:30 am and 6 pm. On Sundays there is an additional service at 3:30 pm. One block away on 4 Hung Vuong Street is a small Protestant church stand-

ing near the intersection of Nguyen Thi Minh Khai Street, which holds Sunday services at 10 am.

Long Xuyen Market occupies the block opposite the Mekong (Hau Giang) River on Le Minh Ngu On Street. The **Luxury Goods Market** is situated two blocks away, in a quadrant bordered by Nguyen Van Cung, Ly Tu Trang, Nguyen He and Hung Vuong streets. Long Xuyen is known for its unglazed black pottery made from diato-mocaolinite – clay formed from the dried remains of living creatures. Once fired, the clay becomes so light that it can float in water.

Depending on which way you drive, Cau Doc is 35 to 55 kilometers (21-34 miles) from Long Xuyen. The town sits on the south bank of the Hau Giang, with about 50,000 inhabitants. The roads between Long Xuyen and Chau Doc are at their most interesting in the early morning, when farmers transport their produce to market in overloaded buses and trucks. A noticeable feature of Chau Doc are the floating houses. Built on empty metal drums, the homes house fish farms underneath.

Chau Phu Temple is on the corner of Gia Long and Bao Ho Thoai streets. It was built in the 1920s to pay homage to Thoai Ngoc Hau, a high ranking official of the Nguyen Dynasty who was responsible for the construction of the nearby Chau Doc Canal. The temple is decorated with a mixture of Chinese and Vietnamese motifs.

Chau Doc Catholic Church, built in 1920 and still active, stands opposite

Phat Lon Pagoda, Rach Gia.

number 459 Le Loi Street. Masses are held from Mondays through Saturdays at 5 am and 5 pm, and on Sundays at 7 am and 4 pm.

Local Muslims worship at the **Chau Giang Mosque** on the opposite side of the river from downtown Chau Doc. Two different ferries cross the river: from a dock in 30 Thang 4 Park near the municipal stadium and from FB Phu Hiep Terminal near the main bus station. The celebrated **Sam Mountain** is about three kilometers (two miles) southwest of Chau Doc, by way of Bao Ho Thoai Street. The hill got its name because it is said to resemble a *sam* (king crab). There are numerous temples, pagodas and monuments to explore. Nearest the main road is the Indian-style **Tay**

An Pagoda which is guarded by black elephants with two tusks and a single white elephant with six tusks. Standing on the roof are images of lions and dragons (fighting for jewels), lotus blossoms and other plants. But, the main feature of this pagoda are the hundreds of intricate wood carvings of religious figures. Situated within the grounds are monks's tombs and a statue of Quan Am Thi Kinh, the Buddhist guardian of mothers and children.

Vietnamese flock to the **Temple of the Goddess Saint** to worship a statue left by the Cambodians. **Cavern Pagoda** stands on the mountain's western face, past Ben Da Market. There are monks' quarters and the tomb of the pagoda's founder (a female tailor called

Le Thi Tho) on the lower level, while the main sanctuary is upstairs. Behind which is a cave with a shrine dedicated to the Goddess of Mercy and statues of the Buddha of the Past and Sakyamuni housed in the main chamber. It is said that Le Thi Tho came here to lead a life of tranquil meditation.

At the foot of the northern side of the mountain is the **Tomb of Thoai Ngoc Hau**. Shortly before his death in 1829, this Nguyen Dynasty *mandarin* ordered the construction of his own tomb as well as the graves of his two wives which stand nearby. Tombs of other officials who served under Thoai Ngoc Hau can be found scattered in the same vicinity.

Gulf of Thailand Coast

Rach Gia, the capital of Kien Giang province, has about 120,000 inhabitants and an agriculture-and-fishing based economy. The city has a number of noteworthy temples and it sits on a small island at the mouth of the Cai Lon River. The Cai Lon descends into the Gulf of Thailand.

Phat Lon is a 200-year-old Cambodian Hinayana Buddhist pagoda. There are eight altars around the exterior of the main hall and in the sanctuary, with numerous statues of Sakyamuni wearing Cambodian and Thai-style pointed hats. The pagoda is open from 4 am to 5 pm during the summer, but the monks are happy to welcome you at

any time. Prayers are held at 4 am and 5 pm daily.

The **Ong Bac De Pagoda** stands in the town center, at 14 Nguyen Du Street. The central altar of this hundred-year-old temple has a representation of Ong

Delta life at Chan Doc.

Bac De, a reincarnation of the Jade Emperor of Heaven. At the corner of Co Bac and Nguyen Van Cu streets is the tiny **Pho Minh Pagoda**. Relatively mod-ern, this temple features a Thai-style Thich Ca Buddha which was a gift from a Buddhist group in Thailand about 20 years ago. Pho Minh is open to visitors

Ha Tien medicine man who has saved his hair for more than 30 years.

from 6 am to 10 pm daily; prayers are held at 3:30 am and 6:30 pm. The gardens of **Tan Bao Pagoda** feature trees pruned in the shape of dragons and other animals. The pagoda is situated on the corner of Thich Thien An Street and Tran Phu Street and is open from 6 am to 8 pm with prayers held at 4:30 am and 5:30 pm.

Nguyen Trung Truc Temple, at 18 Nguyen Cong Tru Street, was named after an important 19th-century leader of the Vietnamese resistance against the French. Nguyen Trung Truc was executed by colonial authorities in 1868 after he turned himself in to protect his mother and the other citizens of Rach Gia whom the French had taken hostage. His portrait adorns the altar of this temple, open from 7 am to 6 pm daily. **Cao Dai Temple**, near the bus station at 189 Nguyen Trung Truc Street, is a small place of worship which was built fairly recently in 1969.

Rach Gia Catholic Church, on the north bank of the Cai Lon River, holds mass at 5 am and 5 pm daily. On Sunday there is also mass at 7 am and 4 pm. There are services at 10 am on Sundays at the **Protestant Church** on Nguyen Trung Truc Street.

Bac Dang Street is the venue of **Vinh Thanh Van Market**, while the bustling Luxury Goods Market is in the block bordered by Nguyen Du, Pham Hong Thai and Bach Dang streets. The **Nhan Dau Theater** on Tran Phu Boulevard and the **Nha Van Hoa Cultural House** on Ho Chi Minh Boulevard provide evening entertainment. You can also visit the small **Rach Gia Museum** at 21 Nguyen Trung Troi Street.

Near Rach Gia, in **Lanh Xuat Khau** district, is a frozen shrimp factory which conducts tours for visitors. Funded by a Norwegian company, the factory processes fish as well as prawns and shrimp for export to the Asia-Pacific region. **Xi Nghiep Dong Tau Shipyard** on the Gulf of Thailand repairs and builds boats from scratch. The management will be glad to show you around.

But, the most important reason to travel to Rach Gia is to visit the ruins of **Oc-Eo**, 11 kilometers (seven miles) inland near Vong village. Oc Eo, rediscovered in the 1940s, thrived between AD 1 to 6 as the capital of a highly devel-

Buddha at Thach Dong Temple, Ha Tien.

oped civilization engaged in trade with what is today's Malaysia, Thailand, Indonesia, Persia and the Roman Empire. Discoveries indicate that it was closely linked with the ancient city of Phu Nam (Funan) in Cambodia. Artifacts excavated from this area can be viewed in the History Museum in Saigon, the Art Museum in Hanoi and the Tong Duc Thong Museum in Long Xuyen.

Between Rach Gia and Ha Tien are a number of duck farms and the **Soc Soai Temple** in Hon Dat district. The temple, set amidst lush tropical vegetation, was completed in 1970 and now houses about 80 monks. Between Hon Soc and Hon Me is **Hon Dat Mountain**. At the base is a gravestone inscribed with the names of local heroes.

There are a number of caves to explore along the coast route. About 30 kilometers (18 miles) before Ha Tien is the **Chua Hang Grotto**. Entrance is gained behind the altar of the pagoda situated at the base of the hill. **Father and Son Island** can be spotted offshore, so named because it is said to resemble a father and son embracing. About five kilometers (three miles) further along is **Hang Tien (Coin) Grotto** which is only accessible by boat. The cave got its name after the army of Nguyen Anh (who later became Emperor Gia Long) discovered coins buried here while they were hiding from the Tay Son forces in the late 18th century.

After travelling for another 15 kilometers (nine miles) you will reach

A typical family tomb in Ha Tien.

Ma So Grotto which has three large chambers and a number of tunnels which you traverse by foot during the dry season.

The **Chua Hang Temple** is situated near the village of Bing An, and is a slight diversion off the main road. A statue of the Goddess of Mercy and two Buddhas are housed within. The Buddhas are rather odd-looking with red lips and nails, and golden garments.

There are also a few beautiful beaches along the Gulf of Thailand. **Duong Beach**, next to Chua Hang

A fruit vendor quite content with life.

Grotto, is one of the nicest with crystal clear water, white sand and shady trees.

The seaport town of **Ha Tien** is situated in the extreme southwest corner of Vietnam, just seven kilometers (four miles) from the Cambodian border. You can enter the city by means of a floating toll bridge over the **To Chau River**. With a population of about 100,000, Ha Tien was founded in the 18th century by Mac Cuu, a Chinese immigrant from Canton.

Today, the city is known for its seafood, pepper plantations and nearby

A goddess stands over the pond at Tam Bao Pagoda, Rach Gia.

Van Son – the Mountain of Clouds.

Tam Bao Pagoda, at 328 Phuong Thanh Street, is said to have been founded by Mac Cuu. Standing outside is a statue of the Goddess of Mercy standing on a lotus and inside, the main statue on the dais is a painted bronze representation of Buddha. Nearby, you can still see a section of the city wall from the same era.

Almost as ancient is the nearby **Phu Dung Pagoda**, on Phuong Thanh Street. On the pagoda's main altar is a glass-enclosed, Chinese bronze of Thich

Ca Buddha and in the center of the main hall is a statue of Buddha as a baby being embraced by nine dragons. It is open from 6 am to 10 pm and prayers are held at 4 am and 7pm daily.

Behind this is the small **Dien Ngoc Hoang Temple**, dedicated to the Jade Emperor. The divinities – the gods of the northern and southern stars, the god of longevity and the like – are made of bamboo and papiermaché. If you wander around the grounds you will find the tomb of Mac Cuu's second wife, who founded this temple.

Built into a cave in the Mountain of Clouds is **Thach Dong Temple** which features a statue of the Goddess of Mercy and Sakyamuni, as well as funerary tablets. Constructed in the 18th century, the temple was last refurbished in 1950. At nearby Thach Dong is the mass grave of 150 Vietnamese peasants massacred by Pol Pot's Khmer Rouge troops during one of their cross-border rampages between 1975 and 1979. After this attack, the area was heavily planted with mines – all of which have yet to be detonated. So be careful where you step!

Not far from town, on the eastern side of Mount Binh San, are the **Tombs of the Mac Cuu Family**. On the approach road is a shrine dedicated to the family and on a slight ridge behind are traditional womb-shaped Chinese tombs decorated with dragons, phoenixes, lions and tigers. Mac Cuu's tomb is easy to spot, being the largest of the group.

Phu Quoc Island lies 45 kilometers (28 miles) off the coast of the Gulf of Thailand, governed from Ha Tien as a district of Kien Gian province. With more than 1,300 square kilometers, the island comprises rugged mountains and lush tropical forests. Fishing and manufacturing *nuoc man* (fish sauce) are the main occupations of the 18,000 inhabitants, who mainly live in the town of **Duong Dong** on the west coast. There are unspoiled beaches, especially in the south, perfect for swimming, snorkelling and fishing. In the 18th century, the island served as a base of operations for the future Emperor Gia Long and later for the French missionary Pigneau de Behaine.

The wild and rugged **Ca Mau Peninsula** sits at the tip of Indochina, the southernmost part of Vietnam and one of the country's most isolated regions. The peninsula comprises the whole of Minh Hai province and parts of the Kien Giang and Hau Giang provinces.

At the heart of the peninsula is the **U-Minh Forest**, the largest mangrove habitat outside of the Amazon. The lush forest – really more of a swamp – provides the locals with timber, charcoal and thatch.

Honey and wax are also derived from the bees that feed on the mangrove flowers. U-Minh was seriously defoliated during the war and despite replanting efforts, about one-quarter of the rotting forest is comprised of tree stumps. Ca Mau is definitely a place to get away from it all, as this area has the lowest population density in southern Vietnam.

Rural sports – like wrestling and rowing – have existed in Vietnam since the dawn of time. But, they were mostly confined to festivals and holidays; the peasants were meant to work, not play. Behind closed doors, the royal families and *mandarins* (high court officials) engaged in various types of games. For instance, children at the imperial court in Hue used to play a game in which the object was to bounce an ivory stick off a flat stone into a copper pot.

Scrambling to place a bet.

The French colonials were great sportsmen, establishing places like the **Cercle Sportif** and **Club Nautique** in Saigon. But, once again, the fun and games were restricted solely to the ruling class. The situation did not change all that much after independence in 1954 and liberation in 1975 as Vietnam was too busy waging war and revolution to bother with other pastimes.

Sports & Recreation

215

Relaxation and recreation by the shores of Vung Tau.

Needless to say, sports and recreational activities are not well developed today. But, this is not to say there is no potential. Vietnam's geographic diversity and unspoilt terrain offers almost limitless potential. But for the time being it is largely a case of "do-it-yourself."

Beaches & Water Sports

Beautiful beaches abound along the entire coast of Vietnam, most of them vacant and completely pollution-free. There are a number of well-established

(which doubles as a fishing port), but watch out for the rough surf. Not far from the city center are the sandy, coco-nut-shaded shores of **Bai Dau Beach**, which are also well worth a visit.

The secluded Con Dau Islands due south of Vung Tau, are ringed by coral reefs and the warm waters of the South China Sea. But there are no organized excursions – you must explore them on your own.

Air Vietnam has a regular helicop-ter service plying between Vung Tau and **Con Son**, the largest island in the archipelago. Alternatively, there is also a 12-hour boat trip leaving from Vung Tau. The Mekong Delta is more than a swamp. There are also some delightful beaches. The small beach resort of **Ha Tien** is only eight kilometers (five miles) from the Cambodian border and **Duong Beach** is 32 kilometers (20 miles) south of Ha Tien, towards Rach Gia. It lies shaded by native *duong* trees and lined with pearly white sands and clear tur-quoise water.

Diving & Snorkelling

beach resorts including **Vung Tau**, **Nha Trang** and **Danang** in the south and **Sam Son** in the north.

Vung Tau's beaches may not be the best, but they are easy to reach from Ho Chi Minh City, just 125 kilometers (80 miles) southeast via Highway 15. You basically have two choices: Back Beach is much more pleasant than Front Beach

Nha Trang, the capital of Khanh Hoa province, is fronted by a broad beach with numerous hotels dotted along the shore. Numerous offshore islands make **Khanh Hoa** province a sealover's play-ground – especially for scuba–diving and snorkelling. The ship chandler at 74 Tran Phu Boulevard (tel: 21195) rents snorkelling and scuba–diving equipment as well as boats.

If you have your own tanks, you can also rent a boat from the docks at Cau Da, six kilometers (four miles) south of central Nha Trang. You do not have to travel far to enjoy calm waters: the waters surrounding the barrier islands off Nha Trang Beach offer some good snorkelling opportunities.

The rest of the central coast has a number of excellent strands. **Mui Ne Beach**, near Phan Tiet, is famous for its sand dunes. Further north, **Ca Na Beach** boasts beautiful blue water and white sand divided by giant boulders. **Lang Co**, just north of the Hai Van Pass, is a long sandy isthmus with a fishing village that is perched on the edge of a turquoise lagoon.

Danang boasts **China Beach**, famous during the Vietnam War as a rest and recreation spot for American GIs, and in more recent times as the venue for a hit television program. The closest shore to Hue is **Thuan An Beach**, near the mouth of the Perfume River.

Moving into what was once North Vietnam, you can find **Nhat Le Beach** at the mouth of a river of the same name in Quang Binh Province, and the often crowded **Sam Son Beaches**, 16 kilometers (10 miles) southeast of Thanh Hoa City, as well as the breathtaking shores of **Ha Long Bay**.

Hiking & Caving

Returning to nature is possible in **Cuc Phuong National Park** which spreads through the provinces of Ha Nam Ninh, Ha Son Binh and Thanh Hoa 140 kilometers (86 miles) south of Hanoi. The park's 222 kilometers of tropical forest are home to nearly 2,000 species of plants, 1,800 species of insects, 137 species of birds, 64 species of mammals and 33 species of reptiles.

Half of **Cat Ba Island** – the largest in Ha Long Bay – and adjacent inshore waters are part of a national park comprising swamps, coral reefs and tropical forests. The park is home to 21 species of mammals, the same number of bird species and more than 600 different types of plants.

The surrounding waters teem with fish, molluscs and arthropods. Marine mammals are also encountered including seals and dolphins. You can catch a boat directly from Haiphong (about three and a half hours) but a much more convenient base to start your travels from is Hong Gai in Quang Ninh province.

Spelunking enthusiasts will not be bored in Vietnam, a landscape marked by myriad *karst* (limestone) formations (porous limestone hills). **Phong Nha Caves**, 45 kilometers (28 miles) northwest of Dong Hoi, consist of thousands of meters of stalactite and stalagmite-lined passages. The caves were Buddhist sanctuaries from the 9th and 10th centuries and you can still find the remains of Cham altars and inscriptions in them.

Exploring these caves requires a combination of boat and foot journeys.

The race track in Ho Chi Minh City.

Ha Long Bay literally has thousands of caves of all sizes waiting to be explored. The most famous caves are **Hang Bo Nau**, **Hang Hanh** and the three-chambered **Hang Dau Go** (Grotto of the Wooden Stakes, which is also called the Cave of Marvels).

At the other end of the country, **Mo So Grotto** is 17 kilometers (10 miles) south of Ha Tien and consists of three large chambers and numerous tunnels. During the wet season the caves are only accessible by boat. If you keep going for eight kilometers (five miles) in the same direction you will come to **Hang Tien Grotto**, which served as a hideout for Emperor Gia Long when he was fleeing from the Tay Son Rebels in 1784.

Horse Racing

One of the few mass spectator sports you can find in Vietnam today is horse racing. Outlawed in 1975 as a decadent, bourgeois activity, racing was reintroduced to Ho Chi Minh City in 1990 by a Chinese-Vietnamese businessman named Philip Chow.

Seven races are held every Saturday and Sunday throughout the year, at **Phu Tho Racecourse** near Cholon district. The meets attract crowds of about 30,000 people. The steeds are small, a result of poor diet and breeding techniques, but so are the jockeys – boys aged between ten and 15 years old who weigh about 35 kilograms (77 pounds).

Lined by a long coast the Vietnamese take to the water quite naturally.

Betting is simple: select the first and second place winners. No odds are posted and stakes are in keeping with the economy, ranging from below US$0.20 cents to about US$1. However, there is no lack of color and enthusiasm.

Theme Parks

If the proposed **Vung Tau Fairy Land Theme Park** is any indication, Vietnam will have ample man-made sports and recreation venues in the future. A Taiwan-Vietnamese joint venture project, Fairy Land is slated to open in late 1993. It will include a 1,500-room resort hotel, aquatic sports centre, golf course, opera house and an ethnic village represent-

ing the various minority groups of Vietnam.

The following is a list of assorted sports, games and recreational activities at the main tourist centers in Vietnam:

Dalat

Billiards

There is a billiard room in the Palace Hotel. Tel: 2203.

Boating

Da Thien Lake in the Valley of Love has paddleboats and canoes which can be rented by the hour.

The lake is five kilometers (three miles) north of the city center by way of

Ho Chi Minh Trail Treks

Highway 9 on the Ho Chi Minh trail.

Many tourists – especially young Western backpackers who have watched too many war movies – think that they can walk the length of the Ho Chi Minh Trail, as if Vietnam was a slightly more tropical version of Nepal. But, their expectations could not be further from the truth. The reality of the situation is that there is not much left of Asia's most famous roadway.

The Ho Chi Minh Trail was not just one road, but a whole network of jungle paths covering more than 20,000 kilometers (12,500 miles). The trail was started in 1959 as an infiltration route for communist troops and supplies into South Vietnam, much of it along ancient caravan routes that ran down through the spine of the Annamite (Truong Son) Mountains. Many of the routes ran through Laos and Cambodia, although this did not seclude them from American bombing. During the hardcore war years (1965-75) as many as 10,000 vehicles were operating along the trail at any one time, including cargo bikes which were dubbed "steel horses" by the Vietnamese. The route was also used to move the dead and wounded back to the North. After liberation in 1975, the Ho Chi Minh Trail largely disappeared back into the jungle from which it was carved. The section along the Da Krang River between Khe Sanh and A Luoi was paved with Cuban aid in the mid-1970s. But, otherwise it is difficult to identify – or travel along – specific parts of the trail.

However, that does not mean that there will be no trekking some day. Tourism authorities at both the national and provincial level are already well aware that trail tourism could be a big cash earner in future, especially for the impoverished rural regions along the Laotian and Cambodian frontiers that have little else going for them except subsistence farming. Two things impeding the evolution of trekking routes are the massive amount of unexploded bombs and other live ordnance that lie hidden along the trail, and the uncertain security situation in the Central Highlands.

An inter-community volley ball match.

Phu Dong Thien Vuong Street.

Paddleboats that resemble gigantic white swans are available for renting near the Tanh Thuy Restaurant on the shores of Xuan Huong Lake in downtown Dalat.

Golf

A small course near the Flower Gardens on the northern shore of Xuan Huong Lake was recently renovated.

Horseback Riding

Horses can be hired by the hour in the Valley of Love and on the banks of the Lake of Sighs, six kilometers (four miles) northeast of downtown Dalat via Phan Chu Trinh Street.

Tennis

Duy Tan Hotel offers excellent tennis facilities. Tel: 2216.

Hanoi

Billiards

If you fancy a game, drop by the Thang Long Hotel. Tel: 258 211.

Cycling

Rent a bicycle at the Thang Long Hotel, Giang Vo Street (tel: 57796) and take off on an exploration of the city.

Jogging/Walking

Join the locals and go for a morning jog or a brisk walk around Hoan Kiem Lake. Six kilometers (four miles) west of Hoan Kiem Lake is another leafy area called Thu Le Park, which also includes the Hanoi Zoo.

Enter on Buoi Street and enjoy the lawns and ponds.

Enter The Dragon: Tay Son Martial Arts

The Vietnamese are deeply interested in martial arts.

Vietnam, like most Asian nations has its own brand of martial arts, developed in the Tay Son region of Binh Ninh province in the late 18th century but now popular throughout the land.

Tay son vo si, as the sport is called in Vietnamese, was developed for personal self-defense and military combat, but today's adherents are more interested in the fitness and artistic aspects. Martial arts demonstrations are often part of any festival and cultural show.

There are a number of specific disciplines, nearly all of them involving some sort of ancient weapon – swords, knives, spears, bamboo canes and other implements of destruction which are used in rapid, acrobatic dance-type movements.

Drumming is an important element of Tay Son martial arts, with specific beats that signal the call to arms, the attack and final victory.

Boys and girls start learning martial arts at the age of nine or ten. But this is not just a young person's sport – there are competitions for each generation, ranging up to 80 years of age. According to tradition, practices in rural districts are conducted on the night of the full moon.

A written code of rules was drafted by Nguyen Hue and Nguyen Lu, two leaders of the Tay Son peasant rebellion, who learned martial arts from an 18th century master. Their original rule book is on display in the Tay Son Museum.

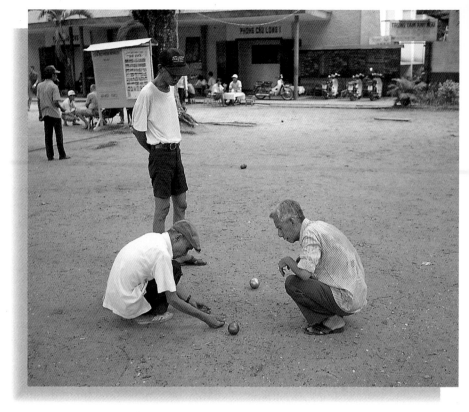

Whiling away time at Petangue.

Swimming

Thang Loi (Victory) Hotel (tel: 258 211) has a swimming pool.

Ho Chi Minh City

Boating

Nowadays, paddleboats, rowboats and sailboats are available for hire in Ho Ky Hoa Park, situated just off Three Thang Two Blvd.

Fishing

Fishing is allowed for part of the year in Ho Ky Hoa Park or try the Saigon River.

Health Club

There is a health club at the Hai Van Hotel (tel: 291 274).

Jogging/Walking

The Botanical Gardens offer a peaceful setting for an early evening walk or jog. You might want to take a stroll through the adjoining zoo. There are gates on Nguyen Binh Khiem and Xo Viet Nghe Tinh streets.

The bench-lined paths of **Cong Vien Van Hoa Park** offer a shaded "track" for jogging and walking. The entrances are on Xo Viet Tinh and Nguyen Du streets. **Artex Saigon Orchid Farm** is primarily a commercial concern, but visitors are welcome to stroll through the beautiful gardens. The farm is at 5/81 Xa Lo Vong Dai Street.

Sauna

The Ben Thanh (Rex) Hotel (tel: 292 185) and the Continental Hotel (tel: 294 456) have saunas.

Swimming

The Ben Thanh (Rex) Hotel (tel: 292 185), the Tan Binh (Airport) Hotel (tel: 441 167) and the Thien Hong (Arc-En-Ciel) Hotel (tel: 552 530) all boast swimming pools. The pool at the Rex is on the roof, adjacent to the outdoor bar.

Tennis

There are tennis courts at the Huong Duong (Central Palace) Hotel (tel: 292 404) and the Tan Binh (Airport) Hotel (tel: 441 167).

Floating Hotel

The most extensive range of recreational activities in one location can be enjoyed at the Saigon Floating Hotel – tennis courts offering racquet hire, outdoor swimming, quoits, indoor table games such as backgammon and chess, health club and fitness centre, saunas, massage and an oriental garden.

Hue

Boating

The Huong Giang (Perfume River) Hotel (tel: 2122) hires boats. You can usually get one of the local fishermen to ferry you around for a modest price.

Cycling

Nha Khach Hue, a small tourist hotel at 2 Le Loi Street, plans to hire bicycles.

Tennis

The Huong Giang (Perfume Hotel) Hotel (tel: 2122) has poorly maintained tennis courts.

Nha Trang

Boating

Bao Dai Villas (tel: 22449) has a private marina from where it hires boats to Nha Trang Bay. Fishermen in the nearby port also offer their boats for hire.

Picnicking

The Ba Ho Falls are 19 kilometers (12 miles) north of Nha Trang, near Phu Huu Village, a forested area with waterfalls and pools set back from the road.

Vung Tau

Cycling

Bicycles can be rented at both Front and Back Beaches, which provide a delightful way to explore the Vung Tau Peninsula.

Hiking

Vung Tao's two mountains offer an easy hike, but the humidity and temperatures can be quite high, so carry lots of water to avoid dehydration.

T hrough most of the 1970s and 1980s, some say the only truly good Vietnamese food was served in Hong Kong, Paris and California. Many of the best chefs had fled the country, many key ingredients were in short supply in the country and bourgeois institutions like restaurants were frowned upon. Eating out in Vietnam was never exciting. However, with the opening up of Vietnam, the resulting economic boom and the emergence of deluxe hotels and restaurants, gourmet Vietnamese food has returned to Vietnam – especially to the south. The same dishes are still on offer as in post-liberation days – but today they are made from better ingredients and under much better conditions.

Making rice wafers in Han Giang Province.

Most meals include *com* (rice) – the staple food of Vietnam – together with meat, vegetables and soup. As with Chinese food, you will be given a bowl full of steamed rice to which you add meats and vegetables selected with chopsticks from central dishes. Do not be too shy to raise the rice bowl to your chin and more or

Jellied health food sold at roadside stalls.

less shovel the food into your mouth with your chopsticks. To get your bill, get the attention of the waiter by pretending you are writing something in the air in an upward movement from left to right.

More Than Rice

Perhaps the best known Vietnamese dish is the spring roll – *cha gio* in the south and *nem* in the north. Spring rolls are usually made from minced pork, shrimp, vermicelli noodles, mushrooms and other fungi wrapped in rice paper and deep fried. *Nem rau* (vegetable spring rolls) are also available. Before eating the spring roll, wrap it in a let-tuce leaf and dip it in *nuoc cham* (a popular sauce made from *nuoc man* (fermented fish and mixed with chili, lime, sugar and garlic). In fact, you will probably come across *nuoc man* and *nuoc cham* at just about every restaurant, as they are considered an integral part of any meal. In addition to its savory flavor, *nuoc man* is also rich in phosphorus, minerals and amino acids.

Perhaps the most popular dish is *pho* (noodle soup), which is eaten at any meal but is most popular for breakfast. The noodles are quickly boiled, strained and placed in the serving bowl with the meat of preference (usually chicken, beef or pork) and some green vegetables. Lastly, *nuoc leo* (hot broth) is added. To further confuse you, noodle soup is also

Vietnamese fast food, market style.

available "dry" with the broth served on the side – ask for *kho pho*.

As soup is served with practically every meal, there are a number of different types to choose from: *xup rau* (mixed vegetable soup), *lau* (fish and vegetable soup) and *mien luon* (soup made from eel, noodles, mushrooms, onions and chicken).

Fresh seafood is abundant in Vietnam. *Cha ca* (barbecued fish fillets served with fried rice) is the most famous dish. You will also find lots of prawns, lobsters and squid. Minced fish cakes are an-

Roasted fare and French rolls in Ho Chi Minh City.

other Vietnamese speciality.

Exotic Meat & Vegetarianism

Exotic (and endangered) meats are considered delicacies and are not hard to find, so if you want to try (or avoid) them, look out for the following menu items: *rua* (turtle), *truc* (pangolin), *nai* (venison), *tran* (python), *ran ho* (cobra), *dong* (gecko lizard) and *doi qua* (bat).

Vegetarian food is widely available. In fact, Vietnam has a long history of vegetarian cuisine as the monks of the Mahayana Buddhist school are strict vegetarians. Ask a local person for the nearest place to find a *tiem com chay* (vegetarian rice shop).

The French influence on food is encountered almost everywhere – French loaves are available in even the smallest markets and a lot of the sandwiches found on the roadside stalls are filled with pâté.

For snacks and dessert there is an abundance of fresh fruit – from *chuoi* (bananas), *dua* (coconuts), *qua buoi* (pomelo), *xam bu che* (rambutans) and *khe* (starfruit). There are also cooked dessert specialties, mostly made from sticky rice, beans and sugar, plus assorted candied fruit and vegetables.

Regional Specialties

Down in the Mekong Delta, especially

Pavement eatery in the old section of Hanoi.

in the town of Can Tho, frog and fresh-water fish are well prepared. For dessert you should try *banh bia* – (wheat flour cake made with mung beans, coconut and candied fruit).

When in My Tho you should try not to miss their special soup dish – *hu tieu my tho* (soup made with vermicelli noodles, fresh and dried seafood, meat and special spices).

Seafood is synonymous with Rach Gia. Dishes to try are dried cuttlefish or dried sliced fish prepared in pepper. Steamed prawns or freshwater crayfish are also delicious. The ultimate delicacy of Chau Doc is small turtles, but many Western visitors cannot bear to eat them as they are served whole in their shells.

With the opening up of the south,

more and more restaurants are popping up every day in Ho Chi Minh City (Saigon). Nowadays, you can find just about any type of cuisine you crave; French, Indian, Thai, all types of Chinese and even good old steak and chips. Traditionally, Saigon food tends to be spicier and contains a lot more coconut milk than the dishes served further north. They are usually served with raw, leafy vegetables which are used to wrap your food within.

Some specific dishes to try in Saigon include *chanh chua* (tamarind soup), *cu lao* (assorted meat and seafood soup), *ca loc kho* (boiled trout with fish sauce) and minced shrimp on a sugarcane stick.

Strawberry lovers can feast on this fruit in cool and fertile Dalat. You can

Fish Sauce

If there is one thing that Vietnamese epicures are passionate about, it is *nuoc man* (fish sauce). You will definitely find a bottle of thick, sticky fish sauce sitting on nearly every dinner table in Vietnam.

The ubiquitous liquid is used as a sauce in which to dip cooked vegetables and meat, or as a raw ingredient in the preparation of chicken, pork and other foods. Sometimes it is even consumed raw as a high protein drink, because *nuoc man* contains 25 percent protein, (as much as blood).

The south central coast of Vietnam is the fulcrum of fish sauce production, with factories at Phan Thiet and Phan Rang in Thuan Hai province. The large, government-run facilities can produce as much as four million liters of fish sauce per year, both for export and domestic consumption.

Fishing boats dock right outside the fish sauce factories in Phan Thiet. A fish sauce factory is basically comprised of a giant warehouse full of wooden vats. Hundreds of whole fish are thrown into the vats, heaps of salt added and the concoction is allowed to ferment for six to 12 months. Each vat contains a different type of fish, because each species produces a unique taste. The best (and most expensive) is said to be blue fin tuna sauce.

Generally speaking, the longer the mixture sits in the vat the better – although a six to seven month period is considered long enough. Sometimes the fish sauce is pumped into cement vats located outside the warehouse, where it is exposed to the sun in order to speed up the fermentation process.

Once the specified date is reached, the *nuoc man* is drawn off by means of a long tube and filtered so that no bones or scales remain in the brew. The fish sauce is then bottled, tasted and graded according to its quality. Waste material from inside the vats is mixed with fertilizer or animal food. Nothing is thrown away.

Thuan Hai province also produces a number of other seafood products including shark's fin, seaweed, dried cuttlefish and frozen fish, crab and shrimp. The main export markets are Japan, Hong Kong and Malaysia. More than 20,000 people are involved in the seafood industry in Thuan Hai, including fishermen and factory workers, which generates an income of between US$8 to $10 million a year.

eat them fresh, made into candy, preserved as jam or made into a refreshing drink. But, do not buy this candy to give to the children living in the area – they seem to have had their fill and will only throw it away.

Other fresh fruit and vegetables grow in abundance, a real vegetarian's delight of yams, spinach, peas, beans, avocados (eaten sliced with sugar or made into ice cream) apples, blackcurrants, cherries and peaches. There is also artichoke syrup and tea. Another Dalat favorite is *dau hu*, (a dessert made from sweetened soya milk, prepared with a hint of ginger).

Phan Rang's specialty is not for the faint hearted – roasted *gecko* (lizard) served with fresh green mango. But if that is not to your taste, the town is also known for its fresh grapes.

Nha Trang is another seafood town, but you should also try a local speciality called *thanh long* (dragon fruit) which is deep red on the outside with white flesh full of little black seeds on the inside. It's said that this fruit is only found here.

Hoi An's specialty is *cao lau* (noodles mixed with bean sprouts, pork, green vegetables and croûtons with rice paper

Mobile noodle shop.

added on top).

Noodles are also considered a specialty in Hue, where they are served with green vegetables, dried meat and fruit, to which is added *nuoc leo* (a sauce made from peanuts and sesame seeds). Hue also boasts of a special crêpe stuffed with bean sprouts, shellfish and meat topped with *nuoc leo*. In Quang Ngai City, ask for *bo gan* (large rice crackers topped with beef and ground peanuts).

The good citizens of Hanoi are proud of their *pho* (noodles) and *mien luon* (soups) together with *nem* (spring rolls).

Familiar labels are available to quench all tastes.

On the slightly more exotic side, they specialize in *oc nhoi* (chopped snail cooked in ginger leaves) and *ech tam bot ran* (frog served in vinegar).

Drinks

Nuoc tra (tea) and *ca phe* (coffee) are probably the most popular local drinks. Both are drunk strong and sweet, either hot or cold. *Nuoc ngot* (soft drinks) are also as popular. However, drink only the imported brands like Coke as the domestic sodas produced by BGI may not be to everyone's taste. The supply of *nuoc suoi* (mineral water) is increasing. Gone are the days when you only had a choice of salty Vinh Hao or an undrink-able Soviet brand. With the abundance of fruit, it is not surprising that fruit juice is a popular way to quench local thirst. You can get your fruit juice fresh or in preserved syrup form.

The most popular types are *soda chanh* (lime soda), *nuoc cam* (orange juice) and *nuoc dua* (coconut milk). Outside of the large hotels, be careful with water – unless boiled it is sometimes not safe enough for drinking. Adding ice is also a risk.

Beer & Liquor

Bia (beer) is found all over Vietnam. The two most popular local brands – Saigon Export® and 333® – are quite good, so

Rice flour crisps, prettily coloured.

there is no need to buy expensive imported beer. Throughout the countryside you will come across a variety of
unnamed local beers. Take your chances
– some are good, others are flat and
tasteless.

Besides the well-known international brands of hard liquor, you can
find some interesting alcohol selections
from the former Eastern Bloc countries
– vodka, brandy, schnapps etc. Vietnam itself produces over 50 varieties of
wine – made from rice and fruit and
Dalat is famous for its strawberry wine.

V ietnam may not be a shopping paradise like Hong Kong or Bangkok, but give it time. The potential is there in terms of both artistic talent and marketing savvy – and so are the bargain prices. All of the major tourist destinations in Vietnam feature an abundance of handicrafts that can be purchased at very reasonable prices – especially if you are paying in US dollars. Bargaining is definitely the rule of thumb.

Local flowers mostly find their way to altars.

Local Ware

Lacquerware is one of the most popular souvenir items, but before you purchase a piece, visit a factory where can see the painstaking process involved in its production. It will make you appreciate your purchase all the more. The raw material is extracted from lacquer trees that grow in the northern provinces of Vietnam and is skillfully applied to each article layer by layer. Some sort of design – animals, people, landscapes, abstracts – is painted on or inlaid during the lac-

A modern shopping complex in Hanoi.

quering process, giving the finished article an almost multi-dimensional effect. The range of lacquerware items is quite diverse, ranging from small vases, boxes and trays to huge wall panels and tables. Chairs and sofas are also available. The most widely-used design feature is the goldfish. If it is not to your liking, you can still find other wonderful designs if you hunt around a bit. Mother-of-pearl inlay is also a very popular way of decorating laquerware.

Ceramic elephants are another ubiquitous souvenir. They make perfect coffee table bases or plant stands – if you can figure out a way to get them home. Pottery pachyderms are a real bargain in Vietnam, costing maybe a tenth of the price they fetch in Hong Kong or Singapore. You should consider buying some of the local basketwork as extra luggage in which to transport the elephants. Some shops will also pack them into wooden crates.

Vietnam also has some wonderful hand embroidery. Some of the most surprisingly modern items are the children's wall hangings, but you can also get the more traditional and exotic motifs like dragons, orchids, pheasants and lotus flowers. The range of hand-embroidered articles also includes tablecloths, kimonos and dressing gowns. Paintings executed on silk, various types of tapestries and curtains fashioned from bamboo or beads also make good souvenirs.

While you can still find tortoise-shell items (mainly in the coastal ar-

Local fruits laid out at markets.

eas), please do not buy them no matter how old the piece may be. Every species of sea turtle is highly endangered and every tortoiseshell piece you buy will be replaced by the killing of another live turtle.

While wandering around Hanoi or Saigon, you will find an abundance of antiques for sale. If you ask the shop owner, he will probably bring out some exquisite pieces from under-the-counter for your selection – old porcelain, clocks, Rolex® watches, silver, ivory and jade objects. Old paper money, coins and stamps can also be found in small antique shops in most major towns.

But, you must be cautious on two counts: first, it is illegal to export too many antiques without a government permit; and secondly the Vietnamese are getting quite good at producing fakes. In many cases, only an expert can tell the difference between a genuine antique and a well-crafted imitation.

Of course, no shopping expedition in Vietnam would be complete without the purchase of the ultimate tourist items – a *non la* (conical hat) and an *ao dai* (traditional silk dress). You can buy these in nearly every city and town, at very reasonable prices. The following is a breakdown of shopping opportunities in the major tourist areas:

Dalat

For a vegetarian's delight of the best

A sharp business of hawking knives.

mountain fruit and vegetables, as well as freshly-baked French bread and beautiful cut flowers, visit Dalat's central market at the northern end of Nguyen Thi Minh Khai Street.

If you are lucky enough, you will also see the *montaguards* (local hilltribe people) wandering around in their traditional dress.

Danang

A variety of hawkers cruise China Beach

– especially around the stretch in front of Non Nuoc Hotel and Marble Mountain selling soft drinks, fresh fruit, conical hats, bamboo souvenirs and old military dogtags. Non Nuoc village specializes in statues and other souvenirs fashioned from marble.

Hanoi

The best craft shopping in Hanoi is along Hang Khay Street, opposite the southern shore of Hoan Kiem Lake. One especially good shop is number 17. You can also try Tran Tien Street for handicraft shops and art galleries.

Material Finds

Pre-printed or custom-designed tee-shirts and hand-painted silk greeting cards are available all around Hanoi. The souvenir shop in the Thang Loi Hotel offers a good selection of silk cards.

Embroidery is abundant in the area around Hang Bong Street, and you will find some interesting antique shops on nearby Kim Lien Street. Tapestry weaving is a relatively new handicraft in Vietnam, which was only introduced by the French in the 1930s. One of the most interesting places to buy your tapestry is at the **Dong Da Tapestry Factory** (also known as Tada) where you can see the tapestries being woven. One of Hanoi's largest markets is the **Dong Xuan Market** on Silk Street in Old Hanoi. Here you

will find lots of kitchenware, wickerware, food and flowers. But, you could stumble onto Russian caviar, vodka and French wine. Stamp collectors should head for the philatelic counter at the General Post Office, 75 Dinh Tien Hoang Street.

Ho Chi Minh City

Saigon's famous lacquerware factories began opening their doors to customers in the mid-1980s when Vietnam began attracting international tourists. They are a good place to learn about the intricate production process from the artists who design the items on drafting tables, to the workers who apply layer after layer of lacquer.

But, it is not necessarily the best place to buy, as prices tend to be quite expensive. However, the factory claims that all their products are properly kiln-dried so that they will not crack when taken to cold climates (shoddy lacquerware *will* crack) and they can also arrange for the packing and export of expensive, bulky items. There are several large factories from which to choose: **Lam Son Lacquerware**, 188 Le Van Street, Phu Nhuan District (tel: 452 235) and **Saigon Lacquerware**, 139 Hai Ba Trung Street (tel: 494 183).

Of Markets & More!

Ben Thanh Market is just a five minute

A prosperous provision shop selling imported packaged goods.

walk from the Rex Hotel, at the junction of the Ham Nghi, Le Loi and Tran Hung Do boulevards. This huge 11,000 square meter market has been around since 1914. Although originally a food mart it now sells all sorts of items including perfumes, watches, tobacco, kitchenware, clothing and consumer electronics, imported from Japan, Taiwan, the US, Europe and Singapore. Hand-embroidered fabric lengths to make the traditional *ao dai* are also available. War buffs – and anyone else looking for military paraphernalia – should try the **Dan Sinh Market**, 104 Nguyen Cong Tu Street. Stalls at the back of the market have a huge selection of new and used military uniforms and supplies originally made for the American, Chinese

and Russian armies. The selection includes flak jackets, canteens, gas masks – even stretchers! Do not look too anxious to buy, as the vendors are apt to wildly-overcharge.

The **Thieves Market** located at the intersection of Huynh Thuc Kang and Ton That Dan streets got its name during the Vietnam War, when stolen US Army goods found their way here.

Today, the market is stocked with goods brought home by Vietnamese sailors or sent home to relatives by Vietnamese living abroad. The best places in Saigon for stamp collectors to choose their souvenirs from are at the two stores run by the post office's philatelic section at 2C Le Loi Boulevard and 12 Ton That Dam Street.

Inside Ben Thanh market.

Traditional Finds

If you are in pursuit of more traditional souvenirs, there are dozens of antique, art and handicraft shops. The greatest concentration being along Dong Khoi Street and Nguyen Hue Boulevard in downtown Saigon.

Saigon Souvenir at 30 Ngo Duc Ke Street (near the Cuu Long Hotel) has a great selection of lacquerware, ceramics, handicrafts and antiques. **My Nghe Viet Nam** at 20 Nguyen Hue specializes in bamboo handicrafts, ceramic elephants and lacquerware. Two of the best hotel handicraft shops are at the Rex (ground floor) and the Cuu Long (first floor).

For tailoring, we recommend that you try the hotel shops, as you can be assured of some kind of standard quality. Ask the tailors at the Rex and Oscar hotels to show you samples of their work. If you are in dire need of western style "personal care" products, head for the **Minimart** at 101 Nam Ky Khoi Nghia Street, or try your hotel shop.

Hue

You will find a large souvenir shop in the Huong Giang Hotel, but less expensive (and often more interesting) items can be bought from artists who frequent the entrances of many tourist attractions like the Noon Gate, Linh Mu Pa-

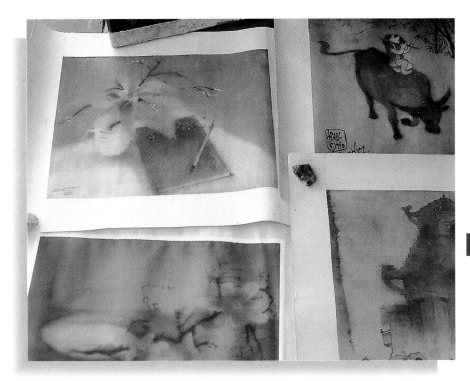

Art students sell their pieces outside Thien Mu Pagoda in Hue.

goda and the royal tombs. Jewelry is sold at the **Gold and Silver Trade Department** at 55 Tran Hung Dao Street.

Hue is home to perhaps the best *non la* (conical hats) in Vietnam. The hats from Hue often contain designs that incorporate poetry, flora and fauna, as well as traditional landscape scenes hidden between the layers of palm leaves, which reveal themselves when held to the light. If you buy directly from the artist you can ask him to sign the hat.

Nha Trang

Seashells and seashell items can be bought along the main beach and near the Oceanographic Institute in Cau Da village.

Vung Tau

Souvenirs from the sea are the focus of shopping activity in Vung Tau. Vendors congregate near the intersection of Le Loi and Ly Tu Trong streets. They sell a range of bleached shells and articles crafted from shells.

Alternatively, you can also buy the same range of sea crafts from the numerous hawkers that ply the beaches, sometimes at unbelievably low prices.

Saigon was the nightlife capital of Southeast Asia back in the 1960s. But that distinction was quickly obliterated after liberation in 1975, as communist authorities launched a massive clean-up drive to rid the city of vice and other bourgeois influences. Saigon – and, in fact all of Vietnam – lapsed into a coma of dreary nightlife in which the primary form of after-dark entertainment was hanging out on street corners listening to party propaganda emanating from loud speakers.

But now things are slowly changing once again. A little bit of capitalism has gone a long way in terms of nightlife. Saigon has regained much of its former vigour with a multitude of new bars, restaurants and dance clubs. And the trend is slowly spreading northwards, with the sound of music punctuating the night air in places like Nha Trang, Danang, Hue

A songstress entertains.

Neons light the way.

and even Hanoi. But, the return of legitimate entertainment has also spurred a revival of vice, especially prostitution and drug abuse, not just in perpetually-decadent Saigon, but also in Hanoi, which had largely remained aloof from the seedy nightlife for so long.

Night Spice

Most of the larger hotels in Saigon offer a variety of after-dark diversions – restaurants, bars, karaoke lounges and cultural shows. But entertainment is alive and well beyond their walls, especially along Dong Khoi Street (the former To Du Street) which is well on its way to rivalling Bangkok's Patpong as the wild-

est nightlife scene in Southeast Asia with a variety of boisterous bars where you can partake of cold beer, rock'n'roll and female companionship.

Two of the trendier places in "new" Saigon are the **Superstar Disco and Nightclub** at 431A/2 Hoang Van Thu Street and the **Down Under Disco** in the Floating Hotel. Some of the better bars include **Apocalypse Now** and **Good Morning Vietnam** on Dong Du Street. Another lively setting is **Tiger Tavern** at 227 Dong Khoi Street.

Slowly but surely the wave of nightlife is sweeping across Vietnam with high-tech entertainment centers which cater to various tastes and thousands of people all at once. **VIP Club** is at the cutting edge with outlets in Hanoi (60-

At the Rex Hotel disco in Saigon.

62 Nguyen Du Street) and Saigon (2D Pham Ngoc Thach Street) boasting cafés, lounges, karaoke and games rooms. The **Shangri-La Complex** at 1196 3/2 Street in Saigon offers all of the above plus a health club and department store.

Ballroom Dancing

Ballroom dancing, which, for decades constituted the main component of Vietnamese nightlife, was virtually banned in 1975 as a bourgeois pastime. But today, ballroom dancing can be found in large towns and cities throughout the country, often existing side-by-side with pop music. On any given night, in any one dance hall, you can hear a medley of rumba, cha-cha-cha, waltzes, tango, bebop and disco music.

Saigon is considered the fulcrum for ballroom dancing in Vietnam. The premier venue being the **Dance Club** at the Cultural Labor House, where you can watch Vietnamese couples doing a number of Saigon-style routines. Indeed, Vietnamese dancing seems to have evolved independent of overseas influence for almost two decades. Famed as the center for the revival of ballroom dancing, the Cultural Labor House was the first club to gain permission to teach dancing in the mid 1980s. There are now nine other dance clubs in Saigon.

Some of the older hotels in Saigon – the Caravelle, the Rex and the Majestic – also feature live bands nightly, usu-

Movie houses enjoy a good following.

ally from about 7 to 11 pm. In fact, these hotels are the only places where dancing never stopped in Vietnam – even in the dark days after liberation – as only foreigners were allowed to engage in this "degenerate" activity.

Hanoi's young and restless crowd head for the privately-owned **Palace Dance Hall** on Pho Nha Trung. Here too, the music alternates between modern and traditional with surprising ease. On some nights the clientele is decidedly older and the music selection more sedate.

There is also dancing at the Thong Nhat Hotel on weekend nights from 8 to 11:30 pm, and at the Bo Ho Hotel on Thursdays. In Dalat there is nightly dancing (except Monday) at the Dalat Hotel, starting at 7:30 pm.

Classical Pursuits

Another popular form of night-time amusement are performances of traditional Vietnamese and Western classical music.

Saigon's celebrated **Conservatory of Music** (112 Nguyen Du Street) features concerts every Monday and Friday at 5:30 pm, from March to May and from October to December. Other conservatories are found in Hanoi and Hue. In Phan Thiet, Cham music is sometimes performed at the Vinh Thuy Hotel on the beach.

Municipal theaters offer a steady

A cafe with some entertainment.

diet of drama, music, dance and alternative entertainment like gymnastics and acrobatics. They are generally open every night except Monday and change their programs from week to week. There are various municipal theaters in Saigon (Dong Khoi Street; tel 291-249), Dalat (Hung Vuong Street), Hanoi (Trang Tien Street) and Hue (Huong Vuong Street).

There is usually something going on at the massive **Hoa Binh Theater** complex in Saigon (143 Thang 2 Blvd, District 10; tel: 255 199). Performances include plays, films, live bands playing Vietnamese and western pop music, acrobatics and circus acts. It also has a disco on the ground floor. The Hanoi equivalent is the **Workers Cultural**

Palace located on Tran Hung Dao Street, east of the railway station, which has a huge theater as well as libraries and sports facilities.

Cinema

Cinema is as popular in Vietnam as elsewhere in Southeast Asia. Cinemas screen movies from Thailand, Taiwan and Hong Kong, as well as domestic productions and some Hollywood films. Look for the word *rap* if you want to see a movie.

Social life in rural areas tends to center around small cafés, usually in the market towns or provincial capitals, where people gather to drink coffee,

Maxim's for the bigger spenders.

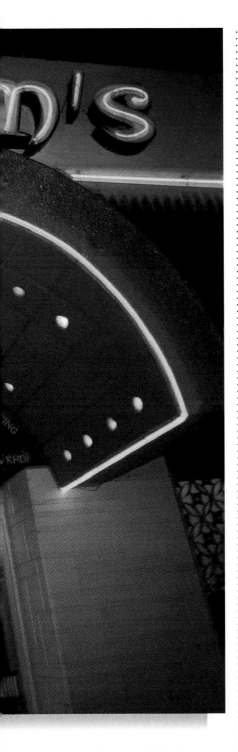

beer or Mekong whisky, chat about the days' events and listen to music. Often the music consists of ancient Western records left over from the war, anything from Patty Paige's "Butterflies" to the Eagles' "Hotel California" blaring from an old gramophone.

In Nha Trang, try the cluster of outdoor cafés situated on the beach along Tran Phu Boulevard where the chairs are comfortable and the stars shine brightly every night.

In Dalat, the cafés around Xuan Huong Lake are the center of action. People say that **Café Tung** (Khu Hoa Binh Street) has not changed since the 1950s when it was a meeting place for local intellectuals who used to come here and expound on key issues while listening to French music. Strangely, no alcohol is served.

Back in the days when there was no western-style nightlife to speak of, embassy personnel in Hanoi used to have to make their own evening entertainment. The German Embassy still has a popular weekly beer garden in the basement (29 Tran Phu Street) and the Australian Embassy still has its famous "Billabong Club" every Friday from 8 pm to midnight. Non-Australians must receive an invitation from embassy personnel to attend.

Or, you can hang out on the streets with young Vietnamese, especially on Dong Khoi Street and Le Loi Boulevard in Saigon on a Sunday night, as thousands of teenagers throng the streets on bicycles and motorbikes.

Vietnam is a natural gateway into Cambodia and the splendors of Angkor. The political and security situations in Cambodia have been highly unstable for more than 20 years. But a United Nations-backed ceasefire, put into effect in 1992 after years of tense negotiations, has brought new hope to a country that has suffered more than its fair share of tragedy over the latter half of the 20th century.

The South gate, Lokesvara at Angkor.

Phnom Penh

The vast majority of visitors heading for Cambodia have one thing in mind – a trip to Angkor. But, nearly everyone has to sojourn in Phnom Penh, the slow-moving and slightly seedy capital of Cambodia. The city was founded in 1434 after the Khmers abandoned Angkor to an advancing Thai army.

They called it Vyadhapura, but the Khmers were never able to re-establish their power base. They spent the next four

centuries letting the Thais and Vietnamese chip away at the edge of their kingdom. By the time the French arrived in 1863, the Khmer monarch was no more than a vassal of the King of Siam. He was easily bullied into signing a treaty that gave France "suzerainty" over Cambodia.

Phnom Penh lies at the strategic water junction where the outlet from Tonle Sap pours into the Mekong River, and where the Mekong breaks into two distinct branches called the Tian Giang and Hau Giang after they reach Vietnam. The city sits on the right (western) bank with the long Quai Karl Marx running along the waterfront. Achar Mean Boulevard is the main street running through the center of town, connecting with Route One to Saigon and Route Five which used to run all the way to Bangkok. Most of the major hotels and night market are situated along Achar Mean.

The **Royal Palace** (Banteay Kev) is the only "must" attraction in Phnom Penh. It was built in 1813 on the site of an earlier royal citadel. After entering through the Chan Chaya Pavilion, the first building that you will see is the ornate Throne Hall (1919) which appears across a broad courtyard. Much of the decor was looted by the Khmer Rouge, but the building is nonetheless impressive with its *Ramayana* murals and 60-meter (180-foot) spire fashioned after the Bayon Temple at Angkor. The fabled **Silver Pagoda** (1892) lies in the adjacent compound, and derives its

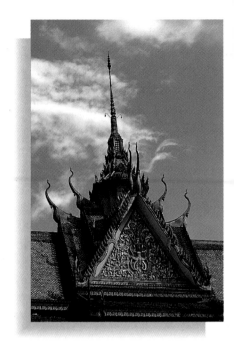

The Silver Pagoda at Phnom Penh.

name from the 5,000 silver tiles that cover the floor.

The nearby **National Museum** (1920) contains priceless works of art from various epochs of Cambodian history including Angkor, but the building itself is in a sorry state. The "killing fields" are recalled at **Tuol Sleng Museum** on the site of the notorious S-21 prison, where more than 17,000 people were tortured and killed by the Khmer Rouge between 1975 and 1978. There are a number of other interesting *wats* (Buddhist temples) around the capital including Wat Ounalom and Wat Phnom. The **Central Market** is a proverbial beehive of activity, but the best place to buy souvenirs is probably the **Tuol Tom Pong Market** on the street of

Bas-relief of Apsaras at Angkor Wat.

the same name. The quickest way to reach Phnom Penh is by air. There are regular flights from Saigon (Air Vietnam and Cambodian Airlines), Bangkok (Bangkok Air and charter services) and Singapore (Silk Air). An alternative mode of transportation is by overland bus from Saigon. The trip takes between 8 and 10 hours, including a long wait at the border. People with enough cash hire a car (and driver) for the journey saving a couple of hours off travelling time.

Angkor: Grandeur Amidst the Jungle

Angkor is one of the earth's great treas-ures, a place of infinite stature that ranks with the Pyramids and the Parthenon as symbols of civilization. Awesome in both its quantity and quality, Angkor's temples were lost amidst the jungle for hundreds of years before their "rediscovery" by French archaeologist and naturalist Henri Mouhot in 1860.

The stones speak of a great nation which flourished between AD 9 to 14, a highly sophisticated Hindu kingdom that drew its cultural inspiration from both India and Java. The roots of Angkor civilization can be traced to two earlier kingdoms – Funan and Kambuja – which occupied an area roughly similar to present-day Cambodia and southern Vietnam. The Khmer Empire was founded in AD 802 by King Jayavarman

II who developed both a powerful army and a religious cult devoted to himself. By the end of the 9th century, construction had started at Angkor, the political and spiritual seat of the empire. The Khmers reached the height of their military and artistic talent during the 12th-century reign of Jayavarman VII. By the early 15th century, Angkor had been captured by the Thais and Khmer culture was in rapid retreat.

Today, many people think of Angkor as one monument, perhaps a single shrine, but the area comprises dozens of separate royal and religious compounds built over a 500-year span. There are more than 70 individual sites, covering an area of nearly 200 square kilometers (75 square miles) on a broad expanse that runs between the northern shore of Tonle Sap Lake and a mountain called Phnom Kulen.

Explore & Discover

With an airport and tourist hotel, **Siem Reap** is a good base for visits to the various antiquities. Cambodian Airlines has daily (one hour) flights from Phnom Penh, but there is a strong rumor that direct flights from Bangkok may start in the near future.

Northwest Cambodia was the scene of bloody fighting in the 1970s and 1980s as various factions waged civil war to gain ultimate control over the entire country. Despite the UN ceasefire, well-armed Khmer Rouge guerrillas con-

tinue to control large tracts of bush in the northwest region, with a constant danger that combat could spill over into Siem Reap or Angkor.

You can explore the main ruins on your own, but you should not wander into the bush, or explore remote areas, without a local guide. The surrounding jungle is littered with live mines and other unexploded ordnance. In early 1992, guides were charging as much as US$100 a day for their services, but the government cracked down hard on touts.

The most famous site is **Angkor Wat**, five kilometers (three miles) north of Siem Reap. This massive structure was built as the funerary temple of King Suryavaraman II (who reigned from AD 1113-1150) during the golden age of the Khmer Empire. Dedicated to the Hindu god Vishnu, the temple complex covers an area of exactly 1.6 square kilometers (one square mile) and its construction marked the start of the classic age of Khmer art and architecture.

The entrance to Angkor Wat faces due west, towards the airport. The shrine is protected by a moat and a thick outer wall with bas-reliefs depicting the life of Suryavaraman II and the *Ramayana* – an epic Hindu story that was later adapted into the Buddhist and Muslim lore of Southeast Asia. Each of the stone panels is a distinct masterpiece – priceless works of art that have been somehow spared the destruction of war and a thousand years of tropical weather. The temple itself is marked by five elaborate *prasats* (towers), with the center one

Nature runs over the ruins at Bayon, Angkor Thom.

built above the actual tomb. Angkor did not become an actual *wat* (Buddhist temple) until the 15th century when it was taken over by Buddhist monks. There is still an active monastery on the site, full of young saffron-robed monks.

Directly behind the temple is **Angkor Thom** (Great City), the remains of the Khmer royal capital which in some way is more impressive than Angkor Wat. The city began to take shape in the late 9th century at the start of the Khmer epoch, but most of the grand architecture dates from the reign of King Jayavarman VII (1181-1218), a powerful monarch who vanquished the Chams who had earlier pillaged his country. He is remembered for having introduced Buddhism to Cambodia.

To reach the royal city, turn right out of the front gate of Angkor Wat and walk 1.5 kilometers (one mile) north along the tree-shaded causeway. On the left, before the city walls, are two relics of the early Khmer Empire. **Bakheng** was erected in the fourth year of the reign of King Yasovarman I (AD 893) and which later served as his funerary temple. A prototype for later structures, the main shrine at Bakheng features seven levels and five towers – a design that was meant to reflect Mount Meru, the sacred peak in Hindu mythology.

Directly behind is **Baksei Chamkrong**, a 10th century temple that is noteworthy as the first Khmer monument made entirely from stone and brick (previous temples like Bakheng were

Giants and nagas at Angkor Thom.

fashioned from sandstone).

The **Royal Causeway** is flanked by dozens of moss-covered statues of stone warriors grappling with a giant snake, a powerful depiction of the Khmer myth of creation. Looming ahead is the mighty **South Gate**, built wide enough to accommodate a parade of ceremonial elephants. The stone faces on the gateway portray Lokesvara, one of Buddha's many reincarnations, but they are also said to resemble Jayavarman VII, who commissioned the city walls.

At the center of Angkor Thom is a stunning temple complex called **Bayon**, which is more awesome than Angkor Wat in terms of pure stone majesty. Two hundred stone heads cover the temple façade, each of them taller than a man.

Once again they render a double image – the divine being Lokesvara and the god-king Jayavarman VII – executed in a deliberate style that was meant to reinforce the indelible union between the heavens and the monarchy. Even today, in an age when mass media and modern science has removed much of the mystery out of life, the stone heads carry a puissant message. Step back and ponder their impact eight centuries ago, when Bayon was first chiselled.

Aztec-like Similiarities

In a design reminiscent of Aztec Mexico, four causeways lead out in the cardinal directions from Bayon. The path from the front of the temple leads to the **East Gate**, also called the Gate of Death, an interesting about-face from the ancient Egyptians who thought the afterlife was in the west. The western causeway leads to a huge artificial *baray* (lake), while the northern causeway passes through the **Royal Terrace**, which lies at the heart of the old imperial precinct, the Angkor equivalent of a forbidden city.

Palaces and temples were arranged on either side of the Royal Terrace. On the east are the **Khleang Temples** and a strange set of monuments called the **Towers of the Tightrope Walkers**, which are now thought to have been royal dungeons and were located opposite the palace so the king could keep a close eye on his enemies. On the left are the remains of the **Royal Palace** itself, fronted by a thick wall with bas-relief like the **Panel of the Five Headed Horse** and a 427-meter (1,500-foot) stone masterpiece called the **Elephant Frieze.**

Two structures inside the palace complex predate Jayavarman VII's reign. **Phimeanakas** is a late-10th century temple constructed by King Jayavarman V as a place where he could worship Naga, the sacred snake from Hindu mythology, considered the spiritual guardian of the Khmer monarchy. It is also called the Celestial Palace, because it was situated on a hill which provided an excellent view of the heavens. Standing nearby is a ruined sandstone temple called **Baphuon**, once a massive structure but now badly in need of renovation. In bygone days it was

also called the Copper Tower, perhaps because it was sheathed in metal.

Another whole set of monuments is located to the east of Angkor Thom, around the shore of the Eastern Baray. You can gain access via another long causeway through the majestic **Gate of Victory**. The most prominent of the temples in this area is the much-photographed **Ta Prohm**, where the roots of giant kapok trees grow up and around the stone walls. Jayavarman VII built Ta Prohm as a memorial to his beloved mother, but today it stands in silent testament to how nature has helped to preserve Angkor from the destructive hand of man. Another temple, **Preah Khan**, is situated north of the city walls and honors the memory of Jayavarman's father. The temple is unusual because it is the only structure at Angkor built with stone columns. There are numerous other antiquities in the Angkor area, but you will need a vehicle to reach them. **Banteay Srei** is 25 kilometers (16 miles) north of the royal city, a fabulous temple almost lost amidst the forest. The pink sandstone friezes show provocative dancing girls and many jungle creatures – leopards and monkeys – not found anywhere else in Angkor. The town of **Rolous** southeast of Siem Reap has two magnificent 9th-century temples, **Prah Ko** and **Bakong.**

Despite its myriad social, political and military quandaries, Cambodia is worth a side trip from Vietnam for no other reason than to see the magnificent ruins of Angor Wat in the flesh.

TRAVEL TIPS

ARRIVING

By Air

Nowadays, most people arrive in Vietnam by air. Many international airlines have direct flights to Hanoi and Ho Chi Minh City. Such as:–

Aeroflot: Moscow to Hanoi and HCMC.

Air France: Paris to HCMC via Bombay and Bangkok.

Cathay Pacific: Hong Kong to Hanoi and HCMC.

Garuda Indonesia: Jakarta to HCMC via Singapore.

Kampuchean Airlines: Phnom Penh to Hanoi and HCMC.

Lao Aviation: Vientiane to Hanoi and HCMC.

Malaysian Airlines: Kuala Lumpur to Hanoi and HCMC.

Philippines Airlines: Manila to HCMC.

Lufthansa: Frankfurt to HCMC via Singapore.

Singapore Airlines: Singapore to Hanoi and HCMC.

Thai Airways: Bangkok to Hanoi and HCMC.

Vietnam Airlines: Hanoi and/or HCMC to Singapore, Bangkok, Phnom Penh and Vientiane.

Japan Airlines has an office in Hanoi but has yet to start its operations to Vietnam.

A taxi from Noi Bai Airport to downtown Hanoi (48 kilometers) is a fixed price (US$33 at press time). The public bus service offers a much

cheaper alternative. A special Vietnam Airlines taxi service is available from Tan Son Nhut Airport to downtown HCMC. The 8 kilometers ride takes about 20 minutes and costs US$10-15. Private taxis are available for about $25. Some hotels have their own motor pool for airport collection, but demand is high, so it is wise to reserve as far in advance as possible.

By Sea

As yet there is no regular passenger ship service to Vietnam. However, some cargo boats will take passengers from ports around Asia (Hong Kong, Thailand, Singapore, etc) to HCMC, Haiphong or Danang.

By Road

This is not really a feasible alternative except if you are arriving from Phnom Penh or other points in Cambodia. Theoretically, the border between Vietnam and southern China is now open to foreigners, but, transportation links remain undeveloped. Roads from Laos remain closed to foreigners.

Domestic Air

Air travel offers the quickest form of in-country travel (once the plane takes off). Vietnam Airlines (Hang Khong Viet Nam) has a monopoly on all domestic flights. However, their services are often subject to delays, changes and cancellations. Another problem is that you can only book for flights originating in the town you are in (unless you want to take your chances by sending a cable to your next destination). The more popular routes tend to be heavily overbooked.

VA uses only Soviet-made aircraft – Tupolev 134 jets (70 seats), Antonov AN-24 prop jets (45 seats) and AK40 prop jets (22 seats). Helicopters also service some routes. Inflight service is kept to a minimum.

Flights can be booked at any local VA offices. There is a 20 kilogram baggage allowance. Foreigners must purchase their tickets in US dollars (cash). Sometimes travelers' checks will be accepted but expect otherwise.

Destinations of flights from Danang (Vietnam Airlines, 35 Tran Phu Street, tel: 21130) are: Buon Ma Thuot, Dalat, Hanoi, HCMC, Nha Trang, Quy Nhon and Pleiku.

Destinations of flights from Hanoi (Vietnam Airlines Domestic Office, 16 Le Thai To Street, tel: 255 283) are: Buon Ma Thuot, Cao Bang, Dalat, Danang, Dien Bien Phu, HCMC, Hue, Nha Trang, Pleiku, Quy Nhon, Son La and Vinh.

Destinations of flights from HCMC (Vietnam Airways Domestic Office, 27B Nguyen Dinh Chieu Street, tel: 299 910/299 980) are: Buon Ma Thuot, Dalat, Danang, Hanoi, Hue, Nha Trang, Phu Quoc Island, Pleiku, Quy Nhon and Rach Gia.

Destinations of flights from Vung Tau (Con Dau Tourism Co, 450 Truong Cong Dinh Street, tel: 2580) are: Con Dau Island (helicopter).

BUSINESS HOURS

The business day starts early in Vietnam – generally from 7 to 8 am – and ends between 4 to 5 pm. Offices close for one or two hours over lunch, between 11 to 2 pm. Many shops close in the late afternoon and then open from about 8 to 11 pm. Government offices are closed on Sundays, museums on Mondays. Banks are open from 8 to 3 pm Monday-Friday and on Saturday mornings.

CLIMATE

The weather in the south does not change much throughout the year with the temperature ranging from 26-32°C (78-90°F). April is the hottest month. You can expect heavy rainfall between June to September with humidity being highest in July, September and October.

Hanoi and the north suffer from more extreme weather with cold, but snowless winters from November to April. January is the coldest month with temperatures averaging 17°C. Summer temperatures reach 38°C (100°F). The rainy season is generally April to October with the possibility of devastating typhoons occurring. Humidity is at a peak in March, April and August.

CLOTHING

Take along light, casual clothes for your stay in the south and for the summer months elsewhere. Simple clothes are best if you do not want to really stand out from the crowd. The further north you go, the more you may need heavier garments for the chilly winter months. If you are heading for Dalat, the Central Highlands or the hilltribe country to the northwest, take along a heavy sweater or jacket.

Protective hats (to block the sun) and modest swimsuits are recommended for sojourns to the shore, while rain apparel is essential for visits during the wet monsoon season. If you are staying in budget hotels or are going to be in the countryside a lot, a pair of rubber slippers will be useful for the shower.

Unless you are staying in a top hotel, only pack what you can comfortably carry as you will probably be lugging your own bags most of the time.

CUSTOMS

On entry you will be required to complete a customs declaration form in duplicate. One copy will be handed back to you. Do not misplace it, as the declaration will be collected at your point of departure.

The customs form is very detailed. You will be required to state the amount of foreign currency you are taking into Vietnam. This figure might be checked – together with your exchange transactions, purchases and residual cash on departure from Vietnam to ensure that you have not been using the black market. You must also list any electronic equipment you are temporarily "importing" into the country. As you have to list their serial numbers, it would be a good idea to make a list of them before packing – otherwise you will have to dig around in your luggage at the airport.

Jewelry, unexposed film, medicine and gifts must also be itemized. Gifts should not exceed US$50 if you are a tourist and US$300 for returning Vietnamese (US$600 per family). As many as 200 cigarettes, 50 cigars, 250 grams of tobacco and 2 liters of alcohol can be brought in duty free. The export of Vietnamese *dong* (currency) and live animals is prohibited. Official permission has to be sought to export antiques.

HEALTH
Vaccinations
Recommended vaccinations include: diphtheria, gamma globulin, meningitis, polio booster and tetanus.

Medical Evacuation

As the standard of medical attention is still lagging far behind the west, it is recommended that you purchase an emergency evacuation service plan. Before your trip, you can purchase such a plan from International SOS Assistance (Far East) Ltd, PO Box 1080, Robinson Road, Singapore 9021. Tel: (65) 221 3981, fax: (65) 226 3937. SOS 24-hour emergency line: (65) 226 3936.

In Vietnam, SOS Assistance has a representative at Interlink Resources Pte Ltd, 134 Ham Nghi Street, District 1, HCMC. Tel: 230 499, fax: 290 583 or at the SOS Vietnam Operations Center: 230 499, 441 182.

Food and Water

As a general rule, (aside from international standard hotels), do not drink any water that is not imported or boiled for ten minutes and do not put any ice in your drinks. Be careful with fruit juices as they may have been watered down. Milk could also be a problem, as it may be unpasteurized. Also stay away from salads and other non-cooked foods. The standard of hygiene at street stalls is suspect, so be very careful when trying Vietnamese snacks. Stay away from food that has been cooked, left to cool and then reheated.

Other Recommended Supplies

Your personal first-aid kit should include disposable syringes, a course of antibiotics, some sort of antiseptic cream, anti-diarrhoea tablets, malaria tablets (a combination of Malarex® and Pyrimethamine® is recommended for Vietnam), water sterilizing and salt tablets along with the usual aspirin, adhesive bandages and gauze. Also include: sunscreen for coastal areas, insect repellent and mosquito coils, a flashlight (because of frequent power cuts), a shortwave radio (if you wish to keep in touch with the "outside world") and biscuits and/or chocolate (for the hunger pangs if you are travelling in remote areas)

INTER-CITY TRAVEL

Buses

There is an extensive network of buses that provides transportation to virtually every corner of Vietnam, but the vehicles are usually old, very slow and unreliable. Cities and larger towns usually have more than one bus station and finding the right one for your destination can be a daunting experience. If you do find the right bus, be prepared for overcrowding, virtually no

legroom and frequent breakdowns. You must have infinite patience, even with the so-called express services.

Most inter-city buses depart in the early morning.

Dalat

Destination:	Express to Dalat, Danang HCMC, Nha Trang and Quy Nhon.
Station:	Ben Xe.
Destination:	Non-express to Danang, Hanoi, HCMC, Phan Rang, Phan Thiet and Quy Nhon .
Station:	Ben Xe Dalat. 100 meters towards market from Xuan Huong Dam.
Destination:	Lam Dong province.
Station:	Ben Xe Khach Noi Thanh.

Danang

Destination:	Express to Buon Ma Thuot, Dalat, Haiphong, HCMC and Nha Trang.
Station:	Ben Xe Khach Da Nang opposite 200 Dien Bien Phu Street.
Destination:	Non-express to Hoi An, Hue, Kontum and Vinh.
Station:	Ben Xe Khach Da Nang opposite 200 Dien Bien Phu Street.

Hanoi

Destination:	Express to Danang, HCMC, Nha Trag, Quy Nhon.
Station:	Ben Xe Kim Lien 100 Le Duan Street.
Destination:	Non-express to Danang, Dong Ha, HCMC, Hoa Binh, Hue, Sam Son, Vinh.
Station:	Ben Xe Kim Lien 100 Le Duan Street.
Destination:	Dien Bien Phu, Hoa Binh, Lai Chau, Mai Chau, Son La, Yen Bai and other destinations northwest of Hanoi.
Station:	Ben Xe Kim Ma opposite 166 Nguyen Thai Hoc Street.
Destination:	Haiphong, Ha Long Bay and

other destinations east of Hanoi.

Station: Ben Xe Long Bien east bank of the Red River.

Ho Chi Minh City
Destination: Dalat, Danang, Hanoi, Haiphong, Hue, Nha Trang, Vinh and Vung Tau.
Station: Ben Xe Mien Dong.

Destination: Ben Tre, Camau, Cuu Long, Dong Thap, Hau Giang, Kien Giang, Long An, My Tho, Tay Ninh, Tien Giang and Vinh Long.
Station: Ben Xe Mien Tay An Lac and Binh Chanh District.

Destination: Vung Tau, Dalat and Nha Trang Cong Ty Dich Vu Du Lich 39 Nguyen Hue Boulevard Cuu Chi, Tay Ninh.
Station: Ben Xe Tay Ninh Tan Binh District.

Destination: Phnom Penh.
Station: 155 Nguyen Hue Boulevard.

Hue
Destination: Buon Ma Thuot, Danang, HCMC, Kontum, Pleiku, Nha Trang, Quy Nhon.
Station: Ben Xe An Cuu corner Hung Vuong/Nguyen Hue streets.

Destination: Dong Ha, Hanoi, Khe Sanh Quang Tri, Vinh.
Station: Ben Xe An Hoa corner Le Duan/ Tang Bat Ho streets.

Long Xuyen
Destination: Camau, Can Tho, Chau Doc, Ha Tien, HCMC and Rach Gia.
Station: Ben Xe Long Xuyen opposite 96/3B Tran Hung Dao street.

Destination: Express to HCMC.
Station: 225/4 Nguyen Street.

Destination: Express to HCMC.
Station: 11 Ngo Gia Tu Street.

My Tho
Destination: Can Tho, Chau Doc, HCMC,

Tay Ninh and Vung Tau.
Station: Ben Xe Khach Tien Giang Highway One west of My Tho.

Nha Trang
Destination: Bien Hoa, Buon Ma Thuot, Dalat, Danang, HCMC, Phan Rang, Quy Nhon and Pleiku.
Station: Ben Xe Lien Tinh opposite 212 Ngo Gia Tu Street.

Destination: Express to Dalat, Danang and HCMC.
Station: Youth Tourism Express Bus Office 6 Hoang Hoa Tham Street.

Destination: Express to Buon Ma Thuot, Dalat, Danang, Hanoi, HCMC, Hue, Quy Nhon and Vinh.
Station: Tram Xe Toc Hanh near 46 Le Thanh Ton Street.

Phan Rang
Destination: Cam Ranh Bay, Dalat, Danang, HCMC, Nha Trang and Phan Thiet.
Station: Ben Xe Thuan Hai opposite 64 Thong Nhat Street.

Phan Thiet–Phan Rang
Destination: Bien Hoa, HCMC and Phan Rang Phu Cuong.
Station: Ben Xe Thuan Hai, Tu Van Tu Street.

Rach Gia
Destination: Can Tho, Dong Thap, HCMC, Ha Tien and Long Xuyen.
Staion: Ben Xe Kien Giang, Nguyen Trung Truc Street.

Destination: Express to Can Tho, Ha Tien and HCMC.
Station: 33 30 Thang 4 Street.

Destination: Express to HCMC.
Station: 78 Nguyen Trung Truc Street.

Vinh
Destination: Express to Danang, Hanoi and HCMC.
Station: Ben Xe Vinh, Le Loi Street.

Destination: Non-express to Cau Lo, Con

Cuong, Hanoi, Ha Tinh, Hue, Pleiku and Quy Chau.

Station: Ben Xe Vinh, Le Loi Street.

Vung Tau

Destination: Bien Hoa, HCMC, My Tho and Tay Ninh.

Station: Ben Xe Khach Vung Tau, 52 Nam Khoi Nghia Street.

Destination: Express to HCMC.

Station: In front of the Hanh Phuoc and Hoa Binh hotels.

INTERNAL TRAVEL PERMITS

If you wish to travel outside the city limits of your port of embarkation on an overnight trip, you must get an **Internal Travel Permit**. The **Immigration Police** are also in charge of these permits but you can also get one from TOSERCO in Hanoi and there are an increasing number of tourist companies who will assist you (see section on **Tourist Offices, Tour and Overland Transport Operators**). Tour group organizers usually obtain them for their members.

MONEY

Vietnam's *dong* is the official currency (abbreviated to "d") and comes in denominations of 5,000, 2,000, 1,000, 500, 200, 100, 50, 30, 20, 10, 5, 2, and 1. Its value fluctuates wildly. The most widely-accepted foreign currency is the US dollar; you will probably have to pay for most major expenses (hotel bills, car rental, etc) in US currency. It is technically illegal for you to pay for goods jn anything but *dong* in non-government retail establishments, restaurants and bars, or to exchange US$ for *dong* anywhere but hotels, banks or authorized money changers.

Travelers' cheques are not widely accepted; you can virtually only use them in hotels. However, they can be cashed in banks for thick wads of *dong*. Credit cards are now accepted in a growing number of establishments – mostly big hotels and restaurants in HCMC – but in most cases it is not advisable to count on their use.

It is a good idea to keep your money exchange receipts as your currency declaration may be checked at the airport upon departure. Money can be transferred into Vietnam via the Overseas Vietnamese Export Company, COSEVINA, 102 Nguyen Hue Boulevard, HCMC. Tel: 92 391/96 648, Telex: 18255 COSEVIN. However, this is a slow and painful process and

you can only collect the money in *dong*.

The acceptance of credit cards is limited mostly to the large hotels, but this will gradually change. Visa and MasterCard have yet to open their own offices but non-US citizens can get cash advances with their MasterCard at The Bank for Foreign Trade (BFT). The branch in Hanoi is at 47-49 Ly Thai To, Tel: 259 859 (see **Banks – Local**, for other branches).

NEWSPAPERS & MAGAZINES

Business Vietnam

Company for Promotion and Development of Industrial Property Activities (INVESTIP).
A monthly newsletter in which Vietnamese experts provide analysis on investment and economics in Vietnam.

International Herald Tribune

This Paris-based "global" newspaper is now available at The Saigon Floating Hotel in Ho Chi Minh City and by postal subscription from Singapore.

National Geographic

Periodically has articles on Vietnam.

Vietnam Business: An Introduction to Import and Export

Vietnam Trade Information Center.
A bi-monthly magazine in English and Vietnamese which features the trading potential of a different province in each issue.

Vietnam Business Handbook, The Birth of Opportunity

Vietcochamber and Chamber Publications.
Eight chapters covering areas such as infrastructure, marketing and media, foreign investment, banking etc. There is also a very useful section which provides a list of the members of the Vietnamese Chamber of Commerce and Industry, including names and contact numbers.

Vietnam Courier

VNA (Vietnam News Agency).
A monthly English magazine that covers political and cultural events from the Vietnamese government's perspective.

Vietnam Investor

Dong Khoi Resources Pte Ltd.
A monthly English-language magazine, published in Singapore, which provides hard-core information on banking, finance, business and industry.

Includes a useful directory to doing business in Vietnam – listing approved joint-venture projects, service companies and relevant government departments.

Vietnam Pictorial
Vietnam News Agency.
A leisure magazine, published monthly in English and quarterly in Mandarin.

Vietnam Today
Communication Indochine Pte Ltd.
An English magazine that calls itself "the only independent magazine totally targeted on the Vietnam market". Covers business and tourism. Published in Singapore.

Vietnam Weekly
VNA.
A weekly foreign language review published by the Vietnamese Information Agency.

PERSONAL SAFETY
Take the normal precautions to protect your passport, money and airline ticket when travelling in Vietnam. If your hotel has safety deposit boxes, use them. A money belt or neck pouch are the safest ways to carry your valuables when on the road.

HCMC has a reputation for pickpockets, so be extra careful when you are there. It is not wise to change money on the streets. There have been very few reports of violent crimes against foreigners, but with the onset of prostitution, massage parlors and the resulting vice, this could change. It would be wise to check with your hotel if there are any areas of HCMC that are dangerous for foreigners. There have been some incidents of luggage being slit and looted when leaving the country from Tan Son Nhat Airport.

Crime is a growing problem in Hanoi, although once again it rarely touches foreign visitors. The government estimates that there are more than 300,000 heroin addicts in northern Vietnam alone (10,000 in Hanoi). Many of the addicts are labelled "known criminals" by the police because they are also involved in other crime-related activities. A spinoff from the drug problem is the rising rate of prostitution and AIDS in the north.

PHOTOGRAPHY
Kodak, Fuji, Konica and Agfa 35mm print film are now readily available in most Vietnamese cities.

When buying film make sure you check the expiry date and only pick film sold in pristine boxes. Well-worn boxes are a sign that the film has probably been sold to the vendor by overland travellers. If possible, buy film from air-conditioned shops as prolonged heat can even damage print film.

Processing of a reasonable standard is available. Japanese one-hour development service is now available for those in a hurry. In HCMC, try 66A Nguyen Hue Blvd and **Eden Color Photo Center** at 4 Le Loi Blvd. In Hanoi, there are many photo developing stores along Hang Khay Street.

Slide film is more difficult to find and there are no processing facilities as yet.

Vietnam's airport x-ray machines are not film-safe. If you want to avoid the heartbreak of having your photographs ruined, make sure not to x-ray any of your film – no matter how low the ASA or Din rating is. Checked luggage is x-rayed when entering and leaving the country, so hand-carry all your film, preferably in a lead-lined bag – just to be sure.

PRIVATE CAR AND MINIBUS
By far the most comfortable and probably the most reliable (but also the most expensive) way to travel is by private car or minibus which can be hired from the land transport tourist companies or arranged through your hotel by the hour, day or week. All vehicles come with drivers (self-drive cars are not yet available in Vietnam). It would be wise to check how experienced your driver is. Rental fees are extremely high by Western standards: about US$100 a day for vehicle, fuel and driver. You will also be expected to pay for the driver's meals, snacks and drinks along the way.

PUBLIC HOLIDAYS & FESTIVAL HOLIDAYS

January 1	New Year's Day
February 3	Founding of Vietnam's Communist Party
April 30	Liberation Day
May 1	Labor Day
May 7	Dien Bien Phu Day
May 19	Ho Chi Minh's Birthday
July 28	War Invalids and Martyrs Day
September 2	National Day
September 3	Anniversary of Ho Chi Minh's death
December 25	Christmas

Festivals that occur according to the Lunar Calendar:

1st to 7th day, 1st month Tet Nhat marks the Lunar New (January to February) Year and the first day of spring.

6th day, 2nd month Trung Sisters Day. (February to March) Celebrates two sisters' actions in fighting the Chinese in AD 40.

5th day, 3rd month Thanh Minh. Graves of deceased relatives are visited and honored.

8th day, 4th month Buddha's birth is celebrated largely in temples and pagodas.

5th day, 5th month Tet Doan Ngo. Beginning of the summer solstice.

7th day, 7th month Weaver & Shepherd Day. Celebrates start of the rainy season.

15th day, 7th month Trung Nguyen. The wandering spirits of the forgotten dead are appeased through offerings.

15th day, 8th month Tet Trung Thu. Mid-Autumn festival marked by lantern processions and moon cakes.

9th day, 9th month Double Nine celebrates the beginning of winter.

28th day, 9th month Confucius' birthday.

RADIO

The Voice of Vietnam broadcasts in English in Hanoi between 6 to 6:30 pm on 1010 kHz AM. This official radio station also broadcasts from Ho Chi Minh City.

The stations in both cities also broadcast in Cantonese, French, Indonesian, Japanese, Khmer, Lao, Mandarin, Russian, Spanish and Thai. International stations can also be heard on shortwave bands.

RAILWAY STATIONS:
Danang
Haiphong Street

Hanoi
Nam Bo Street

Ho Chi Minh City
1 Nguyen Thong Street
District 3

Hue
Le Loi Street

Nha Trang
19 Thai Nguyen Street

REGISTRATION
All visitors are required to register with the **Immigration Police** within 48 hours of entering the country. Visas just get you into the country, **Immigration Police** give you permission to stay where you are. If you change accommodation, you are required to re-register. People travelling in groups do not usually have to worry about this as it is taken care of for them.

All hotels are required to hand over your details upon your checking-in, so do not think you can go unnoticed.

RELIGION
Four religious philosophies dominate Vietnam: – Confucianism, Taoism, Buddhism and Christianity. Like some other Asian countries Confucianism, Taoism and Buddhism have fused together into "The Triple Religion". Vietnamese are likely to call themselves Buddhist yet practice Confucianism when it comes to family duties and Taoism when they desire an understanding of the cosmos. There are an estimated six million practising Catholics in Vietnam today.

SELECTED READING
A Biography of Ho Chi Minh
David Halberstam
Alfred A Knolf, New York, 1987.

The Birth of Vietnam
Keith Weller Taylor
University of California Press, Berkeley, 1983.

Born on the Fourth of July
Ron Kovic

Pocket Books, New York, 1976.

Bright Shining Lie: John Paul Vann and America in Vietnam
Neil Sheehan
Random House, New York, 1988.

Dispatches
Michael Herr
Avon Books, New York, 1978.

A Dragon Apparent – Travels in Indochina
Norman Lewis Charles Scribner's Sons, New York, 1951.

Fire in the Lake
Francis Fitzgerald
Vintage Books, New York, 1972.

The Gentlemen in the Parlour: A Record of a Journey from Rangoon to Haiphong 1930
Somerset Maugham
Oxford Press, London and New York, reprinted 1966.

Henry Mouhot's Diary: Travels in the Central Parts of Siam, Cambodia and Laos During the Years 1958-61
Edited by Christopher Pym
Vintage Books, New York, 1972.

Ho
David Halberstam
Random House, New York, 1971

In the Midst of War — An American's Mission to Southeast Asia
Major General Edward Geary Landsdale
Harper & Row, New York, 1972.

Land of Nine Dragons: Vietnam Today
Joseph R Yogerst and Nevada Weir
Abbeville Press, New York, 1992.

The Montagnards of South Vietnam
Robert L Mole
Tuttle, Tokyo, 1970

The Quiet American
Graham Greene
Viking, New York, 1956.

River Journeys
William Shawcross

Hippocrene Books, London, 1985.

A Rumor of War
Philip Caputo
Ballantine Books, New York, 1977.

Saigon
Anthony Grey
Pan Books, London, 1983

Tradition on Trial 1920-1945
David G Marr
University of California Press, Berkeley, 1981.

The Tunnels of Cu Chi: The Untold Story of Vietnam
Tom Mangold & John Penycate,
Random House, New York, 1987.

Vietnam Business Handbook
Vietcochamber and Chamber Publications

Vietnam: A Complete Account of Vietnam War
Stanley Karnow
Penguin Books, London, 1983

Vietnam: A History
Stanley Karnow
Viking Press, New York, 1983

Vietnam: A Long History
Nguyen Khac Vien
Foreign Languages Publishing House, Hanoi, 1987

Vietnam: Opening Doors to the World
Rick Graetz & Fred Rohrbachh
American Geographical Publishing

Vietnam Revisited
David Dellinger
Southend Press, Boston, 1986.

Vietnam War Almanac
Harry G Summers Jr
Facts On File Publishing, New York, 1985

Vietnamese Anti-Colonialism 1885-1925
David G Marr
University of California, Berkeley, LA & London, 1971.

Why Vietnam?
Archimedes L Patti

University of California Press, Berkeley, LA & London, 1980.

The Yellow Rainmakers
Grant Evans
Thetford Press, 1983.

SHOPPING

An abundance of Vietnamese handicrafts can be purchased at very reasonable prices – especially if you are paying in US Dollars. Bargaining is definitely the rule of thumb.

Lacquerware is very popular with a wide range of items from vases to wall decorations and trays. The most abundant design feature is the goldfish. If they are not to your taste, do not worry as you can find other wonderful designs if you hunt around a bit. Mother-of-pearl inlay is also very popular especially when decorating boxes of all shapes and sizes.

Ceramic elephants are perfect plant stands (if you can figure out a way to get them home). They are a real bargain in Vietnam, where they cost a tenth of the price they fetch in Hong Kong or Singapore. You should consider buying some of the sturdy basketwork as extra luggage. Embroidery, silk paintings and tapestries are all also a good bet.

While you can still find tortoiseshell items (mainly in the coastal areas) try not to buy them no matter how old the piece may be as sea turtles are a highly-endangered species and every piece that is bought will be replaced.

While wandering around, you will also find an abundance of antiques for sale. If you ask the shopowner, he will probably bring out some exquisite under-the-counter pieces for your selection – old porcelain, clocks, Rolex® watches, silver, ivory and jade. But, you must be cautious on two counts: First, it is illegal to export many antiques without a permit and secondly the Vietnamese are getting quite good at manufacturing fakes.

Of course, no shopping expedition in Vietnam would be complete without the purchase of the ultimate tourist items – a *non la* (conical hat) and an *ao dai* (traditional silk dress).

The best souvenir shopping in Hanoi is along Hang Khay Street, opposite the southern shore of Hoan Keim Lake. One especially good shop is at #17. There are dozens of antique, art and handicraft shops along Dong Khoi Street and Nguyen Hue Boulevard in downtown Ho Chi Minh City. In Hue, there is a large souvenir shop in the Huong Giang Hotel. However, less expensive (and often more interesting) items can be bought from artists who frequent the entrances to many tourist attractions like the Noon Gate, Linh Mu Pagoda and the royal tombs. Hawkers ply the beaches at Vung Tau and Danang.

TELECOMMUNICATIONS

Post

International mail is accepted at the larger post offices and an increasing number of hotels. Look for the sign saying Buu Dien.

The postal charges are among the highest in the world. Telegram and telex facilities are available 24 hours, seven days a week in the larger towns and at many hotels. Courier services are available at some post offices. DHL has a desk in the GPO in Ho Chi Minh City (tel: 296 203/290 446).

Selected post offices:
Dalat
14 Tran Phu Street

Danang
46 Bach Dang Street

Haiphong
3 Nguyen Tri Phuong Street

Hanoi
75 Dinh Tien Hoang
Hoan Kiem District
Tel: 254 413

Hue
8 Hoang Hoa Tham Street

Ho Chi Minh City
125 Hai Ba Trung, District 1
Tel: 292 997

Nha Trang
2 Tran Phu Boulevard

Qui Nhon
Corner of Hai Ba Trung and Tran Phu streets

Vinh
Nguyen Thi Minh Khai Street

Vung Tao
4 Ha Long Street
Tel: 2377/ 2689/ 2141

Faxes

All incoming and outgoing faxes in Vietnam have to pass through the post office system – even if you send them from a private fax number. The post office will alert the owner of the private fax number of the arrival of a fax and either hold for collection or refax it. The latter procedure can take up to a day, so if the fax is urgent, it is much better to collect it yourself. The average cost per page to send a fax within Asia is roughly US$12-$14.

Telephones

IDD calls are also very expensive and your charges commence when you start dialling. A three-minute call within the Asia/Pacific region will cost between US$21-$26 and US$30 to Europe.

Electricity

Primarily 220 volts, 50 cycles but can sometimes be 110 volts. Check the voltage on the sockets or ask at the hotel front desk. It is recommended that you protect your electrical equipment with surge suppressors. Vietnam suffers frequent electricity blackouts.

TELEVISION

Television was first launched in Vietnam in 1970. Programming largely consists of local Vietnamese shows and local or Russian documentaries. It is better to rely on your hotel videos.

TIME

GMT + 7 hours. There are no daylight savings time changes.

Time differences between Vietnam and other major cities are as follows:

City	Hours
Amsterdam	- 6
Athens	- 5
Auckland	+ 5
Bahrain	- 4
Bangkok	0
Bombay	- 1½
Brussels	- 6
Cairo	- 5
Chicago	- 13
Colombo	- 1½
Darwin	+ 2½
Frankfurt	- 6
Geneva	- 6
Helsinki	- 5
Hong Kong	- 1
Honolulu	- 17
Jakarta	0
Karachi	- 2
Kuala Lumpur	- 1
Lisbon	- 7
London	- 7
Los Angeles	- 15
Madrid	- 6
Manila	- 1
Montreal	- 12
Moscow	- 4
Nairobi	- 4
New Delhi	- 1½
New York	- 12
Osaka	+ 2
Oslo	- 6
Paris	- 6
Rio de Janeiro	- 10
Rome	- 6
Seoul	+ 2
Singapore	- 1
Stockholm	- 6
Sydney	+ 4
Taipei	- 1
Tel Aviv	- 5
Tokyo	+ 2
Vancouver	- 15

TIPPING

Tipping is not the norm in Vietnam. In fact, if you leave a tip on the table in the countryside, the vendors will almost certainly run after you to return your forgotten money. In the city, tipping is still not expected but would be enormously appreciated. In the larger international hotels, a 10 percent service charge is usually added to the bill.

TRANSPORTATION WITHIN TOWNS

Taxis

Taxis are virtually non-existent except for airports and hotel fleets. But, the number of taxis is expected to escalate in both HCMC and Hanoi by the end of the 1990s.

Bicycles

Bicycles are still the most popular form of transportation for locals. If you intend to stay in Vietnam for any length of time, you may want to consider buying a cheap, Vietnamese-made bicycle. You can probably get one for less than US$40, although top flight models can run for as high as US$100.

Bargain for bicycles at one of the numerous bicycle shops along Hue Street in Hanoi or the corner of Cach Mang Thang Tam and Le Thanh Ton streets in HCMC. In Hanoi, you can rent bicycles at the Thang Long Hotel, Giang Vo Street (tel: 257 796).

Cyclos
The most abundant form of urban transportation is the *cyclo* (a trishaw where the driver peddles from behind with the passenger reclining in a seat mounted on the front). Be sure to agree on a price before you set off and never accept the first price offered as haggling is expected.

Trains
Vietnam's passenger railway system runs between HCMC and Hanoi, and between Hanoi and Haiphong. The fastest service between Hanoi and HCMC runs twice weekly and covers the 1,730 kilometers in about 48 hours (the slow train takes about 70 hours). There is only one set of tracks and trains have to pass at limited sidings. If a train coming in the opposite direction is late, you just have to wait – and so it snowballs.

USEFUL WORDS AND PHRASES
Hello:

to an older man	*Chao ong*
to an older lady	*Chao da*
to a younger man	*Chao anh*
to a younger woman	*Chau co*
to small children	*Chao chau*
What's your name?	*Ten ong la gi?*
My name is...	*Toi ten la...*
How are you?	*Bach co khoe khong?*
I'm fine thanks	*Cam on binh thuong*
Goodbye	*Tam biet*
See you again	*Hen gap lai*
Please	*Xin moi*
Thank you	*Cam on*
I'm sorry	*Xin loi*
Excuse me	*Xin Toi*
How much?	*Bao Nhieu?*
Expensive	*Mac dat*
Cheap	*Re khong dat*
What is this?	*Cai nay la cai gi?*
I need/want	*Toi can/toi muon*
I don't want	*Toi khong can*
I like	*Toi thich*
I don't like	*Toi khong thich*
I'm hungry	*Toi doi*
this	*Cai nay*
that	*Cay do*

yes	*Khong*
no	*Da (ya in the north)*
today	*Hom nay*
tomorrow	*Ngay mai*
Where is the...	*...o dau*
hotel	*Khach san*
(Where is the hotel?)	*(Khach san o dau?)*
air-conditioning	*may lanh*
bed	*giuong*
hot water	*nuoc lanh*
laundry	*giat quan ao*
first class room	*phong hang nhat*
second class room	*phong hang nhi*
mosquito net	*mung*
sheet	*ra trai giuong*
blanket	*chan (north)*
blanket	*men (south)*
shower	*bong sen*
toilet	*nha ve sinh*
towel	*khan tam*
bus station	*Ben xe*
train station	*Ga xe lua*
taxi rank	*Ben xe tac xi*
airport	*San bay*
post office	*Nha buu dien*
bookshop	*Hieu sach*
stamp	*tem thu*
film	*phim*
hospital	*Benh vien*
dentist	*Nha si*
doctor	*Bac si*
(I need a doctor)	*(Toi can gap bac si)*
pharmacy	*Nha thuoc*
I am sick	*Toi binh*
I have a toothache	*Toi bi rang*
right	*phai*
left	*trai*
(Turn left)	*(Re ben trai)*
straight ahead	*Hay di thang*
street	*Pho/duong*
district	*Quan*
I'm not Russian	*Khong phai Lien Xo*
I'm a Singaporean	*Toi la nguoi Xingapua*
American	*My*
Australian	*Uc*
Chinese	*Trung Hoa*
English	*Anh*
Hong Konger	*Hong Cong*
Japanese	*Nhat Ban*
Malaysian	*Ma Lai A*
New Zealander	*Niu Dilan*
Filipino	*Philippin*
Thai	*Thai Lan*
fruit	*Trai cay*

bread	*Banh mi*
tea	*Nuoc che*
coffee	*Ca Phe*
beer	*Bia*
boiled water	*Nuoc soi*
rice	*Com trang*
noodle soup	*Pho*
beef	*Bo*
fish	*Ca*
chicken	*Ga*
one	*mot*
two	*hai*
three	*ba*
four	*bon*
five	*nam*
six	*sau*
seven	*bay*
eight	*tam*
nine	*chin*
ten	*chuc*
eleven	*muoi mot*
twenty	*hai muoi*
twenty-one	*hai muoi mot*
thirty	*ba muoi*
fifty	*nam muoi*
one hundred	*mot tram*
two hundred	*hai tram*
one thousand	*mot nghin*
ten thousand	*muoi nghin*
one hundred thousand	*tram nghin*
one million	*mot trieu*
Monday	*Thu hai*
Tuesday	*Thu ba*
Wednesday	*Thu tu*
Thursday	*Thu nam*
Friday	*Thu sau*
Saturday	*Thu bay*
Sunday	*Thu nhat*

VISAS & OTHER ENTRY REQUIREMENTS

Everyone entering Vietnam must be the holder of a valid passport and an entry visa. In the past, obtaining a visa has been a frustrating experience, but as Vietnam gets more tourists and visiting businessmen, and sees their benefit, it will continue to get easier. However, the rules seem to change almost daily, so what a friend was able to do a few months ago may no longer apply.

There are a number of different categories of visa you can apply for: tourist, business, official, multiple-entry business, family visit and journalist. The latter is probably the most difficult to obtain.

Tourist Visa

By far the easiest way to get a tourist visa is to join an organized tour group and let your travel agent handle all the paperwork for you. Vietnam does not encourage independent travelers. But, if you do want to travel alone, Manila and Bangkok are the two best places to try for a speedy result. If you give them enough lead time, the Vietnam Tourist Office in your home country may be able to help. Alternatively, you can apply directly to the official tourist organization in Hanoi, Ho Chi Minh City or Bangkok and state which Vietnam diplomatic mission you wish to deal with.

In your application you must provide all the usual particulars like your full name, address, date and place of birth, nationality, profession, passport number and duration of stay. Not forgetting your port of entry and departure and the areas you intend to visit. If your application does not include these, you will be expected to stay within the area of your arrival and you could face real trouble if you try to enter or leave from alternative ports.

Prior permission must be granted and stamped on your visa by the Foreign Ministry Office in either Ho Chi Minh City or Hanoi if you wish to change your point of departure.

Recently, visitors have been able to register an application for a visa with the Immigration Authorities through an approved travel company inside Vietnam or with a business travel consultant overseas. They then obtain their visa upon entry. This visa will cost twice as much for people arriving from countries where there is a Vietnamese embassy as the Vietnamese feel you are wasting the funds they spend to provide the mission. This route is not to be chosen by the faint hearted as sometimes the names of applicants get mislaid (this system is not computerized) and you are fined and taken under escort to stay overnight in a special hotel. The next day you will be allowed to transfer to the hotel of your original choice.

Business Visa

To obtain a business visa, you will probably have to have a letter of invitation from a local sponsor. If you can arrange it, it is better to get this invitation sent to your office or hotel directly because if you get it sent straight to the visa issuing body, you run the risk of having it mislaid. If you do not have local business contacts, you can engage the services of a business travel consultant or Vietcochamber (Vietnam's Chamber of Commerce) who can supply you with details of a local-state run company in your field of business. Alternatively, the book *"Vietnam Business Handbook, The Birth of Opportunity"* has a directory of Chamber of Commerce members and the magazine *"Vietnam Investor"* usually has a list of approved projects for foreign investment (see **Newspaper & Magazines**).

Overseas Vietnamese

Vietnamese returning home for a visit must supply the same information as a regular tourist plus the date, reason, means of exit and details of their relatives living in Vietnam.

Other Visas

Ministerial authorization from Hanoi is usually needed for other classes of visas, in addition to a local invitation.

Do not think that you can merely overstay your visa without getting into trouble. Get a visa extension through your travel company or directly from the **Immigration Police** if you are travelling alone. In Hanoi the **Immigration Police** are located at 83 Tran Hung Dao. The **Police Office for the Registration of Foreign Visitors** is at 63 Tran Hung Dao. In Ho Chi Minh the **Immigration Police** are at 258 Nguyen Trai and the **Ho Chi Minh City Police Station** is at 161 Nguyen Du, District 1.

DIRECTORY

AIRLINES

Aeroflot
4 Trang Thi Street
Hanoi
Tel: 56184

4B Le Loi Blvd
District 1, HCMC
Tel: 293 489

Air Hong Kong (cargo)
Tan Son Nhat Airport
Tel: 445 050, ext: 3749

Air France
1 Ba Trieu Street
Hanoi
Reservations & Reconfirmations
Tel: 253 484

130 Dong Khoi Street
District 1, HCMC
Reservations & Reconfirmations
Tel: 290 982

Cathay Pacific
Ground Floor
27 Ly Thai To Street
Hoan Kiem District
Hanoi
Reservations & Reconfirmations
Tel: 267 213

49 Le Phanh Ton Street
District 1, HCMC
Reservations & Reconfirmations
Tel: 223 252

China Southern Airlines
27 Le Thai To

Bin Minh Hotel
Tel: 266 441
Fax: 257 725

52B Duong Pham Hong Thai
Tel: 291 172
Fax: 291 470

Garuda
Rooms 67-68
International Terminal
Tan Son Nhat Airport, HCMC
Reservations & Reconfirmations
Tel: 241 740/242 696

106 Nguyen Hue Boulevard
District 1
Tel: 293 644/293 645
Fax: 293 688

Japan Airlines
CTSC Building
1 Ba Trieu Street
Hanoi
Tel: 266 693
Fax: 266 698

Lufthansa
GSA Vietnam Airlines
116 Nguyen Hue Boulevard
District 1, HCMC
Reservations & Reconfirmations
Tel:440 101/443 179

Malaysian Airlines
Pullman Metropole Hotel
15 Ngo Quyen Street
Hoan Kiem District
Hanoi

Tel: 266 441/268 820

116 Nguyen Hue Boulevard
District 1, HCMC
Reservations & Reconfirmations
Tel: 230 695

Philippines Airlines
116 Nguyen Hue Boulevard
District 1, HCMC
Reservations & Reconfirmations
Tel: 225 538

4A Le Loi Boulevard
District 1
Tel: 811 496

Quantas
120 Cach Mang Thang
Tam St
District 1
Tel: 291 135
Fax: 291 135

Singapore Airlines
Pullman Metropole Hotel
15 Ngo Quyen Street
Hoan Kiem District
Hanoi
Reservations & Reconfirmations
Tel: 266 920/268 888

6 Le Loi Blvd
District 1, HCMC
Reservations & Reconfirmations
Tel: 231 583/231 586/231 588
Fax: 231 554

Thai Airways

Quang Rung Street
Hanoi
Reservations & Reconfirmations
Tel: 257 021/266 893
Fax: 267 394

116 Ngu Yen Hue Street
District 1, HCMC
Reservations & Reconfirmations
Tel: 292 118

Vietnam Airlines
Corner of Trang Thi and Quang
Trung streets
Hoan Kiem District
Hanoi
Reservations & Reconfirmations
Tel: 271 513/271 420
Fax: 259 222
Telex: 412260 TCHK VT

116 Nguyen Hue Boulevard
District 1, HCMC
Reservations & Reconfirmations
Tel: 440 101/443 179

BANKS
Bank for Foreign Trade (BFT)
47-49 Ly Thai To Street
Hanoi
Tel: 252 831/252 832
Fax: 258 385
Cable: VIETCOMBANK HANOI

29 Ben Chuong Duong Street
District 1, HCMC
Tel: 811 234/811 235
Cable: VIETCOMBANK HCM

4 Nguyen Tri Phuong Street
Haiphong
Tel: 245 227
Cable: VIETCOMBANK
HAIPHONG

77-81 Trung Trac Street
Vung Tau

**Bank for Investment and
Reconstruction**
10 Phan Huy Chu Street, Hanoi

**Industrial and Commercial Bank
of Vietnam**

79A Ham Nghi Street
District 1, HCMC
Tel: 290 491/297 268
Fax: 295 342
Telex: 812266 NHCH VT

**Saigon Bank for Industry and
Trade**
144 Chau Van Liem Street
Cholon District, HCMC
Tel: 553 824/553 660
Fax: 253 660
Telex: 812386 SGBANK

State Bank of Vietnam
49 Ly Thai To Street
Hoan Kiem District
Hanoi
Tel: 252 833
Fax: 258 385

Vietnam Export-Import Bank
7 Le Thi Hong Gam Street
District 1, HCMC
Tel: 293 938
Fax: 296 063
Telex: 812 690 EIB

Invovina Bank
36 Ton That Dam Street
District 1, HCMC
Tel: 224 995/293 096
Fax: 230 131
Telex: 811515 IVB VT

18B Le Thanh Tong Street
Hanoi
Tel: 265 516/266 321
Fax: 266 320

VID Public Bank
194 Tran Quang Khai Street
Hanoi
Tel: 268 307/266 965
Fax: 266 965
Telex: 412241 VPB VT

FOREIGN BANKS
Anzbank
c/o Hotel Pullman Metropole
15 Ngo Quyen Street
Hoan Kiem District
Hanoi
Tel: 266 919

Fax: 266 920

Bangkok Bank Limited
117 Nguyen Hue Boulevard
District 1, HCMC
Tel: 223 424/223 425
Fax: 223 421
Telex: 813080 BBLHCM VT

**Banque Française Du Com-
merce Exterieur (BFCE)**
27 Nguyen Huy Tu Street
Hanoi
Tel: 259 820/259 813
Telex: 411253 KS

10 Ham Nghi Street
District 1, HCMC
Tel: 294 144/294 134
Fax: 299 126
Telex: 811 563 BFCE

Banque Indosuez
Q1, Ba Trieu Street
Hanoi
Tel: 265 323
Fax: 265 322

4 Dong Khoi Street
District 1, HCMC
Tel: 295 048/296 061
Fax: 296 065
Telex: 812 688 INDOS

Banque Nationale De Paris
8 Tran Hung Dao Street
Hanoi
Tel; 253 175
Fax: 259 617
Telex: 412234 TTXVN

Credit Lyonnais
8 Tran Hung Dao Street
Hanoi
Tel: 259 625
Telex: 411250 CREDHN

17 Ton Duc Thang
District 1, HCMC
Tel: 299 236/299 226
Fax: 296 465
Telex: 812742 CRED VT

Deutsche Bank AG

25 Tran Binh Trong Street
PO Box 88
Hanoi
Tel: 268 554/268 555
Fax: 268 652
Telex: 411225 DBHAN

HongKong Bank
1st Floor
Vietnam EXIM Bank Building
7 Le Thi Hong Gam Street
District 1, HCMC
Tel: 223 348
Fax: 296 063
Telex: 812690 EIBVT

Societe Generale
Suite 158
Hotel Thang Loi
Yen Phu Street
Hanoi
Tel: 193 384
Telex: 411276 KS TL

Standard Chartered
134 Dong Khoi Street
District 1, HCMC
Tel: 298 335/298 383
Fax: 298 426
Telex: 811411 SCBH CM VT

Thai Military Bank
78 Nguyen Hue Boulevard
District 1, HCMC
Tel: 223 289

BUSINESS CENTERS
Boss Hotel
60 Nguyen Du St
Central
Hanoi
Tel: 252 690/265 859
Fax: 257 634

Megabiz
39 Hai ba Trung
HCMC
Tel: 230 499
Fax: 230 464

Metropole Hotel
15 Ngo Quyen St
Central
Hanoi

Tel: 266 919
Fax: 266 920

Phu Tho Enterprises
Shangri-La Complex 1196
3-2 Street
District 11
HCMC
Tel: 556 831/559 471

Saigon Star Hotel
204 Nguyen Thi Minh Khai
District 3
HCMC
Tel: 230 260
Fax: 230 255

Saigon Business Centre
49-57 Dong Du Street
District 1, HCMC
Tel: 298 777
Fax: 298 155

Saigon Floating Hotel Business Centre
1a Me Linh Square
District 1, HCMC
Tel: 290 783

HOTELS
$ - less than or equal to US$30
$$ - US$30-60
$$$ - $60-90
$$$$ - $90 upwards

CAN THO
Quoc Te Hotel $
12 Hai Ba Trung Street
Tel: 20973/35793
41 air conditioned rooms, three restaurants, souvenir shop, laundry and video room. Beside the Can Tho River.

DALAT
Duy Tan Hotel $
823 Thang Street
Tel: 2216
40 rooms divided into three classes. Tennis court.

Khach San Da Lat (Dalat Hotel)$
7 Tran Phu
Tel: 2363

67 rooms, restaurant, bar, souvenir shop and laundry.

Minh Tam Hotel $-$$
20A Khe San
Tel: 2447
17 rooms, situated 3 kilometers from the town center. Pleasant garden surroundings with great views. Renovated in 1984.

Ngoc Lan Hotel $
54 Nguyen Tri Phuong
Tel: 2136
Near the bus station.

Palace $-$$
2 Tran Phu
Tel: 2203
42 rooms with high ceilings and fireplaces, restaurant, billiard room and banquet facility. Good view of the lake.

DANANG
Danang Hotel $
1 Dong Da Street
Tel: 21179
With 100 rooms, the Danang was built in the late 1960's to house American personnel, it is in need of renovation but is appropriately priced for budget travellers. Restaurant.

Dong Da Hotel (Khach San Huu Nghi) $
7 Dong Da Street
Tel: 22563
68 rooms, restaurant.

Hai Chau Hotel $-$$
215 Tran Phu Street
Tel: 21101/22722
Air-conditioned rooms. Souvenir shop, laundry and dancing.

Hai Van Hotel $
2 Nguyen Thi Minh Khai Street
Tel: 21300
47 rooms with air-conditioning.

Huu Nghi Hotel $
7 Dong Da Street

Tel: 22563/21101
Souvenir shop, dancing and restaurant.

Non Nuoc Hotel $-$$
10 Ly Thuong Kiet
Hua Nghi
Tel: 21470/22137
40 rooms with air-conditioning and fans, situated right on China Beach. Beach restaurant and bar. A new, 60-room extension under construction.

Peace Hotel $
3 Tran Quy Cap Street
Danang City
Tel: 23984/23161
Television available on request.

Phuong Dong (Oriental) Hotel $$
93 Phan Chu Trinh
Tel: 21266/22854
36 air-conditioned rooms, centrally located, restaurant bar, souvenir shop, laundry and international direct dialing (IDD).

Song An Hotel $
24 Bach Dang Street
Tel: 22540
30 rooms, some air-conditioned. Situated along the Han River.

Thai Binh Duong (Pacific) Hotel $
80 Phan Chu Trinh
Tel: 22137/22931
60 air-conditioned rooms, restaurant, bar and laundry.

DONG HA
Dong Truong Son Hotel $
Tran Phu Street
Tel: 239
75 rooms.

Nha Khach Dong Ha $
Tran Phu Street
Tel: 361
24 rooms. A comfortable government guest house.

HAIPHONG/HA LONG BAY
Bach Dang Hotel $$
40 Dien Bien Phu
Haiphong
Tel: 247 486/247 206/249 244
30 air-conditioned rooms, two restaurants, bar and souvenir shop.

Bach Long Hotel $-$$
Bay Chay Town
Halong Bay
Tel: 281
Situated on the beach. Souvenir shop, video room, laundry and dancing.

Ha Long Hotel $$
Bai Chay Town
Halong Bay
Tel: 238
100 air-conditioned rooms. Great view. Restaurant and laundry.

Hoang Long Hotel $$
Bai Chay Town
Halong Bay
Tel: 264
On the beach.

Huu Nghi Hotel $-$$
62 Dien Bien Phu
Haiphong
Tel: 247 486/247 206
French era hotel with 30 rooms, half are air-conditioned. Restaurant and laundry.

Son Long Hotel $$
Bai Chay Town
Halong Bay
Tel: 254

Villa Hotel $
Bai Chay Town
Halong Bay
Tel: 235

HANOI
Airport Hotel $$-$$$
Noi Bai International Airport
Tel: 254 745

Bac Nam Hotel $$
20 Ngo Quyen
Tel: 257 067
Newly-renovated, friendly staff, centrally located. Good and inexpensive restaurant.

Bo Ho Hotel $
1 Ba Trieu
Tel: 252 075

Boss Hotel $$$
60 Nguyen Du St
Central
Tel: 252 690/265 859
Fax: 257 634
Restaurant, bar, lounge, business centre, karaoke and car rental service.

Dan Chu Hotel $$
29 Trang Tien
Tel: 254 937/253 323/254 344
28 air-conditioned rooms with traditional decor. Good, inexpensive restaurant, bar and laundry.

Dong Loi $$
94 Ly Thoung Kiet St
Tel: 257 796
Fax: 259 209
Restaurant, bar and karaoke.

Giang Vo $
Giang Vo Road
Ba Dinh District
Tel: 253 407

Hoa Binh Hotel $-$$
27 Ly Thuong Kiet
Tel: 253 315
59 air-conditioned rooms, centrally-located, laundry, souvenir shop and video room.

Hoa Hong (Rose) $$
20 Phan Boi Chau
Tel: 254 439

Hoan Kiem Hotel $$-$$$
25 Tran Hung Dao
Tel: 254 204
15 air conditioned rooms, res-

taurant, bar and laundry.

Metropole $$$$
15 Ngo Quyen St
Central
Tel: 266 919
Fax: 266 920
French and Vietnamese restaurant, bar with live music from 6 pm nightly, business centre, convention facilities, swimming pool and souvenir shops.

Military Guest House $$$
33 Pham Ngu Lao
Tel: 254 593/252 896
Fax: 259 276
Well-run government guest house on a quiet street near the river where many foreign correspondents stay. The small lobby bar can be quite lively in the evenings.

Nha Khach Cua Dang (Communist Party Guest House) $$$
off Nghi Tam Street
North shore, West Lake
Tel: 258 241/254 165
Previously these spacious villas were solely-used by top party officials but have recently been made available to tourists. Set in beautiful landscaped gardens, the food is good and the staff helpful. Location could be a problem if you do not have private transportation as it is a 5.5-kilometer trip from downtown.

Nan Luong (Energy Guest House) $$$
30 Ly Thai To
Tel: 253 167
Fax: 259 226

Orient Hotel $$$-$$$$
Lang Ha St
Tel: 245 397
Fax: 245 396
Laundry, car rental and tourist guide service.

State (Government) Guest House $$$
2 Le Thach
Tel: 255 801/255 853
Fax: 255 855
Centrally located in downtown Hanoi, this relatively-modern guest house plays host to many visiting diplomats and dignitaries.

Thang Loi (Victory) Hotel $$-$$$
Dupng Yen Phu
Tel: 258 211/258 215
160 air-conditioned rooms, two restaurants, three bars, swimming pool, souvenir shop, laundry, hair salon, postal services and ballroom.

Thang Long Hotel $-$$
Giang Vo Road
Ba Dinh District
Tel: 257 796/252 270
61 air-conditioned rooms, 2 restaurants, bar, souvenir shop, postal services and billiard room.

Thong Nhat (Metropole) Hotel $$-$$$
15 Ngo Quyen
Tel: 252 785/252 755/266 919
Fax: 266 920
192 rooms with or without air-conditioning, newly renovated. Souvenir shop, restaurant, bar, laundry, hair salon. Evening Vietnamese cultural shows. Conference facilities.

HO CHI MINH CITY (SAIGON)
Ben Thanh (Rex) Hotel $$-$$$
141 Nguyen Hue Blvd
District 1
Tel: 292 185/292 187/292 186
Fax: 291 469
87 air-conditioned rooms. Centrally located, two restaurants, swimming pool, cinema, shops, roof garden, conference facilities. Hair salon, sauna, massage, acupuncture and postal services.

Bong Hong (Rose) $$
123 Dong Khoi
District 1
Tel: 290 613/225 418
Fax: 298 076

Bong Sen (Miramar) Hotel $-$$
117-119 Dong Khoi Street (or 115-119)
District 1
Tel: 291 516/299 127
Fax: 299 744
85 modern, air-conditioned, recently-refurbished rooms. Vietnamese/French restaurant, bar, souvenir shop and disco.

Boss Mini Hotel $$
60-62 Nguyen Van Troi
Phu Nhuan District
Northern HCMC
Tel: 443 093
Fax: 443 264

Century Saigon Hotel $$$$
68A Nguyen Hue Boulevard
District 1
Tel: 293 168/230 542
Fax: 292 732
The first land-based international hotel in HCMC. 109 rooms and suites on eleven floors with facilities including three restaurants, rooftop nightclub, karaoke lounge, banquet facilities, health club and business center. Targeted mainly at businessmen.

Continental Hotel $$
132 Dong Khoi Street
District 1
Tel: 294 456/299 255
Fax: 290 936
72 air-conditioned rooms, recently renovated. Centrally-located, three restaurants, souvenir shop, conference facilities, car service, hair salon, massage and sauna.

Cu'u Long (Majestic) Hotel $$-$$$
1 Dong Khoi Street
District 1

Tel: 291 375/295 515
Fax: 291 470
91 air-conditioned rooms, centrally-located, restaurant, Cyclo Bar, shops, laundry, conference facilities, dance hall and massage.

Doc Lap (Caravelle) Hotel $$
19-23 Cong Truong Lam Son (or 19-23 Lam Son Square)
District 1
Tel: 293 704/293 705/293 706
Fax: 299 902
113 air-conditioned rooms. Centrally-located, restaurants, bar, laundry, banquet and conference facilities, disco and massage.

Hai Van Hotel $$
69 Huynh Thuc Khang
District 1
Tel: 291 274
20 international standard rooms. European and Asian restaurant, conference facilities in 200-seat hall, health club and cultural performances.

Huong Duong (Central Palace) Hotel $$-$$$
150 Nguyen Thi Minh Khai Street
District 1
Tel: 292 404
80 air-conditioned rooms. Close to the Town Hall. Restaurant, bar and tennis court.

Huong Sen (Lotus) Hotel $$
66-70 Dong Khoi Street
District 1
Tel: 291 415
Fax: 299 744
50 air-conditioned rooms. Restaurant, bar and shop.

Huu Nghi (Palace) Hotel $-$$
56-64 Nguyen Hue Boulevard
District 1
Tel: 297 284/294 722
Fax: 299 872
112 air-conditioned rooms, restaurant, bar, swimming pool,

souvenir shop and laundry.

International Hotel $$$-$$$$
19 Vo Van Tan
District 3
Tel: 290 009
In-room safety boxes and in-house movies, Chinese seafood restaurant, café, bar, business center, laundry service and beauty salon.

Majestic Saigon $$-$$$$
1 Dong Khoi Street
District 1
Tel: 955 155/95 517
Fax: 291 470
120 rooms including 25 suites. Situated in the heart of the business district on the Saigon River.

Mondial Hotel $$$-$$$$
109 Dong Khoi Street
District 1
Tel: 296 291
Fax: 296 324
40 air-conditioned rooms with 24-hour room service, in-house movies, mini bars. French and Vietnamese restaurant and lounge.

New Ky Hoa Hotel $$$-$$$$
12-14 Ba Thang Hai Street
District 11
Tel: 653 332
Only 20 minutes from the airport. Set in a 25-hectare landscaped park near Cholon. Business facilities

Norfolk Hotel $$$
117 Le Thanh Ton
District 1
Tel: 295 368
Fax: 293 415
All rooms air-conditioned. Centrally located, restaurants, bars, conference facilities, business center and satellite television.

Phong Lan (Orchid) Hotel
29A Don Dat Street
District 1

Tel: 231 810
Fax: 292 245
Air-conditioned rooms, centrally-located, European and Chinese restaurant, coffee shop, karaoke lounge and business center.

Saigon Floating Hotel $$$$
1A Me Linh Square
District 1
Tel: 290 783/290 624
Fax: 290 783/290 784
201 air-conditioned rooms, restaurants, bars, business center, swimming pool, tennis courts, in-house video, laundry, conference facilities, disco and sauna. Berthed at Hero Square in the city center.

Saigon Star $$$-$$$$
204 Nguyen Thi Minh Khai
District 3
Tel: 230 260
Fax: 230 255
Rooms have a view of the city park, restaurant, lounge, business centre, conference facilities, disco and an airport pick-up service.

Tan Binh (Airport) Hotel $$
201 Hoang Van Thu Street
Tan Binh District
Tel: 441 167/441 175/444 207
52 rooms, with or without air-conditioning. Five minutes from the airport. Restaurants, swimming pool, tennis court, shops and massage.

Thang Long (Oscar) Hotel $-$$
68A Nguyen Hue Boulevard
District 1
Tel: 293 416
70 rooms, most only have fans. Restaurant and bar.

Thien Hong (Arc-En-Ciel) Hotel
52-56 Tan Da Street
Cholon District
Tel: 552 550

90 rooms. Situated in Chinatown. Restaurant which specializes in Chinese food, bar, handicraft shop, sauna and massage.

Vinh Loi Hotel $
129-133 Ham Nghi Street
District 1
Tel: 223 184
30 rooms, some air-conditioned. Restaurant.

Yuco Hotel $$
28-34 Nguyen Thi
Minh Khai
District 1
Tel: 295 947
Fax: 295 913

HOA BINH
Hoa Binh Tourist Hotel $
Tel: 01 Hoa Binh
On a bluff overlooking Highway 6, just south of the city center. Clean and simple typical government guest house. Friendly and helpful staff.

HUE
Hang Be Hotel $
173 Huynh Thuc Khang Street
Tel: 3752
Fronts a canal. Restaurant.

Huong Giang (Perfume River) Hotel $$-$$$
52 Le Loi Street
Tel: 2122/2288
42 air-conditioned rooms, restaurant, souvenir shop, tennis courts, dance hall and massage. Great view of the Perfume River. Boat rental from private marina. Royal dances are performed on request.

Nha Khach Chinh Phu Hotel $
5 Le Loi Street
Tel: 2153
Villa accommodation, conveniently located near the train station, on the river.

Thuan Hoa Hotel $

7B Nguyen Tri Phuong
Tel: 2553/2576
66 rooms with and without air-conditioning. Restaurant, bar and shop.

Nua Thu Hotel $
26 Nguyen Thi Phuong Street
Tel: 3929
Recently-renovated, good restaurant.

NHA TRANG
Bao Dai's Villa $$-$$$$
Cau Da
Tel: 22449/21124
Former seaside retreat of Bao Dai, the last emperor of Vietnam, who abdicated in 1954 and went into exile in France. Superb setting on a bluff overlooking Nha Trang Bay and the offshore islands. The five villas are set in lush tropical surroundings. You can rent individual rooms for as little as US$35 a night or the entire Royal Villa for US$120. Six kilometers south of central Nha Trang. Boat rentals from private marina.

Hai Yen Hotel $-$$
40 Tran Phu Blvd
Tel: 22974/22828
104 air-conditioned rooms, restaurant, bar, souvenir shop, laundry and disco. Across the street from the beach.

Thang Loi Hotel $-$$
4 Rue Pasteur
Tel: 22241/22226
70 rooms, television, fridge and air-conditioning available. Restaurant, souvenir shop and laundry. Simple holiday hotel situated one block from the beach.

Thong Nhat Hotel $
18 Duong Thong Nhat
Thanh Pho
Tel: 22966
70 rooms, restaurant, souvenir and art shop and laundry. Across

the street from the beach.

PHAN THIET
Vinh Thuy Hotel
Ton Tuc Thang Street $
Tel: 2622/2655
38 rooms, restaurant. The seashore offers good swimming.

QUI NHON
Quy Nhon Tourist Hotel $-$$
8 Nguyen Hue Street
Tel: 2401/2329
On the beach but a little out of the town center.

VINH
Nghe Tinh Guest House $
Dinh Cong Truong Street
Tel: 3175
The older wing is much more pleasant to stay in.

VUNG TAU
Canadian Hotel
48 Quang Trung Street
Vung Tau City
Tel: 459 852/452 321/452 523
Fax: 459 851
It may not have the ambience of Montreal but this three-storey hotel boasts a sea view and a fairly good seafood restaurant.

Hoa Binh Hotel $-$$
11 Nguyen Trai Street
Chau Thanh
Tel: 2265/2411
Well-run hotel in downtown Vung Tau, half a block from Front Beach.

Lam Son Hotel $$
94 Thanh Thai
Chau Thanh
Tel: 2588

Thang Loi Hotel $-$$
1 Duy Tan Street
Chau Thanh
Tel: 2135
80 rooms with and without air-conditioning. Restaurant. Located one block from Front

Beach in the old Russian Compound.

Thang Muoi Hotel $
5 Thuy Van
Tam Thang
Tel: 2665
Modest motel run by the Oil Services Company (OSC). Across the street from Back Beach.

Truong Son Hotel $$
2 Phan Dinh Phung
Chau Thanh
Tel: 2486

FOREIGN MISSIONS
Afghanistan
Khu Van Phuc
District 1
Tel: 253 249

Albania
49 Dien Bien Phu St
Tel: 254 490

Algeria
13 Phan Chu Trinh St
Tel: 253 865

Australia
66 Ly Thoung Kiet
Tel: 252 703/252 763

Belgium
Khu Van Phuc
B3, suites 201-2
Tel: 252 263

Bulgaria
41-43 Tran Phu St
Tel: 257 923

Cambodia
71 Tran Hung Dao St
Tel: 253 789

China
46 Hoang Dieu St
Tel: 253 737

Cuba
65 Ly Thuong Kiet St
Tel: 252 281

Egypt
26 Ly Thuong Kiet St
Tel: 252 944

England
16 Ly Thuong Kiet
Tel: 252 510/252 349

Finland
133b Giang Vo Area
Tel: 257 096

France
49 Ba Trieu
Tel: 254 367/254 368

Germany
29 Tran Phu
Tel: 253 663/255 402

Hungary
47 Dien Bien Phu
Tel: 252 748/252 858

India
58-60 Tran Hung Dao
Tel: 253 406/255 975

Indonesia
50 Ngo Quyen St
Tel: 253 353

Iran
54 Tran Phu
Tel: 232 068/232 069

Iraq
66 Tran Hung Dao
Tel: 254 141

Italy
9 Le Phung Hieu
Tel: 253 388/256 256

Japan
Khu Trung Tu, E3
Tel: 257 902

Korea (North)
25 Cao Ba Quat St
Tel: 253 008

Laos
22 Tran Binh Trong St

Egypt
Tel: 254 576

Libya
Khu Van Phuc, A3
Tel: 253 379

Malaysia
Khu Van Phuc, A3
Tel: 253 371

Mongolia
39 Tran Phu St
Tel: 252 151

Myanmar (Burma)
Khu Van Phuc, A3
Tel: 253 369

Nicaragua
Khu Trung Tu, E1
Tel: 262 214/262 216

Philippines
Khu Trung Tu, E1
Tel: 257 948

Sweden
So2, Duong 358
Khu Van Phuc
Ba Dinh District
Tel: 254 824

Switzerland
27 Quang Trung
Tel: 254 751

Thailand
Khu Trung Tu, E1
Tel: 256 043

CONSULATES
Ho Chi Minh City
Bulgaria
6 Phung Khac Khoan
District 1
Tel: 295 075

Cambodia
124-126 Nguyen Dinh Chieu
Tel: 295 818/297 351

Cuba
23 Phung Khac Khoan

District 1
Tel: 297 350
France
27 Xo Viet Nghe Tinh
Tel: 297 231/297 235

Germany
45 Phung Khac Khoan
District 1
Tel: 292 455

Hungary
53 Nguyen Dinh Chieu
Tel: 299 027/299 023

RESTAURANTS, BARS & NIGHTCLUBS

Dalat
La Tulipe Rouge Restaurant
1 Nguyen Thi Minh
Tel: 2394
European, Chinese and Vietnamese dishes.

The Shanghai Restaurant
8 Khu Hoa Binh Quarter
Chinese, Vietnamese and French food is available throughout the day.

Thuy Ta Restaurant
Xuan Huong Lake
Tel: 2268
Built of stilts over the lake, this restaurant offers a wonderful view.

DANANG
Chin Den Restaurant
32 Ngo Gia Tu Street
Good for a traditional breakfast of fried eggs, beef, french bread and salad.

Tu Do Restaurant
180 Tran Phu Street
Open-air restaurant with an extensive Vietnamese, Chinese and European menu. Popular with tourists. Reasonably priced.

Thanh Lich Restaurant
42 Bach Dang Street
English, French and Vietnamese

menu. Popular with foreign businessmen.

HANOI
Art Cafe Cocktails
57 Hang Non Street
Hoan Kiem District
New bar in the heart of old Hanoi, on the street where they used to make hats.

Australian Embassy
66 Ly Thoung Kiet
Tel: 252 703
Every Friday night is Billabong Club night from 8pm to midnight. Australian passport holders have right of admittance; all other nationalities need an invitation.

Cafe Pastry Shop
252 Hang Bong Street
Hoan Kiem District
Not quite Fauchon, but one of the most tasty establishments in town. Mr Le Hun Chi, the friendly proprietor, spent 13 years in New Caledonia before returning to Vietnam. The cafe features French-style coffee (with fresh milk biked in from the countryside each day), homemade yoghurt and French bread sandwiches with cheese, tomato and onion.

Cha Ca La Vong Restaurant
14 Cha Ca Street
Tel: 253 929
Fish-and-rice *cha ca* served in sizzling skillet is the specialty of the house. Popular with local businessmen, aid workers and tourists. Reasonably priced.

German Embassy Basement
29 Tran Phu Street
Tel: 253 663
German beer garden serving food once a week.

International Club
11 Le Hong Phong Street

Tel: 257 758/252 820
The paragon of high society in Hanoi, the Inter Club has a somewhat dour cafe. But the club supermarket is packed with Western goods: Kraft® macaroni and cheese, Pabst® Blue Ribbon beer, peanut butter, marshmallows, Nestles® hot chocolate powder, Heinz® ketchup and Japanese instant noodles.

Piano Bar Restaurant
93 Phung Hung Street
Hoan Kiem District
Tel: 259 425/232 423
Good though relatively expensive Vietnamese food. Menu includes fried squid, grilled king prawns, stuffed crab, spring rolls and noodles with vegetables. Live classical music and Vietnamese folk tunes each night. Ask Madame Tong to sing. Relaxed, cozy atmosphere. Popular with the expat community.

Restaurant 202
202 Pho Hue Street
Hai Ba Trung District
Delicious food at a reasonable price served in modest surroundings. The kitchen turns out tasty *coq au vin*, roast rabbit, crab farci, fried vermicelli noodles, three different types of fried shrimp, *wiener schnitzel*, papaya and carrot salad and banana flambé.

Tay Ho Floating Restaurant
West Lake (Ho Tay)
Tel: 257 884
Vietnamese variation of the ubiquitous Asian floating restaurant. A little on the pricey side, but the atmosphere is unique for Hanoi.

Viet Phuong Restaurant
4 Mai Hac De Street
One of the city's gourmet secrets. This place is hard to find, but worth the effort. The menu

features roast rabbit, snails dipped in garlic and pepper sauce, eel soup and superb soft-shelled crabs.

VIP Club
60-62 Nguyen Du Street
Tel: 252 690
Fax: 257 634
Multi-media entertainment center with dancing, karaoke lounge, games room and bar.

HO CHI MINH CITY
Appocalypse Now Bar
Dong Du Street
District 1
Relive Saigon of the 1960s at this little dive bar near the waterfront. Drink Saigon Export Beer against a background of tunes from the movie "Good Morning Vietnam".

City Bar and Grill
63 Dong Khoi
District 1
Tel: 298 006

Dong Que Restaurant
905 Hau Giang St
Chinatown
District 6
Tel: 50578
Home cooked Vietnamese food.

Down-under Disco
Saigon Floating Hotel
1A Me Linh Square
District 1
Tel: 290 783
Where many of the young and trendy cash rich children of the new elite hang out.

Givral Restaurant
169 Dong Khoi St
District 1
Tel: 292 747
Old-style French restaurant and coffee house.

Good Morning Vietnam Bar
Dong Du Street

District 1
Noisy, lively bar featuring Western rock music.

International Tourist Club
76 Le Lai
District 1
Tel: 259 134

La Bibliotheque
84A Nguyen Du Street
District 1
Located in the house of former Upper House Opposition Vice President Madame Nguen Phuoc Dai. Meals are served in Madam Dai's library where old French law books line the walls. You can choose between set Vietnamese meals with lots of courses or an extensive *a la carte* French menu. The clientele is mainly expatriates and tourists. Reasonably priced.

Liberty Restaurant
80 Dong Khoi St
District 1
Tel: 299 820
Vietnamese cuisine with nightly live entertainment.

Lobby Bar
Saigon Floating Hotel
1A Me Linh Square
District 1
Tel: 290 783
Typical hotel cocktail bar popular with expatriates and visiting businessmen. Live entertainment and snacks.

Marina Café
Saigon Floating Hotel
1A Me Linh Square
District 1
Coffee shop with a bistro atmosphere serving everything from snacks to full meals. Indoor or outdoor dining available.

Maxim's
13-17 Dong Choi Street
Tel: 296 676

The French and Chinese menu used to be the talk of the town before the recent tourist surge introduced heated competition. Live cabaret and classical music are featured from 7 pm nightly.

Mini Rex Restaurant (Tennis Restaurant)
86 Le Thanh Ton
District 1
Tel: 292 186
Vietnamese, Chinese and European food. Situated in a spacious garden inside a former presidential palace, behind the Rex Hotel next to the tennis courts. Fairly expensive but pleasant atmosphere in the *al fresco* section. The **Revolutionary History Museum** where old tanks and helicopters are on display within the grounds is in the adjoining building. The dining room and garden are available for barbecue parties or other functions. Happy hours start from 5 to 8 pm daily.

My Phung Restaurant
Me Linh (Hero) Square
District 1
For the adventurous eater as this menu features pigeon, turtlê, armadillo and live cobra. It is located opposite the Floating Hotel.

Nihon Bashi Restaurant
Rex Hotel
4-6 Le Loi St
District 1
Foreign-managed Japanese restaurant.

Orient Dancing Restaurant
104 Hai Ba Trung
District 1
Tel: 225 478
Vietnamese, Chinese and Western food in a beautifully-restored, French colonial building from the art deco period. Disco dance on the top floor to entertainment

provided by a well-known local band.

Oriental Club
Saigon Floating Hotel
1A Me Linh Square
District 1
Tel: 290 784
The Hotel's premier restaurant, specializing in Asian dishes.

Oriental Gourmet Restaurant
472-474 Tran Hung Dao
Cholon District
Tel: 359 619
The Oriental's Hong Kong chef serves up Cantonese and Taiwanese cuisine, Vietnamese seafood and wild game.

Queen Bee
104-106 Nguyen Hue Boulevard
District 1
Tel: 229 860
Restaurant with nightly dancing and karaoke.

Ritz Taiwanese Restaurant, Café and Karaoke
333 Tran Hung Dao Boulevard
District 1
Tel: 324 325
Taiwanese and Cantonese dishes. Open for lunch and dinner; breakfast is available in the cafe from 7 am. Karaoke from 6 pm to midnight.

Seoul Restaurant
37 Ngo Duc Ke St
District 1
Tel: 294 297
Korean cooking.

Sky View Restaurant
Mondial Hotel
109 Dong Khoi Street
District 1
Tel: 296 291
Vietnamese cuisine and a great view of Ho Chi Minh City at this penthouse restaurant in the Mondial Hotel. Cultural shows are featured three times a week.

Shangri-la Complex
1196, 3/2 Street
District 11
Tel: 556 831
Fax: 559 471
One of Vietnam's largest and most complete entertainment complexes which includes the **Pink Cadillac Disco**, the **Saigon Café**, a karaoke bar, music lounge, a business center, health club and a department store.

Siren Floating Restaurant
Boardat Bachdang Quay
District 1
Tel: 225 402
Open 6 - 11 pm.
Enjoy fresh seafood while cruising down the Saigon River.

Starlight Disco
Century Saigon Hotel
2D Pham Ngoc
Thach St
District 1
Tel: 231 818
The latest in entertainment on the hotel's 11th floor.

Superstar Disco and Nightclub
431A/2 Hoang Van Thu Street
Tan Binh District
Tel: 440 242
One of the city's largest nightclubs with an imported lighting and sound system. Live house band and overseas deejays provide the entertainment. Located a mere ten minutes from the city center and close to the airport.

Thanh The Restaurant
5-7-9 Nguyen Trung Truc St
Tel: 291 214
Vietnamese food served the traditional way.

Tiger Tavern
227 Dong Khoi Street
District 1
Tel: 222 738
Centrally-located bar, lounge, restaurant with fairly good Viet-

namese and Western food at reasonable prices. Popular with expatriate businessmen. There is also a library corner stocked with foreign newspapers, books and magazines.

Vietnam House
93-95 Dong Khoi Street
District 1
Tel: 291 623
Good but expensive Vietnamese food. Traditional musical entertainment. Lounge on the ground floor.

VIP Club
2D Pham Ngoc Thach Street
District 1
Tel: 231 187
Fax: 231 024
Multi-media entertainment complex which features disco, karaoke lounge, games room and bar.

Volvo
52-56 Tan Da Street
Cholon District
Tel: 556 924

Vy Restaurant
Two locations: 164 Pasteur & 105 Bacssi Yersin Streets
District 1
Tel: 296 210 (Pasteur)
        294 567 (Bacssi Yersin)
Vietnamese breakfasts, seafood dinners and all-day snacks. Al fresco do-it-yourself barbecues or indoor private rooms with chamber music.

West Villa Club
2B Le Duan St
District 1
Tel: 231 652
Cantonese and Vietnamese food in air-conditioned comfort.

HUE
Ban Khoai Thuonng Tu
6 Dinh Tien Hoang Street
Features traditional Hue speci-

alities.

The Café
51 Phan Dinh Phung Street
Drinks served in the ambience
of an interesting old building.

Huong Giang Hotel Restaurant
51 Le Loi Street
Tel: 2122
Banh khoai, huong giang, nem
and other specialties of Hue,
together with seafood; Western
dishes and vegetarian food are
usually available here. Reasonable prices.

Nam Son Huong Restaurant
7 Huong Hoa Tham Street
Specializes in soups and egg-
rolls.

Song Huong Floating
 Restaurant
Near the intersection of Le Loi
and Hung Vuong streets
Tel: 3738
Just north of Trang Tien Bridge,
a pleasant restaurant situated on
the banks of the Perfume River.

Nha Trang
Cafe Restaurant Lys
117A Hoang Van Thu Street
Tel: 22006
Popular rooftop restaurant serving tasty seafood and a glass
cabinet full of exotic delights
like French cheese, Spanish ol-
ives and imported liquor. The
huge color television in the dining room plays a constant stream
of Vietnamese pop videos.

VIETNAM TOUR
OPERATORS OVERSEAS
Canada
New Asia Tours
Tour Nouvelle Asia Inc
210 Quest Rue Chabanel Que
Canada HZN IG2
Tel: (514) 4180

Discovery Tours

Cathay Pacific Airways
18 fl, 650 Georgia St
Vancouver
Tel: 682 9747

France
Hit Voyages
21 Rue des Bernadins
Paris 75005
Tel: 43 54 17 17

Discovery Tours
Cathay Pacific Airways
267 Bld Pereire
75017 Paris
Tel: 42 27 75 21

Germany
Indoculture Tours
Bismarckplaz 1 d-7000
Stuttgart 1
Tel: 0711/61

Discovery Tours
Cathay Pacific Airways
Feuerbachstrasse 26,
6000 Frankfurt am Main 1
Tel: 069/720900

Hong Kong
Abercrombie & Kent
27th floor, Tai Sang Commer-
 cial Building
24-34 Henessy Road
Wanchai, Hong Kong
Tel: 865 7818
Fax: 866 0556

Chu & Associates
Unit E, 5 Floor
8 Thomson Road
Hong Kong
Tel: 527 8828

Traveler Services
Room 704, Metropole Building
57 Peking Road
Tsim Sha Tsui, Kowloon
Tel: 367 4127

Vietnam Tours & Trading
Room 302, Loader Commercial
Building
54 Hillwood Road

Tsim Sha Tsui, Kowloon
Tel: 368 2493
Fax: 576 6635

Philippines
Discovery Tours
Cathay Pacific Airways
Manila Gammon Center
126 Alfaro Street
Salcedo Village
Makati, Metro Manila
Tel: 815 9401

Impex International
Suite 201, Centrum Bldg
104 Perea St
Lagaspi Village
Makati, Metro Manila
Tel: 816 4865/813 4865

Singapore
Chan Brothers
150 South Bridge Road
Fook Hai Building, #07-01
Singapore 0105
Tel: 535 5333

Discovery Tours
Cathay Pacific Airways
16-03 Ocean Building
10 Collyer Quay
Singapore 0104
Tel: 530 5650

Taiwan
Discovery Tours
Cathay Pacific Airways
12 Floor, Worldwide House
683 Min Sheng E Road
Taipei
Tel: 712 8228

Cathay Pacific Airways
3rd Floor
21 Chung Hwa 3rd Road
Kaohsiung
Tel: 201 3166

Stone International Dev Co Ltd
Unit 1, 4 Floor, Pao Chiao Road
Msien Tien, Taipei
Tel: 918 6556
Fax: 918 6373

Thailand
Abercrombie & Kent
491/29-30, 4th Floor
Silom Plaza, Silom Road
Bangkok 10500
Tel: 235 3545
Fax: 233 1864

Air People Tour and Travel
307 Sa La Daeng Road
Bangkok 10500
Tel: 235 2668
Fax: 240 9003

Diethelm Travel
Kian Gwan Building II
140/1 Wireless Road
Bangkok 10500
Tel: 255 9150/60/70
Fax: 256 0248/9

Discovery Tours
Cathay Pacific Airways
5th Floor, Charn Issara Tower
942/136 Rama IV Road
Bangkok 10500
Tel: 237 6161

Vista Travel
24/4 Kaosan Road
Banglumpoo
Bangkok 10200
Tel: 281 0786/281 3208

USA
Discovery Travel
Cathay Pacific Airways
300 North Continental Blvd
Suite 500
El Segundo
California 90245
Tel: 800-233-ASIA

Mekong Travel
151 First Avenue, Suite 172
New York, NY 10003
Tel: (212) 420 1586

HOSPITALS
(BEHN VIEN)
Danang
Hospital C (Polyclinic)
74 Hai Phong Street (at Ngo Gia
Tu Street)

Hanoi
The French and Swedish embassies each have a doctor on staff.

Bach Mai Hospital
Nam Bo Street
Dong Da District
Tel: 253 731

E Hospital
Co Nhue Street
Tel: 253 561

Hospital of Traditional Medicine
29 Nguyen Binh Khiem Street
Tel: 252 850

Institute of Ophthamology
38 Tran Nhan Tong Street
Tel: 253 967

International Hospital (Behn Vien Quoc Te)
Kiem Lien Street
Dong Da District
Tel: 254 373/262 042

K Hospital (Cancer)
43 Quan Su Street
Hoan Kiem District
Tel: 252 143

Viet Duc (German) Hospital
47 Tran Thi Street (at Quan Su Street)
Hoan Kiem District
Tel: 253 531

Haiphong
Traditional Medicine Hospital (Benh Vien Dong Y)
Nguyen Duc Canh Street (near Xe Lua Bridge)
An Duong District

Vietnam-Czchoslovakia Friendship Hospital (Benh Vien Viet-Tiep)
Nha Thuong Street (off Hai Ba Trung Street)
An Duong District

Ho Chi Minh City
Cho Quan Hospital
Tran Hung Dao Boulevard
Cholon

Cho Ray Hospital (Benh Vien Cho Ray)
201B Nguyen Chi Thanh Boulevard
Cholon District
Tel: 255 137/255 138

Nhi Dong 2 (Grall) Hospital
Ly Tu Trong Street

Thong Nhat Hospital
Corner of Ly Thuong Kiet Blvd and Cach Mang Thang Tam Blvd
Tan Binh District (near the airport).

Hue
Hue General Hospital
16 Le Loi Street
(south bank near Phu Xuan Bridge)
Tel: 2325/ 2326

Nha Trang
Tinh Hospital (Bien Vien Tinh)
Yersin Street (at Dien Tien Hoang Street)
Tel: 22175/22168

Quy Nhon
Quy Nhon Hospital
102 Nguyen Hue Street
Thanh Pho District
Tel: 2708

Vung Tao
Veteran's Clinic
Down the alley opposite 99 Le Loi Boulevard
Tel: 7348/2573

PHARMACIES
(NHA THUOC)
Hanoi
International Hospital
Benh Vien Quoc Te
Kiem Lien Street
On-site pharmacy

Pharmacy
52 Trang Tien Street

Ho Chi Minh City
Hieu Thuoc Dong Khoi
201 Dong Khoi Street
Tel: 290 577
English speaking pharmacist
Open 7 am till 12 noon and
from 1 - 5 pm.

Pharmacy
105 Nguyen Hue Boulevard
Open from 8 till 11:30 am and
from 2 to 6 pm.

**Pharmacy of Traditional Viet-
namese Medicine**
34 Nguyen Hue Boulevard
Open 6 - 7:30 pm.

VIETNAMESE
EMBASSIES
Albania
Tirana
Tel: 2556

Algeria
30 Rue Chenoua Hydra
Algeria
Tel: 600 752

Australia
6 Timbarra Crescent
O'Malley
Canberra
ACT 2603
Tel: (062) 866059

Bulgaria
Sofia - 1113
Ulitsa Ilia Petrovl
Tel: 639043/658486

Cambodia
Son Ngoc Minh area
Phnom Penh
Tel: 25481

China
32 Guang Hua Lu St
Jian Gguo Men Wai
Beijing
Tel: 532 1125/532 1155

Congo
BP 988
Brazzaville

Cuba
5a Avenida No 1802
Mirmar
Ciudad de La Habana
Tel: 296 262/25214

Egypt
47 Noned Heshmet Street
Zamalak, Cairo
Tel: 340 2401

England
12-14 Victoria Rd
London W8 5RD
Tel: 937 1912

Ethiopia
Kebele No12
House No 161-123
Addis Ababa
Tel: 201 147

France
62-66 Rue Boileau
Paris 16E
Tel: 75016

62 Rue de Boileau
75016 Paris
Tel: 452 450 63

Germany
Konstantinstr 37
5300 Bonn 2
Tel: (0228) 357022

37 Konstantin-Strasse
5300-Bonn
Tel: (0228) 357 0201

Hong Kong
Representative of the National
Export-Import Corporation of the
Socialist Republic of Vietnam
17/F Golden Building
20-24 Lockhart Road
Tel: 528 3361

Hungary
Benczur U18

Budapest
Tel: 429 943

India
42F, South Extension
New Delhi Part 1
Tel: 624 586

Indonesia
Jalan Teuku Umiar 25
Jakarta
Tel: 347 325

Iraq
Dawoodi al-Mansour
No 71/7/17
Baghdad
Tel: 551 1388

Italy
Piazza Barberini 12
00187 Rome
Tel: (06) 475 4098

Japan
50-11 Moto Yoyogi-Cho
Shibuya-ku
Tokyo 151
Tel: (3) 466 3311

Korea (North)
7 Munxu Street
Pyongyang
Tel: 291

Laos
Thanon That Luang
Tel: 5578

Libya
Sharia Addhu 1/Bin Ashun
Tripoli
Tel: 45753

Malaysia
4 Pesiaran Stonor
Kuala Lumpur
Tel: (03) 248 4036

Mexico
Sierra Ventana 255
Col Lomas de Chapultepec
11000 Mexico, DF
Tel: 540 1612

Mongolia
Enkhe-Taivan Oudomjni 47
Ulanbator
Tel: 50465/50547

Mozambique
Av Julius Nyerere No 1555
Maputo
Tel: 741 948

Myanmar
40 Kmin Kochin Road
Yangon
Tel: 50361

Nicaragua
Calle Saturno No 40
Zona Residencial la Planetarium
Managua
Tel: 52168

Pakistan
60 Embassy Rd
Ramna 6/3
Islamabad

Philippines
554 Vito Cruz
Malate
Metro Manila
Tel: (02) 500 364

Singapore
10 Leedon Park
Singapore
Tel: (65) 462 5938
(All visitors' visas must be applied for through a travel agent)

Sweden
Orby Slottsvag 26
125 36 Alvsjo
Tel: (8) 861 218

Syria
Mezzeh Villas West E1
Aksan Ben Saifi Street
Damascus
Tel: 667 026

Thailand
83/1 Wireless Rd
Bangkok
Tel: (02) 251 7201

USA
Vietnamese Mission to the United Nations
20 Waterside Plaza
New York, NY 10010
Tel: (212) 685 8001

TOURIST OFFICES, TOUR & LAND TRANSPORT OPERATORS

Ben Tre
Ben Tre Province Tourism
(government tourist office)
65 Dong Khoi Street

Can Tho
Hau Giang Province Tourism
(government tourist office)
27 Chau Van Liem Street
Tel: 20147/35275

Cholon
Cholon Tourist (government tourist office)
192-194 Su Van Hanh Street
District 5, HCMC
Tel: 557 100
Fax: 555 375

Dalat
Lan Dong Province Tourism
(government tourist office)
12 Tran Phu Street
Tel: 2125/2366

Lam Dong Youth Tourism
Company (sightseeing, camping and trekking trips)
2nd Floor, Lang Bian Youth Hostel
Nguyen Thi Minh Khai Street
Tel: 2136/2318

Danang
Danang Tourism (government tourist office)
48 Bach Dang Street
Danang
Tel: 21423

Quan Nam Danang Province Tourism (government tourist office)
48 Bach Dang Street
Danang
Tel: 21423

Vicarrent (car rental)
53 Tran Phu
Danang
Tel: 21681

Dong Ha
Quang Tri Province Tourism
(government tourist office)
Dong Truong Son Hotel
Tran Phu Street
Tel: 239

Haiphong
Haiphong Tourism (government tourist office)
15 Le Dai Hanh Street
Tel: 47486

Hanoi
Hanoi Car Services (car rental)
5 Le Than Tong Street
Tel: 254 074/253 668
Telex: 412 410 CARCONM

Hanoi Tourism
18 Ly Thuong Kiet Street
Tel: 254 209/257 886

Hanoi Tourism & Service Company (Toserco)
8 To Hien Thanh Street
Hai Ba Trung District
Hanoi
Tel: 252 937/263 541
(run by the Hanoi People's Committee; a good place for visa extensions and internal travel permits)

Tourist Transportation Company (car rental)
16 Nguyen Cong Tru Street
Tel: 257 335
Fax: 252 707
Telex: 252707

Vicarrent (car rental)
39 Ngo Quyen Street
Tel: 264 007/259 027

Vietnam Tourism (national government tourist office)
54 Nguyen Du Street
Hoan Kiem District
Tel: 257 080/252 986

Ho Chi Minh City
Ben Thanh Tourist
86 Ly Tu Trong Street
District 1, HCMC
Tel: 291 616

Cosevine (car rental)
Saigon Salon Auto
102 Nguyen Hue Boulevard
District 1, HCMC
Tel: 291 505/292 391

Fidi Tourist (car rental)
71 Dong Khoi
District 1, HCMC
Tel: 296 264/222 941
Fax: 225 950/299 891

Riverway Transport Incorporation (car rental)
94 Nam Ky Khoi Nghia Street
District 1, HCMC
Tel: 224 342

Saigon Railway Tourist (railway tours)
275C Pham Ngu Lao Street
District 1, HCMC
Tel: 223 747

Saigon Tourist (government tour agency)
39 Le Thanh Ton Street
District 1, HCMC
Tel: 295 000/298 914

Saigon Tourist Association
112 Cach Mang Thang Tam Street
District 3, HCMC
Tel: 238 653

Saigon Tourist Automobile Corp (car rental)
34 Ton Duc Thang Street
District 1, HCMC
Tel: 295 925/295 866

Saigon Tourist's Guide Office
49 Le Thanh Ton Street
HCMC
Tel: 224 987/298 914

Sataxi (Saigon Taxi Pte Co Ltd) (car rental)
75 Ham Nghi Boulevard
District 1, HCMC
Tel: 398 016/296 624

Sp Tour Services (private local and special interest tours)
66-68 Nguyen Trai Street
District 1, HCMC
Tel: 391 141
Fax: 391 141

Tourist Automobile Company (car rental)
131 Nguyen Hue Boulevard
District 1, HCMC
Tel: 222 531

Tourist Car Company (car rental)
151 Nguyen Hue Boulevard
District 1, HCMC
Tel: 296 992

Trung Tam Du Lich Thanh Vietnam
31 Cao Thang Street
Cholon District, HCMC
Tel: 590 553

Vicarrent (car rental)
29 Dong Du Street
District 1, HCMC
Tel: 290 415

Vietnam Tourism (government tourist office)
61-71 Nguyen Hue Boulevard
District 1, HCMC
Tel: 290 772/290 776

Voiles Vietnam (boat cruises)
17 Pham Ngoc Thach
District 1, HCMC
Tel: 296 750

Hoi An
Hoi An Tourist Service (government tourist office)

100 Tran Phu Street
Tel: K72

Hue
Hue City Tourism (Cong Ty Du Lich Thanh Pho Hue) (accommodation, cultural shows, car rentals)
18 Le Loi Street
Tel: 3577

Thua Thien-Hue Province Tourism (government tourist office)
51 Le Loi Street
Tel: 2288/2355

Long Xuyen
An Giang Province Tourism (government tourist office)
6 Ngo Gia Tu Street
Tel: 52888/52086

Tourism Services Company (tours and car rentals)
93 Nguyen Trai Street

My Tho
Tien Giang Province Tourism (government tourism office)
56 Hung Vuong Boulevard
Tel: 3591/3154

Nha Trang
Khanh Hoa Province Tourism (Cong Ty Du Lich Khanh Hoa) (government tourist office)
Hai Yen Hotel
40 Tran Phu Boulevard
Tel: 22753

Phan Thiet
Thuan Hai Province Tourism (government tourist office)
82 Trung Trac Street
Tel: 2474/2475

Phan Rang
Thuan Hai Province Tourism (government tourist office)
Huu Nghi Hotel
1 Huong Vuong Street
·Tel: 74

Quy Nhon
Binh Dinh Province Tourism &
Ship Chandler Co (Du Lich
Cung Ung Tau Bien Binh Dinh)
(government tourist office)
opposite 78 Tran Hung Dao
Street
Tel: 2329

Rach Gia
Kien Giang Province Tourism
(government tourist office)
12 Ly Tu Trong Street
Tel: 2081

Vinh
Nghe Tinh Province Tourism
(Cong Ty Du Lich Nghe Tinh)
(government tourist office)
3rd Floor, Public Housing
Project
Quang Trung Street
Tel: 4692/2285

PLACES OF WORSHIP
Chau Doc
Catholic
Chan Doc Church
opposite 459 Le Loi Street

Muslim
Chau Giang Mosque
Chau Giang District

Dalat
Catholic
Dalat Cathedral
Tran Phu Street
(beside the Dalat Hotel)

Domaine De Marie Convent
6 Ngo Quyen Street

Du Sinh Church
Huyen Tran Cong Chua Street

Protestant
Vietnamese Evangelical Church
72 Nguyen Van Troi Street

Buddhist
Lam Ty Ni Pagoda
2 Thien My Street

Linh Son Pagoda
120 Nguyen Van Troi Street
Minh Nguyet Cu Sy Lam
Pagoda
Along the path which starts op-
posite the gate of Thien Vuong
Pagoda

Thien Vuong Pagoda
Khe Sanh Street

Danang
Catholic
Danang Cathedral (Chinh Toa
Da Nang)
Tran Phu Street

Cao Dai
Cao Dai Temple (Chua Cao Dai)
Opposite Hospital C, 74 Hai
Phong Street

Buddhist
Pho Da Pagoda
opposite 293 Phan Chu Trinh
Street

Hanoi
Catholic
St Joseph's Cathedral
40 Nha Chung Street
Hoan Kiem District

Buddhist
Ambassador's Pagoda
73 Quan Su Street
Tel: 252 427

Tran Quoc Pagoda
Tranh Nien Street
West Lake

Trung Sisters Pagoda
Tho Lao Street
Hai Ba Trung District

Ho Chi Minh City
Catholic
Notre Dame Cathedral
Dong Khoi Street

Hindu
Mariamman Hindu Temple
(Chau Ba Mariamman)

45 Truong Dinh Street

Muslim
Saigon Central Mosque
66 Dong Du Street

Buddhist
Chua Go (Phung Son) Pagoda
1408 3 Thang 2 Boulevard
District 11 (near Cholon)

Phuoc Hai Tu (Emperor of Jade)
Pagoda
73 Mai Thi Luu Street
Da Kao Section, District 1

Giac Lam Pagoda
118 Lac Long Quan Street
Tan Binh District

Giac Vien Pagoda
Next to Dam Sen Lake
District 11

Hue
Catholic
Notre Dame Cathedral
80 Nguyen Hue Street

Phu Cam Cathedral
20 Doan Huu Trinh Street

Buddhist
Linh Mu Pagoda
Banks of the Perfume River, 4
kilometers southwest of the Citadel

Tu Dam Pagoda
Corner of Dien Bien Phu and Tu
Dam Streets

Long Xuyen
Catholic
Long Xuyen Catholic Church
Between Tran Hung Dao, Hung
Vuong & Nguyen Hue Streets

Protestant
Long Xuyen Protestant Church
4 Hung Vuong Street

Buddhist
Quan Thanh De Pagoda

Le Minh Ngu On St

Nha Trang
Catholic
Nha Trang Cathedral
Thai Nguyen Street
Cham Hindu
Po Nagar Cham Towers
Banks of Cai River, 2 kilometers
north of central Nha Trang

Buddhist
Long Son Pagoda
off 23 Thang 10 Street
west of central Nha Trang

SHOPPING
Hanoi
Bach Hoa Tong Hop
Hang Bai Street
Hanoi's largest department store.
State-run.

Cultrimex
22B Ha Ba Trung
Arts and crafts. State-run.

Fine Arts Shop
25 Hang Khay

International Bookshop
61 Trang Tien Street
Stocks books in English, Russian, French and Spanish.

Craft Shop
17 Hang Khay Street

Han Art
43 Trang Tien
Old craft items - ceramics, carpets, lacquerware etc.

Souvenirs of Vietnam
30A Ly Thuong Kiet
Good for ceramics and lacquerware.

Tan My
109 Hang Gai Street
Embroidered items.

Xunhasaba
32 Hai Ba Trung

English language publications published in Vietnam, stamps and handicrafts.

Ho Chi Minh City
Art Gallery Particulier
43 Dong Khoi Street
District 1
Tel: 298 802
Features the work of famous Vietnamese artists.

Artexport Saigon Company
159 Dong Khoi Street
District 1
Tel: 295 459
Fine arts and handicrafts. State-run.

Ben Thanh (Rex) Hotel
141 Nguyen Hue Boulevard
A ground floor arcade with a variety of souvenir shops.

Ben Thanh Market
Junction of Ham Nghi, Le Loi and Tran Hung Do boulevards.
Food, clothes, electronics.

Cua Hang Bach Hoa
Le Loi Boulevard
HCMC's largest department store. Three stories.

Cultrimex ˙
94 Dong Khoi
Tel: 292 574/292 896
Arts and crafts. State-run. Closed on Sundays.

Dan Sinh Market
104 Nguyen Cong Tu Street
New and used, authentic and imitation military goods.

Fahasa Bookshop
185 Dong Knoi
English, French and Russian language books.

Fine Arts Product Import-Export Company
160 Pasteur
District 1

Tel: 294 913
Retailer and exporter of art and handicrafts. Several showrooms around HCMC. Call to find out the nearest one to you.

GPO Philatelic Section
2 Le Loi Blvd and 12 Ton That Dam Street
Stamps.

Hoang Minh
103 Dong Khoi Street
District 1
Tel: 222907
Antique watches, pens and jewelry. Money back if found to be fake.

Lac Long's
143 Le Thanh Ton St
Leather goods are among this store's offerings.

Lam Son Lacquerware
188 Le Van St
Phu Nhuan District
Tel: 452 235

Lena
107 Dong Khoi Street
District 1
Tel: 291 146
Russian amber jewelry and antique porcelain.

Minimart
2nd floor
101 Nam Ky Khoi Nghia Street
Western personal care products.

Ngo An
12 Dong Khoi Street
District 1
Tel: 296 359
Lacquerware, silk paintings and hand-painted ties.

Phuong Tranh Art Arcade
151 Dong Du Street

Saigon Lacquerware Factory
139 Hai Ba Thrung St
Tel: 494 183

Son Mai Lam Son Lacquerware Factory
Duong Le Van Si
Quan Phu Nhuan
Tel: 245 2235

"Thieves Market"
Huynh Thuc Kang and Ton That Dan Streets
Stocked mainly with goods brought home by Vietnamese sailors or sent home to relatives by Vietnamese living abroad.

Viet Silk
43 Dong Khoi St
District 1
Tel: 231 186
Vietnamese silk fabrics, garments, hand-made embroidery and silk artwork. Export production facilities.

Vietnam Jewelery & Fine Handicraft Association
56 Mac Thi Buoi Street and 51 Dong Khoi Street
Antiques sold with guarantees, as well as handicrafts and jewelry.

USEFUL ADDRESSES & PHONE NUMBERS

Customs
125 Ham Nghi Boulevard
District 1, HCMC
Tel: 290 095/290 096

Export Development Center
92-96 Nguyen Hue Boulevard
District 1, HCMC
Tel: 290 072

Foreign Investment Service Company
35-37 Ben Chuong Duong Street
District 1, HCMC
Tel: 295 806

Foreign Office
6 Thai Van Lung Street
District 1, HCMC
Tel: 224 127

Foreign Office
136 Ong Ich Khiem Street
Danang
Tel: 21092

Immigration Office/HCMC Police Immigration
161 Nguyen Du Street
District 1, HCMC

Immigration Office/Ministry of Interior International
35-337 Nguyen Trai Street
District 1, HCMC

IMEXCO
Import-Export Company
8 Nguyen Hue Boulevard
District 1, HCMC
Tel: 297 424

Investment Management Consulting Company
1 Nam Ky Khoi Nghia Street
District 1, HCMC
Tel: 291 902

Ministry of Commerce and Tourism
31 Trang Tien
Hanoi
Tel: 262 521

Ministry of Foreign Affairs
1 Ton That Dam
Hanoi
Tel: 258 201

Ministry of Foreign Affairs
(Foreign Press Center)
10 Le Phung Hieu Street
Hanoi
Tel: 254 697

Ministry of Foreign Affairs
(North America Department)
1 Ton That Street
Hanoi
Tel: 257 279/228 201

Ministry of Foreign Economic Relations
406 Nguyen Tat Thanh Street
District 4, HCMC

Tel: 222 415

Office for the Control of Cultural Items' Import and Export
178 Nam Ky Khoi Nghia Street
District 1, HCMC
Tel: 243 250

Ministry of Information
(International Relations Department)
58 Quan Su Street
Hanoi
Tel: 253 152

Office of Foreign Registration
161-163 Nguyen Du Street
HCMC

Office of Foreign Registration
63 Tran Hung Dao Street
Hanoi

Quarantine Office
40 Nguyen Van Troi, QPN

Service of Foreign Affairs
6 Thai Van Lung
HCMC
Tel: 224 127

Service of Foreign Affairs
Tan Son Nhat Airport
HCMC
Tel: 243 250/242 339

State Committee for Cooperation and Investment
56 Quoc Tu Giam
Hanoi
Tel: 254 970/253 666

VNA (Vietnamese Information Agency)
120 Xo Viet Nghe Tinh Street
HCMC

Vietcochamber (Chamber of Commerce and Industry)
69 Dong Khoi Street
District 1, HCMC
Tel: 220 101

Vietcochamber (Chamber of Commerce and Industry)
33 Ba Trieu Street
Hanoi
Tel: 225 961/225 962/253 023

Vietcochamber (Chamber of Commerce and Industry)
c/o Foreign Economic Relations
  Department
Quang Nam-Danang Province
136 Ong Ich Khiem Street
Danang
Tel: 221 092

PHOTO CREDITS

INDEX